GENOMICS IN ASIA

T0346688

The work focuses on issues dealing with the development
and application of molecular biology and bioengineering
technologies in Asian societies and cultures. The workshop,
on which this book proposal is based, aimed to gain an
insight into bioethical issues with relation to the dynamics
of Asian societies, cultures and religions. It was to generate
debate on Asian Genomics and create a basis for
comparative research into the relationship between the
development and application of modern genetics, cultural
values and local interests in Asian societies. The papers
first of all reflect a great variety of bioethical views
discussed from the angle of different disciplinary and
cultural backgrounds, creating a basis on which a further
comparison between different local knowledge systems in
relation to genomic practices will be feasible.

Studies in Anthropology, Economy and Society

~

GENOMICS IN ASIA

A Clash of Bioethical Interests?

EDITED BY MARGARET SLEEBOOM

Routledge
Taylor & Francis Group

LONDON AND NEW YORK

First published in 2004 by
Kegan Paul Limited

This edition first published in 2009 by
Routledge

2 Park Square, Milton Park, Abingdon, Oxon OX14 4RN
Simultaneously published in the USA and Canada by Routledge
711 Third Avenue, New York, NY 10017

Routledge is an imprint of the Taylor & Francis Group, an informa business

First issued in paperback 2012

© Kegan Paul, 2004

Transferred to Digital Printing 2009

British Library Cataloguing in Publication Data
A catalogue record for this book is available from the British Library

ISBN13: 978-0-415-56064-1 (pbk)
ISBN13: 978-0-7103-0943-3 (hbk)

Publisher's Note
The publisher has gone to great lengths to ensure the quality of this reprint
but points out that some imperfections in the original copies may be
apparent. The publisher has made every effort to contact original copyright
holders and would welcome correspondence from those they have been
unable to trace.

TABLE OF CONTENTS

II Cultural and Philosophical Perspectives

III Genomics and Practices in Asia

ACKNOWLEDGEMENTS

This collection of papers is the result of collaborative efforts of an international group of scientists and thinkers studying the impact of new genetics on society. However, the volume would not have come about without the support and encouragement of the International Institute for Asian Studies in Leiden (IIAS). The IIAS shouldered a large part of the co-ordination and expenses of the conference entitled *Genomics in Asia* (28-29 March 2002), co-sponsored by the CNWS, out of which this book has grown. It was also made possible by the generosity of Baywood Publishing, which gave permission to republish a shorter version of chapter fifteen, appearing in *New Solutions: A Journal of Environmental & Occupational Health Policy*. Finally, without the enormous effort exerted by the book's English copy-editor, Dr Sean Taudin Chabot, and the help of Vincent Traag this volume would not have reached the publishers.

Chapter 1

Genomics in Asia: Cultural Values and Bioethical Practices

Margaret Sleeboom

Genomics in Asia focuses on issues dealing with the development and application of molecular biology and bioengineering technologies in Asian societies and cultures.[1] The workshop, on which this book is based, aimed at gaining insight into bioethical issues related to the dynamics of Asian societies, cultures and religions. We hoped to generate debate on Asian genomics and create a basis for comparative research on the relationship between the development and application of modern genetics, cultural values and local interests in Asian societies. The chapters reflect a great variety of bioethical views discussed from the perspective of different disciplinary and cultural backgrounds, creating a basis for further comparison between different local knowledge systems regarding genomic practices.

Most of the authors pay attention to the marginal position of bioethics in academic discourse. As part of a discourse on Western bioethics, it has carried a specific cultural baggage, which the increased application of new bio-medical technologies is putting to question: not only in Asia, but also in the West. The different levels of access to the new medical technologies, the cultural and ethical problems engendered by their application, and political pronouncements on concepts related to the biomedical field—such as cloning, stem cell research, eugenics and euthanasia—are only a few examples of the issues raised in this volume.

Contributors to this book provide insight into some social, political and ethical aspects of genomics, reflecting the bioethical experiences of researchers from Japan, China, the Filippines, Thailand, Taiwan, Pakistan, India and Malaysia. The topics under consideration vary from debates about genetics in China to religious perspectives on cloning and genetic therapy. The themes of the various chapters revolve around the commercial and medical application of new bioengineering technologies, such as the impact of preventive genetic medicine, genetic counselling, genetically modified organisms (GMOs) and stem cell research on wealth distribution, cultural traditions, social well-being, regulations and institutions. This study of bioengineering in Asia brings various points of view together at a concrete research level. It illustrates that there is still a dichotomy between East and West over the meaning of macro-concepts. To attain a more profound understanding of bioethical questions in daily practice, we clearly need new insights into the relationship between local knowledge systems, cultures and interests groups, on the one hand, and a constellation of the various interests of scientific research, governments and multinational companies (MNCs), on the other.

To this end we asked the following questions:
- To what extent can we speak of an Asian attitude toward the application and science associated with bioengineering technologies?
- Which national factors (state religions and ideologies, education, and national culture) are involved in shaping people's ideas and behaviour with regards to bioethical issues?
- Do specific social, political and economic groups across Asian borders have interests in common?

In attempting to answer these questions, this volume considers the following factors:

- The relevance of knowledge and culture: The interplay between local knowledge and culture, religion and scientific paradigms form the cognitive basis influencing the decisions of communities and individuals when faced with decisions to apply treatment. How do the various views on the relationship between mind and body, individuals and collectivity, affect such decision-making in practice?

- Access to the new biomedical and genetic technologies and their politico-economic consequences: What factors determine access to medical care (education, financial choice, social stigma)? How do these factors influence the distribution of the socio-economic advantages and costs engendered by biomedical technologies and agricultural genetic engineering?

- The formulation processes of bioethical policies: The process of formulating bioethical policies by religious and secular regimes is of great importance for the extent and ways in which biotechnology is applied. For instance, to what extent does prenatal screening affect the social-economic make-up of the population? How do religious and political authorities come to decisions on these matters, and on what ethical basis do they formulate their regulations and advice? How are they linked to population policies (e.g., birth control, genetic counselling)? Does the application and validation of biomedicine as a consequence of these policies lead to social-cultural marginalisation?

Worth emphasising here is the great diversity in authors' backgrounds, which makes for a rich amalgam of contrasting views on bioethics in Asia and shows that it is difficult, if not impossible, to make generalisations about 'Asian genomics'. Although this point may seem obsolete, some still make (or defend) rash generalisations about 'Asian beliefs'. In bringing into focus the extent of authors' diversity, the contributors to this book differ in the following important ways:

The cultural and religious backgrounds of the authors vary enormously: Islam, Hindu, Sikh, Confucian, Shinto, Buddhist;

The academic backgrounds of the contributors range from philosophy, genetics, biochemistry, biology and medicine to political science, sociology, international relations and ethics;

The linguistic backgrounds of the authors cover many languages, including Malay, English, Hindi, Japanese, Chinese, Cantonese, Thai, Urdu and Tagalog;

The academic status of the authors ranges from graduate student to professor, from beginning researcher to the founding president of the Asian Association for Bioethics;

The authors come from countries and universities that have unequal access to financial resources, influencing the quality and kind of facilities, the selection of academic research problems and the time and materials available for conducting research;

The authors vary considerably in terms of age and gender.

All these differences are part and parcel of the ideas found in this volume. Some differences remain latent, while others (the various disciplinary backgrounds, for example) are salient. Thus differences in the interpretations of bioethical problems differ more according to the respective disciplines from which authors set out (genetics, biochemistry, medicine, philosophy and international relations) than their cultural and regional backgrounds (Sikh, Islam, Christian, Hindu, Confucian, Shinto, Theravada Buddhism,

Japanese Buddhism, secular). Especially prominent are differences of view on the 'correct' meaning and significance of frequently used concepts such as 'human rights' and 'individualism' (Sakamoto Hyakudai) and 'autonomy' and 'harm' (Lee Shui Chuen). These disagreements lead to heated discussions about the validity of arguments made about the need for a paradigmatic change in favour of so-called Asian bioethics.

The aim of this study is to generate debate and comparative research on the bioethical problems and benefits that have arisen from the development and application of modern biotechnologies in Asian societies. Inspiration and solutions to bioethical problems come from various areas: education (Fujiki Norio), politics and government (Chee Khoon Chan; Mary Ann Chen Ng and Darryl Macer), medical technology and regulation (Wang Yanguang), science and technology (Min Jiayin), individual ethics (Mary Ann Chen Ng; Santishree Pandit), religion (Anwar Nasim), economic redistribution and development (Chee Khoon Chan) and a global paradigmatic change of thought and behaviour (Sakamoto Hyakudai; Morioka Masahiro; Lee Shui Chuen).

The book is divided into three parts, those concerning Religious Perspectives (I), Cultural and Philosophical Perspectives (II) and Genomics and Asian Practices (III). Part I deals mainly with bioethical issues from an Islamic (Anwar Nasim), a Hindu (Santishree Pandit), a Sikh (Gursatej Gandhi), a Thai Buddhist (Soraj Hongladarom) and a Shinto Buddhist and Christian point of view (Tanida Noritoshi).

In chapter one, Anwar Nasim, a senior geneticist from Islamabad, discusses ethical issues from an Islamic perspective. He shows how the Koran deals with issues of infertility and the conditions under which (human) cloning and stem cell research are acceptable in Islam.[2] Nasim also discerns a need for an alternative, Islamic perspective, arguing that 'the questions raised for Europe and North America such as discrimination by insurance companies and employers based on genetic testing—though important issues— may not necessarily be the ones that deserve highest priority in our (Islamic) societies'. To see how views put forward in the Koran are put into practice in society and how views vary within Islam are very important issues. Nasim's paper is more than a first step in this direction (Aksoy 1998; Anees 1995; Ludjito 1997; Nor 1999; Sachedina 2003).

In her 'Hindu Bioethics—The Concept of Dharma' (Chapter 2), Santishree Pandit explores what she calls 'the nature-centred attitude' in Hindu thought. She explains its central concept of Dharma as 'the whole body of rules that declare what are the proper desires one should entertain and the proper ways and means to acquire the material pleasure desired'. Pandit criticises Western hegemonic discourses and Western civilisation, arguing that 'Western civilisation has always believed in man's control over nature, which has meant his/her unravelling the mysteries of nature and exploiting it to man's need and greed'. At the same time, however, Pandit identifies a contradiction between the ideal and the practice of Hindu thought, exemplified by female infanticide in India: 'Nowhere does the concept of Dharma permit the use of medical methods to discriminate and kill the female infants'.

Science cannot be the solution to this problem, Pandit argues, as 'science can describe what is', but 'science cannot tell us what should be'. As a result, in India, which is a secular state, interpretations of Dharma are left to the individual.[3] Questions could be raised, however, as to the exact nature of this privatised concept of Dharma. For if bioethics is left to the individual, how does society decide the norms for the treatment of human life against which behaviour is judged. Furthermore, is it not the case that by privatising bioethical codes it becomes easier for 'hegemonic powers' - those embodied in multinational pharmaceutical conglomerates - to conduct experiments without any limitations at all? Pandit's paper indicates that the ideal concept of Dharma may clash with what actually happens in practice, which diminishes the hope that Dharma, as a religious and communal notion, could deal with bioethical problems in everyday life. In fact, the paper shows the complexity of any concept that endeavours to encompass the notion of society as a holistic body and of interpretation of that complex body by individuals. In this case, however, the author manages to avert the fallacy of equating Dharma with the East and individualism with the West.[4]

In her article on the 'Impact of Modern Genetics: A Sikh Perspective' (Chapter 3), the Sikh geneticist, Gusatej Gandhi, considers the implications of the use of bioengineering techniques, such as prenatal genetic diagnosis and sex selection, cloning, stem cell research and genetically manipulated organisms (GMOs) from a Sikh perspective. Sikhism is a relatively young religion (a little over 500 years old) and largely synthetic in character. Its founders rejected ritualism, formalism, and parochialism in favour of the moral and spiritual discipline and well-being of humanity. To this end, Sikhism spreads the awareness that the laws of God are omnipresent, i.e., they exist in the physical, moral and spiritual spheres.

Gandhi's discussion of prenatal sex selection in favour of males (by means of amniocentesis) among the Sikh is especially interesting. It proves wrong the widespread notion that a preference for baby boys is particularly prevalent among the poor and uneducated,[5] and that sex selection is related to the need for a male successor in societies considered to be underdeveloped. Gandhi demonstrates, however, that the occurrence of sex selection and infanticide of baby-girls is also practised among the educated and wealthy Sikh population. The formal Sikh ideal of non-discrimination and human harmony did not seem to hinder the 'bad' 'neo-Sikh' ethics of gender discrimination. In this case, the solution to bioethical problems was not thought to lie in religious ethics at all. The next chapter is concerned with another area of the new reproductive technologies, that is, nuclear transplantation, or more popularly, cloning (Humber and Almeder 1998; Cole-Turner 1997; Ginsburg and Rapp 1995).

Soraj Hongladarom, a philosopher from Chulalongkorn University, discusses a recent Thai best-seller, Amata (Immortal), by Wimon Sainimnuan (Chapter 4). This science-fiction novel sets off Buddhist values against those accompanying modern technologies and reveals several aspects of the interrelationship between Thai culture, Buddhism, and modern biotechnologies (Ratanakul 2000; Ratanakul and Deepudong 1998). Hongladarom analyses the novel's underlying meanings, especially in terms of how Thai culture and Theravada Buddhism view cloning technologies (see also, Keown 1995). Amata features a business tycoon and his family. The tycoon has cloned several copies of himself in order to harvest their bodily parts for his own use, aiming to become immortal. However, a conflict ensues when one of his clone-sons discovers the truth that he is simply a pool of spare-body parts.

Amata reflects critically upon Western science and technology. It reveals a Thai view of science and technology as being tied up with business and selfish interests rather than as serving the majority of people.[6] Hongladarom relates this pessimistic view of biotechnology to the economic crisis of 1997 and to issues of national identity in a globalising world. Finally, he shows that these issues are crucial to any attempt at articulating systems of local knowledge and culture with Western science and technology.

Hongladarom also argues that Thailand and other Asian countries should find a way to integrate science and technology into their cultural fabric without destroying the collective identity of their culture. Here a distinction should be made between those authors who regard religion as a private matter (e.g., Pandit and Ghandi) and those who regard religion as a collective phenomenon (e.g., Nasim and Lee). The latter worry about the lack of common standards for judging the status of a foetus: left to the individual, murder could turn into an act of convenience. The former authors have no such qualms and leave these matters to the conscience of the individual and the dynamics of society. However, it is this friction between the alternative perspectives that causes major problems with regards to policy-making and the regulation of science and technology. These difficulties are expressed in Part III of the book, where attitudes towards eugenics, biotechnology and pharmaceutical industries are related to the interests and practical issues faced by society.

In his analysis of a survey among Shinto, Buddhist, and Christian religious corporations in Japan, Dr. Noritoshi Tanida (Chapter 5), a physician and teacher of medical ethics, shows how, despite the great differences between religion and medicine, both institutions claim to be devoted to people's well-being. Tanida compares the ways in which various religious institutions aspire to live up to this claim in relation to the use of life-sustaining technologies and euthanasia. Here Tanida examines the views of students and health-care professionals with regard to voluntary and non-voluntary, passive and active euthanasia. Among secular people in Japan the discussion about euthanasia appears to be at a standstill, with two opposing camps: those who would allow active euthanasia and those who deny even passive euthanasia. A closer appreciation of the views of religionists, Tanida expects, may sharpen public debate.

Tanida's data on various religious attitudes towards euthanasia (Buddhist, Shinto, Christian) indicate a certain correlation between religious background and its ethical stance. However, as Hongladarom argues, surveys do not necessarily reflect actual behaviour. Furthermore, Gandhi's paper on Sikh perspectives and Pandit's paper on Dharma show that religious ideals and practices do not always converge. Nevertheless, it would be interesting to study whether this is also the case elsewhere. Hongladarom's discussion of the unique characteristics of Theravada Buddhism, for example, suggests that different views on euthanasia exist among Buddhists in Thailand and Japan—another example of the complexity and diversity of opinion in this field.

Part II, on Cultural and Philosophical Perspectives, deals with bioethical issues from Asian (Sakamoto Hyakudai), cross-cultural (Morioka Masahiro), Confucian (Lee Shui Chuen; Yu Kam Por) and materialist (Min Jiayin) points of view. As will become clear, the exact nature of the regional denomination of these perspectives is problematic. Though the reader may not develop an unambiguous view of Asian bioethics, the variety of cultural and philosophical interpretations of 'Asia', and the ideas associated with dichotomies of East and West will contribute to a deeper understanding of the cultural aspects of bioethics in Asia. In this sense, bioethics in Asia raises questions we all face with regards to human reproduction, such as the influence of germ-line therapy on future generations and the way we treat the natural environment and employ eugenic practices in our attempts to keep populations healthy and happy.

Sakamoto Hyakudai, in 'Human Genome, Artificial Evolution and Global Community' (Chapter 6), is concerned with recent advances in research relating to the Human Genome Project (HGP).[7] The result of this project may generate critical problems in global policy-making, the future status of human beings as well as the whole life system on earth. Sakamoto believes that sooner or later we will apply gene therapy to germ-line cells,[8] which in the long run suggests the possibility of an "artificial evolution" instead of the "natural evolution" of the past (Nordgren 1999). Sakamoto therefore asks how this new concept of 'artificial evolution' could be justified ethically. Such man-made evolution, he argues, may be the only way for human beings to survive. Though Sakamoto cannot find any serious ethical objections to the idea of artificial evolution, he does find it necessary to abolish an essential part of modern humanism and devise an alternative philosophy, one that incorporates an Asian perspective, to befit the new Millennium.

Morioka Masahiro's 'Cross-cultural Approaches to the Philosophy of Life in the Contemporary World' (Chapter 7) proposes the opposite, that is, to move away from Asian bioethics to a more universal approach in the study of life. In analysing the cultural dimensions of bioethics, Morioka argues, we must go beyond the East/West dichotomy as prevalent among ordinary people and scholars in Japan (Kazumasa 1997). Morioka illustrates this trend with the distinction made by Sakamoto Hyakudai between 'Asian bioethics' and 'Western bioethics'. Morioka criticizes Sakamoto, who believes that a sense of 'human rights' is very weak in East and Southeast Asia, and who advocates that Asian bioethics should be built on an Asian ethos, and global bioethics on a 'communitarian' and 'holistic' ethos.

Morioka criticises Sakamoto for his distinction between Eastern and Western bioethics, arguing that a great variety of views exist in both Asia and Europe. Thus, in Japan people's rights movements have existed since the 19th century, and in the US we find so-called 'communitarian bioethics'. The concepts of 'symbiosis' and 'community' associated with this approach, Morioka argues, are not the patent ownership of Confucius or of East Asia.[9] Morioka believes that medical ethics should not be separated from environmental ethics and that psychological and sociological approaches should be incorporated into 'life studies' as an alternative to traditional bioethics.

The discussion highlights a deep schism between those who believe in a 'regional' solution to global bioethical issues and those who want to articulate local practices in terms of global questions relating to the deployment of the new biomedical technologies. Especially the way in which 'the East' is defined forms an obstacle in the various approaches by authors from Asia, and is complicated by the fact that, according to Chan Chee Khoon, Asian and African values are often suspiciously similar. Two other Asian views, described in the next two chapters on Confucian bioethics, however, show that within a certain 'cultural' perspective there is scope for both variety and universality.

In chapter eight, <u>Lee</u> Shui Chuen from the National Central University (Taiwan) presents his Confucian perspective on 'Biotechnology and Responsibility to Future Generations'. Lee refers to the far-reaching effects of the application of germ-line therapy on future generations. He criticises the way in which the problem of responsibility to future generations is defined through the notion of harm as person-affecting (by for instance Derek Parfit), reflecting a Kantian over-emphasis on the interest of the individual and individual autonomy. Instead, Lee proposes a wider conception of harm, based on the principle of non-maleficence along the Hippocratic tradition of medical ethics, the Confucian conception of jen and the human capacity for empathy (De Bary, Chan and Watson 1964). The concept of the moral mind covers both the autonomy and the commiseration towards the sufferings of others (human beings as well as other forms of life). In approaching bioethical problems, commiseration provides the ground for the supremacy of the principle of 'doing-no-harm' over that of 'autonomy'. This 'paradigm shift', Lee demonstrates, delineates our responsibility to future generations with regards to the development and applications of biotechnology and the way in which it accords with our moral intuitions (Doering 2001).

Yu Kam Por from the Hong Kong Polytechnic University provides us with a Confucian perspective with regard to 'Respecting Nature and Using Human Intelligence' (Chapter 9). In the Confucian view, Yu argues, human intelligence should supplement the work of nature, and not replace it. This position, he suggests, could make an important contribution to global bioethics. Intervention in nature, then, is justified in cases of remedy, but not for the pursuit of maximal results. For example, genetic therapy is acceptable but eugenics is not. This view represents an intermediate position in the contemporary debate on genetic engineering. It aims at finding the right balance between respecting nature and making use of human intelligence. However, situations in which bioethical problems arise are not always clear-cut, as will become clear in Wang Yanguang's contribution on new eugenics in China (Chapter 11). For it is not easy to strike this balance between respecting nature and applying human intelligence when the meaning of the concepts that are expected to set the limits of 'remedy' and 'ulitarianism' themselves are afloat and changing, as is the case with the concept of eugenics.

Min Jiayin, in his 'Philosophical Meditation on Genomics' (Chapter 10), presents us with a more positivist approach than those of Lee and Yu. In itself this contribution shows that utilitarian views have no uncomplicated, if any, regional boundaries. Though many of Min's views are idiosyncratic, some of his views on evolution are alive and kicking among academics that try to base their views of society on theoretical models used in science. Their approaches are sometimes heavily influenced by Chinese concepts of enlightenment (Kwok 1965; Brugger and Kelly 1990; Goldman 1994; Miller and Lyman 1996; Lin, Min and Galikowski 1999). Min maintains that the human physique, in general, is degenerating, especially among the young generation raised in the modern city with its comforts. For example, body hair has virtually disappeared together with cold resistance and the human body today requires clothes, quilts, houses and heating facilities to keep it warm. Furthermore, mankind has long lost the ability of eating raw animal meat and grass roots and tree bark, and the intake of refined food is pushing up the incidence of diabetes and other 'illnesses of the wealthy'.[10] The only way to keep up the quality of the human stock, according to Min, is with resort to artificial human reproduction.

Min discusses the idea of 'women's liberation from childbirth' and proposes that 'only when women are freed from childbirth, are they truly free'. Here Min pins his hopes on experimentation with and popularisation of the technology of 'artificial wombs'. In theory, Min argues, it is correct and necessary for mankind to explore eugenic approaches, for systematic scientific approaches inevitably seek to optimise the system to achieve optimal structures and functions. After all, Min observes, mankind throughout its history has never stopped improving crops and livestock—through seed selection, breeding, hybridisation, and so on. Then why should mankind not seek the optimisation of itself?

Regarding this issue of the optimisation of mankind, Chapter 11 makes clear that in China intentions to improve the human stock are part and parcel of the national policy of improving the quality of the population. What is important here is that the questions faced by the Chinese government are very similar to those faced by other governments, which may or may not explicate their policies (Hengleng and Khoon 1984; Hodges 1999; Otsubo 1998; Chung 2002). Other countries may engage in eugenic population policies through other means, such as systems of stimulation and reward at the level of the individual, instead of at the collective and social levels.[11] For this reason, it is important to understand the cultures and philosophies through which concepts of health, nature and social ideals are mediated.

Part III of this book focuses on empirical approaches to genomics-related practices and considers 'the definition, practice and cultural values of eugenics in China' (Wang Yanguang), a survey of 'attitudes toward biotechnology and bioethics in the Philippines' (Mary Ann Chen Ng and Darryl Macer), 'medical genetics in Japan' (Norio Fujiki) and 'a view from the South on Genomics, health and society in Malaysia' (Chee Chan Khoon). Each chapter, besides describing bioethical issues and perspectives, also attempts to define the practice and context in which bioethical views are formed.

Wang Yanguang gives us a definition, and defends the 'practice and cultural values' of 'eugenics' in China (Chapter 11). Eugenics in China is a sensitive issue and discussion on the subject, both inside and outside China, exploded after the announcement of the 'Law of The People's Republic of China on Maternal and Infant Health Care', which was enacted in 1994.[12] This 'eugenic' law places constraints on severely handicapped adults who want to have children (Croll 1993; Mao 1997; Mao and Wertz 1997; Dikötter 1998; Mao 1998; Chan, Chen, Qiu and Du 1999). In its defence, Wang explains that in China the concept of eugenics is not associated with the ideas and practices that it implies in other countries.

The definition of Chinese eugenics grew out of medical-ethical practices wherein distinctions are made between preventive genetic medicine and 'negative eugenics', voluntary and mandatory screening and testing, and directive and non-directive counselling. Furthermore, in this medical practice, the issues of informed consent and access to genetic services are widely debated. Significantly, Yang claims that there is proof that the

Chinese have strong social views on genetic information, that is, it is not only the patient's privacy that is important but also the patient's family and society at large.

Wang contrasts this situation with that of Europe. Here, Wang emphasises that every bioethical issue must be understood within the context of particular societies, cultures and religions. However, insight into the ethical basis for the practices that in China are called 'eugenics' and cultural interpretations of situations in which these ethical issues arise might be valuable, not only for China, but also for other developing countries in Asia and other parts of the world. This, Wang argues, is because Chinese authorities seek to develop and apply new advances in genetics to benefit their populations.

Both Min and Wang express great trust in the power of science and technology as a tool for population policy-making. In Min's eyes, modern technology is capable of solving fertility problems by means of 'artificial wombs', while Wang advocates a new Chinese concept of eugenics that relies on government policies to correctly execute guidelines for technological solutions to matters of public health. It may be worthwhile complementing these studies with anthropological investigations into the views and interpretations of such policies and laws by the female patients and their families, since many studies leave these out of the picture (Downey and Dumit 1997; Kleinman 1999; Lock et al. 2000).

Moreover, a study of people's trust in politicians, as the one conducted by Ms. Ng in the Philippines, may significantly influence whether a new concept of Chinese eugenics is endorsed and put into practice or not. Mary Ann Chen Ng's and Darryl Macer's contribution on 'Attitudes Toward Biotechnology and Bioethics in the Philippines' (Chapter 12) explores the relationship between public concerns and some of the ethical issues raised by various applications of biotechnology in the Philippines. Ng compares a public opinion survey conducted in the Philippines with previous surveys held by the Eubios Ethics Institute in Japan.[13] The study focuses on perceptions of the risk involved in biotechnology and genetic engineering with regards to food production, health care and other ways of improving society. At the same time, it also takes into account moral and religious factors.

Specific items of research concern biotechnological applications using genetically modified organisms (GMOs) such as pest resistant crops and xenotransplantation,[14] the use of gene therapy for curative and enhancement purposes, and the potential of biotechnology to solve crime, increase food production and improve public health. A comparison with wealthier countries, such as Japan, shows a trend of increasingly negative attitudes towards biotechnology in general, which has important implications for national policies toward science and technology. An important factor with regards to the regulation of science and technology research and the development of biotechnological applications is the factor of public trust in regulatory procedures and public authorities.

Fujiki Norio provides us with insights into Japanese attitudes toward abortion and medical treatment of the severely handicapped (Chapter 13). For almost two decades, Fujiki has organised international conferences and seminars on genetic technologies and on the responsibility of medical scientists with regards to bioethical issues. Furthermore, for over forty years, Fujiki has conducted research on handicapped children in the Kyoto Prefectural University of Medicine, in the Aichi Prefectural Colony for the Handicapped and at Fukui Medical University in Japan. He has dealt especially with the thorny question of treatment for newly born infants (neonatals) with severe congenital defects and related issues of human dignity. Opinion surveys on prenatal diagnosis and selective abortion among the general public and health personnel suggest that Japanese attitudes towards these issues are similar to those in other wealthy countries.

However, explicit differences exist regarding the determinants of attitudes to abortion and sex selection. Interestingly, the dividing line is not between Japan and Western societies, as is often assumed to be the case, but between Japan and other Asian countries. This difference, Fujiki believes, is probably caused by religious and social factors. On the whole, the surveys he refers to found an increasing level of agreement on issues regarding selective abortion of a foetus with Down syndrome and an increasing level of disagreement regarding withholding treatment in the case of severely handicapped infants. Fujiki also discusses surveys focusing on prenatal diagnosis, selective abortion and new insights regarding thalassemia,[15] the human supremacy over animals, as well as on the issue of withholding treatment from severely handicapped infants.

Chee Khoon Chan from the Citizens' Health Initiative (CHI) in Malaysia contributes 'A View from the South' on genomics, health and society (Chapter 14). Chan's paper proceeds from the interests of economically vulnerable groups in Asia. It emphasises the neglected health priorities of the South, intellectual property rights and patents, risk management, genetically manipulated crops (GMCs), health insurance and discrimination, predictive testing, reproductive choice, and eugenics. Chan argues for the necessity of adequate, effective and credible representation of popular organisations and transparent, publicly owned and publicly managed institutions committed to a needs-based perspective.

The CHI's stance is that no less important than scientific and technological assessment of the implications of genomics for human health as emphasised by the World Health Organization (WHO) is a perspective that gives due attention to the social context and political economy of scientific/technological development and its deployment. CHI contends that hypothetical scenarios of 'rationally' behaving social agents, acting in accordance with a detached technocratic rationality, is more akin to diplomacy than to rigorous social analysis or illuminating policy science.

Chan also points to problems that are common to developing countries and people from various cultures, and that have a great impact on the health and survival of great numbers of people. Here, Chan observes a correlation between the genome project and the commercial potential of applied technologies, and describes its consequences for the economy, health and agricultural traditions of the 'South' (Bankowski and Levine 1993).

The question of representation therefore is of great importance when we study problems in genomics. Whose problems are we talking about? Anwar Nasim suspected, and quite rightly so, that the problems important to Muslims might differ from those important to Western people. But this issue is extremely complex. The same question also came up when, during the conference, <u>Min</u> Jiayin presented his views as his own and <u>Wang</u> Yanguang claimed that hers were representative of China as a whole. Neither seems accurate. Min expressed his private preference for tailor-made children by using 'artificial wombs', ignoring the fact that others would have to live with the consequences. Wang's introduction of the Chinese view, on the other hand, was obviously (and understandably) not based on an opinion survey of all Chinese people. This issue of generalisation also surfaces in Nasim's Islamic perspective, which at first sight appears to represent the views of 1.2 billion Muslims.

Interestingly, nearly all the contributions to this volume are critical of Western views of nature and society and, of its hegemonic practices. Often, however, the idea of 'the West' is used as a platform for discussion in order to generate alternatives to particular modes of world organisation and distasteful phenomena that are rejected by the authors: individualism, instrumentalism, utilitarianism, replacing nature with forms of biotechnological control, imperialist exploitation, and so on. Ironically, all of these practices are equally rejected by various 'Western' groups of people and supported by some 'Eastern' groups. Therefore, without understanding which groups, in what location and under what circumstances they adhere to certain viewpoints, it makes little sense to make grand generalisations. Of course, adequate political representation is necessary for many kinds of collective interests, especially the vulnerable, among women, or the poor for instance, or among animals. Adequate academic analysis, however, has to rely on the specific problems we are trying to solve. Thus, in order to gain a better understanding of the intertwined bioethical interests of social, economic, cultural and religious groups in Asia, we must conduct more qualitative research and gather more empirical data from a comparative perspective.

NOTES

[1] Genomics pertains to the study of the 'genome', the total genetic makeup of an individual or organism. In other words, it refers to a set of all the genes of an organism.

[2] Cloning refers to the practice of artificially producing two or more genetically identical organisms from the cells of another organism (note that the identity here pertains only to nucleic DNA); stem cells are relatively undifferentiated cells that have the ability to give rise to more differentiated or specialized cells. By cloning stem cells scientists can grow organs and tissues, which can be used for transplantation.

[3] For discussions on biotechnology, life and death, biodiversity , medical and science ethics, and religion and human values in India, see *Bioethics in India* (Azariah, Azariah, & Macer 1998).

[4] According to Dumont, 'Hindu society is organised around the concept of *dharma* in a roughly similar way as modern society is organised around that of the individual' (Dumont 1967: 236; quoted in Celterl 2001).

[5] For a thorough analysis of the new reproductive technologies in India and a comparative study of its practice in India and the Netherlands, see Gupta (2000).

[6] The practice of cloning persons is defended for various reasons. Michael Tooley (1999) lists the following benefits of cloning of persons:
1. It would yield scientific advances in psychology. Cloning could give insights into the heredity vs. environment issue. It could help raise children with desirable traits so that individuals would have a better chance of realizing their potential. The study of twins has been important here; clones could become more important;
2. Cloning could benefit society. The argument that Einstein could be cloned is too radical, but it is possible at least to clone intelligent people and at the same time control the environment;
3. Happier and healthier individuals could be generated, to the extent that mood and health are genetically determined;
4. It could yield individuals with desirable traits and lead to more satisfying child-rearing (following on point 3);
5. As a result of greater psychological similarity with one of the parents, it is possible to use knowledge about one's own rearing in raising a child;
6. It would solve infertility by means of cloning or embryo splitting;
7. Homosexual couples could have children;
8. Cloning could save lives by developing organ and tissue banks.

[7] Information from research on the Human Genome Project (HGP) led to an immense improvement of genetic technologies. In 1990, the HGP was designed to be a 15-year, 3 billion-dollar project conducted under the auspices of the National Institutes of Health (NIH) and the Department of Energy to map and sequence all the DNA of a human prototype. (Of course, since every person's genetic makeup

is different, what is really being mapped out is supposed to be an 'average' genome). As a result of this effort and that of Craig Venter's Celera institute, papers announced in 2000, in the scientific journals *Nature* and *Science*, that there were 30-40.000 genes. According to Eric Landau, the actual number of genes is probably closer to 25.000, and, it is estimated that only 1,5 per cent of the genome consists of genetic code.

[8] Germ-line gene therapy refers to genetic manipulation that changes the germ cells of an organism, as well as those of the person's biological descendants. Germ-line cells include sperm or ova; the cells of the germ-line (unlike somatic cells) bridge the gap between generations.

[9] Even though this seems to be the case according to discussions in for instance Fan Ruiping (1999).

[10] The examples provided could be explained from different angles and one could argue about the temporal accuracy of these statements. Although a sociobiologist looks at functional and evolutionary questions in explaining the characteristics of an organism, others look at the immediate environment and at developmental processes, regarding the individual and the environment as mutually constitutive. For instance Goodman and Leatherman, in *Building a Biocultural Synthesis* (1998), offer a biocultural anthropology that is opposed to what they call the 'biosocial perspective'.

[11] For instance, how does one view the fact that severely handicapped children in developing countries do not survive? If resources are not allocated toward their aid for economic reasons, then, can we speak of 'negative' eugenic policy-making?

[12] See for instance *Law of the PRC on Maternal and Infant Health Care*, printed by the Ministry of Public Health of the PRC, 1994. Provincial regulations also require one spouse to be sterilised if one or both partners suffer from a 'serious hereditary' disease. For example, the Henan Eugenics Law requires sterilisation of at least one spouse if a married couple suffers from 'chronic mental disorders' such as schizophrenia and manic depression (*Henan Eugenics Law, supra* note 45, at Article 8). In addition, provincial regulations, such as those of Gansu Province, require the sterilization of married 'mentally retarded' persons ('Chinese Sterilizing Retarded Who Marry', *Chicago Tribune*, August 15, 1991: 58). For more information

on the eugenic laws at the provincial level, see Women of the World: Formal Laws and Policies Affecting Their Reproductive Lives (a report on East and South-East Asia, coming out in 2003, that will include a chapter on China) and http://www.crlp.org/pub_bo_wowlaw_china.html.

[13] The Eubios Ethics Institute is located in the biology department of Tsukuba University (Japan), and is headed by Darryl Macer. It has an excellent website on bioethics in Asia, displaying a wealth of information on conferences, publications, and links: http://www.biol.tsukuba.ac.jp/~macer/index.html.

[14] Xenotransplantation comprises the modification of the DNA of one organism by inserting the genetic material of another. For example, animals, such as pigs, are bred as organ-donors for human patients. This may also involve the introduction of human genes to the pig to reduce the likelihood of a pig organ being rejected when transplanted into a human patient. Critics are concerned that the technology will expose humans to new viruses that, until now, have only affected animals.

[15] Thalassaemia is a haemoglobinopathy or a disease of the blood, a rare form of hereditary anaemia. It leads to chronic anaemia, bone deformities and an early death. A child born with this condition requires periodic blood transfusions or bone marrow transplantation in a series of operations. Preconceptional screening can help diagnose whether parents carry the traits. The condition is common in Southeast Asia, West Africa and the Mediterranean.

BIBLIOGRAPHY

Aksoy, S. (1998) 'Can Islamic Texts Help to Resolve the Problem of the Moral Status of the Prenate?' *Eubios Journal of Asian and International Bioethics* (EJAIB), 8: 76-79.

Anees, M.A. (1995) 'Anti-cloning on basis of Quran; no abortion (except necessity)', *EJAIB*, 5: 36-37.

Azariah, J., Hilda, A. and Macer, D.R.J. (1998) *Bioethics in India*, Tsukuba: Eubios Ethics Institute.

Bankowski, Z. and Levine, R.J. (eds) (1993) *Ethics and Research on Human Subjects. International Guidelines*, Geneva: The Council for International Organizations of Medical Sciences (CIOMS).

Boyd, A., Pinit R., Deepudong, A. (1998) 'Compassion as Common Ground', *EJAIB*, 8: 34-37.

Brugger, B. and David, K. (1990) *Chinese Marxism in the Post-Mao Era*, Stanford: Stanford University Press.

Burgio, G. R, and Lanton, J.D. (eds) (1994) *Primum Non Nocere Today. A Symposium on Pediatric Bioethics*, International Congress Series 1071, Amsterdam: Elsevier.

Carson, R.A. and Burns, C.R. (eds)(1997) *Philosophy Of Medicine And Bioethics: A Twenty-Year Retrospective And Critical Appraisal*, Dordrecht: Kluwer Academic Publishers.

Celtel, A. (2001) *Louis Dumont and the 'Category of the Individual' A Study in Anthropological Theory*, Ph.D. dissertation, Oxford University.

Chen Z., Chen R., Qiu R. and Du, R, (1999) 'Chinese geneticists are far from eugenic   movement', *American Journal of Human Genetics*, 64: 1199.

Cole-Turner, R. (ed.) (1997) *Human Cloning. Religious Responses*, Louisville: Knox Press.

Croll, E.J. (1993) 'A Commentary on the New Draft Law on Eugenics and Health Protection', *China Information*, Leiden VIII, no. 3: 32-37.

Daniels, N., Kennedy, B.P. and Kawachi, I. (1999) 'Why Justice is Good for Our health: The Social Determinants of Health Inequalities', in A. Kleinman (ed.) *Daedalus*, 128, no. 4 (Summer).

De Bary, W. T., Chan, W. and Watson, B. (1964) *Sources of Chinese Tradition*, New York: Columbia University Press.

Dikötter, F. (1998) *Imperfect Conceptions. Medical Knowledge, Birth Defects and Eugenics in China*, London: C. Hurst & Co.

Doering, O. (2001) *Technischer Fortschritt und kulturelle Werte in China. Humangenetik und Ethik in Taiwan, Hongkong und der Volksrepublik China*, 280 Mitteilungen des Instituts für Asienkunde, Hamburg.

Downey, G.L. and Dumit, J. (1997) *Cyborgs & Citadels. Anthropological Interventions in Emerging Sciences and Technologies*, Santa Fe: School of American Research Press.

Dua, K.K. (2000) 'The Bhagavad Gita on Genetics and Behaviour', in N. Fujiki and D.R.J. Macer (eds) *Bioethics in Asia*, Tsukuba: Eubios Ethics Institute.

Dumont, L. (1967) 'The Individual as an Impediment to Sociological Comparison and Indian History', in V.B. Singh and B. Singh (eds) *Social and Economic Change: Essays in Honour of D. P. Mukherji*, Bombay: Allied Publishers.

Fan R. (ed.) (1999) *Confucian Bioethics*. Dordrecht: Kluwer Academic Publishers.

Fujiki, N. and Macer, D.R.J. (eds) (2000) *Bioethics in Asia*, Tsukuba: Eubios Ethics Institute.

Ginsburg, F. D and Rapp, R. (eds) (1995) *Conceiving the New World Order. The Global Politics of Reproduction*, Berkeley: California University Press.

Goldman, M. (1994) *Sowing the Seeds of Democracy in China*, Cambridge: Harvard University Press.

Goodman, A.H. and Leatherman, T.L. (1998) *Building a Biocultural Synthesis: Political-economic Perspectives on Human Biology*, Ann Arbor: University of Michigan Press.

Gupta, J.A. (2000*) New Reproductive Technologies, Women's Health and Autonomy: Freedom or Dependency?* New Delhi: Sage Publications.

Hengleng, C. and Cheekhoon, C. (1984) *Designer Genes: I.Q., Ideology and Biology,* Selangor.

Hoshino K. (ed.) (1997) *Japanese and Western Bioethics. Studies in Moral Diversity,* Dordrecht: Kluwer Academic Publishers.

Humber, J. and Almeder, R. (1998) *Human Cloning,* Totowa: Humana Press.

Keown, D. (1995) *Buddhism and Bioethics,* New York: St. Martin's Press.

Kimura, R. (1999) 'Genetic Diagnosis and Gene Therapy in the Cultural Context: social and Bioethical Implications in Japan', in Nordgren (ed.) *Gene Therapy and Ethics,* Uppsala: Acta Universitatis Upsaliensis.

Kleinman, A. (ed.) (1999) 'Bioethics and beyond', *Daedalus,* 128, no. 4 (Summer).

Kwok, D.W.T. (1965) *Scientism in Chinese Thought, 1900-1950.* New Haven: Yale University Press.

Lin, M. and Galikowski, M. (1999) *The Search for Modernity. Chinese Intellectuals and Cultural Discourse in the Post-Mao Era,* New York: St. Martin's Press.

Ludjito, A. (1997) 'The Role of Ulama (Islamic Scholars) in Dealing with Bioethical Issues in Indonesia', *EJAIB,* 7.

Lock, M. *et al.* (2000) *Living and Working with the New Medical Technologies, Intersection of Inquiry,* Cambridge: Cambridge University Press.

Mao X. (1997) 'Ethics and genetics in China: an inside story', *Nature Genetics,* 17, no. 20.

Mao X. (1998) 'Chinese geneticists' view of ethical issues in genetic testing and screening: evidence for eugenics in China', *American Journal of Human Genetics,* 63: 688-695.

Mao X. and Wertz, D.C. (1997) 'China's genetics services provider's attitudes towards several ethical issues: A cross-cultural survey', *Clinical Genetics,* 52: 100-109.

Miller, H.L. (1996) *Science and Dissent in Post-Mao China: The Politics of Knowledge*, Seattle: University of Washington Press.

Nor, S.N.M. (1999) 'New Reproductive Biotechnology, Values and Society', *EJAIB*, 9: 166-169.

Nordgren, A. (ed.) 1999. *Gene Therapy and Ethics*, Uppsala: Acta Universitatis Upsaliensis.

Ratanakul, P. (2000) 'Bioethics in Thailand, in N. Fujiki and D.R.J. Macer (eds) *Bioethics in Asia*, Tsukuba: Eubios Ethics Institute.

Rozman, G. (ed.) (1993) *The East Asian Region, Confucian Heritage and Its Modern Adaptation*, New Jersey: Princeton University Press.

Sachedina, A. (forthcoming, 2003) 'End of Life Decisions from an Islamic Perspective, *Lancet*.

Tooley, M. (1998) 'The Moral Status of the Cloning of Humans', in J. Humber and R. Almeder (eds) *Human Cloning*, Totowa: Humana Press.

Toulmin, S. (1997) 'The Primacy of Practice: Medicine and Postmodernism', in Burns (ed.) *Philosophy of Medicine and Bioethics: A Twenty-Year Retrospective and Critical Appraisal*, Dordrecht: Kluwer Academic Publishers.

Wertz, D.C. and Fletcher, J.C. (eds) (1989) *Ethics and Human Genetics. A Cross-Cultural Perspective*, Berlin: Springer-Verlag

Chapter 2

Ethical Issues: An Islamic Perspective[1]

Anwar Nasim

INTRODUCTION

As a geneticist I want to highlight some of the recent breakthroughs in such areas as cloning, gene therapy, stem cell research, artificial insemination and other kinds of human reproductive biology. A search for answers to these extremely complex questions also leads to other issues such as the patenting of DNA fragments, genetic prescreening for insurance and employment, screening of human populations for early diagnosis and the individual's right to privacy. There are also some specific issues related to the human genome project that merit serious discussion.

It is important to emphasise that moral pronouncements and ethical values are intimately related to the beliefs, values and composition of any society. With the Muslim World consisting of nearly twenty percent of the total human population, ethical issues will obviously be examined in the light of the Holy Quran. For Muslims there are two major sources of guidance: firstly, the holy book which gives a complete code of life including economic, social, legal and ethical principles; and secondly, Hadith, which represents the sayings and the way of life of the holy prophet Muhammad (PBUH).

Recent studies in the field of stem cell research will be used to illustrate possible future approaches to deal with ethical issues and questions. The onus for this kind of in-depth analysis is upon academicians, religious scholars and scientists. It is important to appreciate that the required infrastructure for such dialogue and discussion is presently lacking in the Muslim World. The questions raised in Europe and North America, such as discrimination by insurance companies and employers based on genetic testing, though important issues, may not necessarily be the ones that deserve highest priority in our societies. The socio-economic situation demands that, in view of these breath-taking scientific developments, the situation is examined within specific prevailing scenarios. This, in turn, obviously points to the need for public awareness and for Genetics to become an integral part of our educational system. Dialogues, debates or discussions based on ignorance are an exercise in futility. The need to develop an Islamic perspective by mutual discussion and appropriate research needs to be emphasised.

Asia as a continent has enormous cultural and religious diversity, and its philosophical ideas are deeply rooted in centuries of historical events. It is within this richness and diversity that one needs to look for answers to the challenges posed by the revolutionary breakthroughs in bioengineering and molecular biology. Equally important are the issues that relate to the economic impact and social consequences of this revolution in biotechnology, which has obviously given rise to the dynamic interplay of new equations and relationships different participating interest groups and communities. The way human diseases will be diagnosed and treated in the future is obviously going to be radically different from the practices of earlier days. Gene therapy, cloning of human embryos and other current medical devices are just a few examples that illustrate this new scenario.

There are a few basic realities and accompanying notions that need to be stated at the very outset. Firstly, the pace at which new knowledge is being generated has indeed no parallel in history. The ease with which one can access available information is just as impressive. It has been estimated that whereas the total knowledge pool in other areas will double in six to seven years, for life sciences such doubling time is estimated to be nearly three years. This new scenario not only provides an extremely rich and almost unmanageable store of data, but also poses a serious challenge for effective, concrete and meaningful discussion. The ethical challenges that come with these exciting new findings can perhaps best be conveyed by reproducing the following news items.

Chinese claims to have cloned a human embryo
(Dawn, 8 March 2002)
London, March 7. A Chinese scientist claims to have leapt ahead of Western scientists by cloning a human embryo in 1999. Lu Guangxiu, of Xiangya medical college in the southeastern city of Changsha, says she and her team have since grown cloned human embryos to the stage where stem cells could be harvested and then cultured. The Wall Street Journal reported that Professor Lu's work has not been subject to peer review, the usual form of scientific scrutiny, by scientists outside of China. However, she has published a paper in a Chinese journal.

Alongside her research, Prof Lu runs an IVF clinic. Access to human embryos and human eggs are prerequisites of stem cell and cloning research. Her aim is to use early stage cloned embryos to create a line of embryonic stem cells. These would ultimately be a resource from which to cultivate spare parts for transplantation. The point of cloning in this case—therapeutic cloning, as it is sometimes called—is to avoid rejection of the transplant by cloning the cells from the host's own body. Labs around the world have produced human embryonic stem cell lines from surplus IVF embryos, but none has yet cloned a human embryo. Doubts have been thrown on the claims of ACT, a U.S. firm, to have done so last year.

Prof Lu told the Wall Street Journal that her researchers had initially based their cloning on the technique described by Ian Wilmut from the Roslin Institute near Edinburgh, after those scientists cloned Dolly the sheep in 1997. This involves removing the DNA carrying nucleus of an egg, injecting DNA from an adult cell into the hollowed-out space, and applying a tiny jolt of electricity to fuse cell and nucleus together. However, this method produced few embryos living long enough to grow to blastocysts, the ball of a couple of hundred cells from which stem cells can be harvested. Prof. Lu said that they had achieved more success with a new technique: injecting the donor DNA into the egg, leaving it for a time, and then removing the egg DNA.

As described, however, the procedure remains enormously unreliable and wasteful with donated eggs. Only five per cent of the embryos that were cloned in Prof. Lu's lab developed to the blastocyst stage. Not only that, the cloned, harvested stem cells die after dividing for a short time, instead of dividing indefinitely. There is certainly going to be skepticism about Prof Lu's claims outside of China. But China has been investing heavily in biotechnology for years, and has number of other stem cell research labs.

Lords give go-ahead to cloning research
(Sciencedotcom, 8 March 2002)
London: Scientists in the UK have been given the go-ahead to create human embryo clones under strictly controlled conditions. A House of Lords committee set up last year to examine claims that making the clones was unnecessary has decided that the Human Fertilization and Embryology Authority (HFEA) can issue research licences, according to a BBC report.

The HFEA, the body that regulates embryology research in Britain, is likely to issue licences to begin experimenting with human embryonic material almost immediately. The UK's controls on cloning under the 1990 Human Fertilization and Embryology Act were designed to place barriers in the way of anyone wanting to produce a child copy of a human being. The 'Pro-life' lobby then secured a High Court ruling that highlighted an apparent legal loophole and derailed the legislation, but the decision was successfully challenged by the government at the Court of Appeal in January. Reverend Richard Harries, Bishop of Oxford and chairman of the committee, said: 'After looking at all the issues very carefully, the Committee was not persuaded that it would be right to prohibit all research on early embryos, which has been permitted since 1990 and regulated effectively by the Human Fertilization and Embryology Authority since then'.

These news items have been reproduced here to convey the widespread global activity, debate and intellectual excitement that currently prevail. Secondly, it is essential to fully appreciate that the questions that need to be answered are exactly the same for different religions and societies. One could use the example of the new techniques and interventions in 'Human Reproductive Biology' to further emphasise this point. The biological composition of a human body (quite apart and distinct from religious beliefs, cultural traditions and the way we think) is surprisingly uniform. This is a message convincingly conveyed by the completion of the sequencing of the Human Genome in June 2000. The basic biological units that constitute a human being, the magic molecule of DNA, and the fact that DNA from different societies and communities shows 99 per cent similarity, need to be clearly kept in mind as we deal with ethical questions. The basic biological facts are graphically depicted below.

The Human Genome Project has uncovered the exact makeup of every human gene. Based on this information, scientists should be able to generate new medicines, dovetail drugs to suit every individual on Earth, unravel the complexities of the mind and understand our physiology as never before. This information also allows us to address issues like intellectual property rights, patenting of specific human DNA fragments, multinationals and indigenous knowledge of local communities, in search of a consensus. It is with this scenario in mind that I want to share some thoughts on how attempts have been made to answer these questions from an Islamic perspective. My approach is to elucidate only the broad fundamental principles and guidelines that Islam offers to answer these ethical questions.

As stated earlier, for Muslims there are two major sources of guidance: firstly, the holy book, which gives a complete code of life including economic social, legal and ethical principles; and secondly, Hadith, which represents the sayings and the way of life of the holy prophet Muhammad (PBUH). Islam is an Arabic term with two root words: the first, Salm, refers to peace and the other, Silm, means submission. Islam stands for 'a commitment to surrender one's will to the will of God and thus to be at peace with the Creator and with all that has been created by Him'. It is through submission to the Will of God that the harmonisation of different spheres of life under an all-embracing ideal becomes possible.

Islam is a worldview and an outlook on life. It is based on the recognition of the unity of the Creator and of our submission to His will. Everything originates from one God, and everybody is ultimately responsible to Him. Thus the unity of the Creator has as its corollary the Oneness of His creation and distinctions of race, colour, caste, wealth and power disappear in our relations with other persons. Islam assumes total equality by virtue of the common Creator. Henceforth, our mission becomes dedication, worship and obedience to our Creator, who becomes our purpose in life. The following quotation from the holy Quran further illustrates the statements above:

> We created man of an extraction of clay, then we set him, a drop in a safe lodging, then We created of the drop a clot, then We created of the clot a tissue, then We created of the tissue bones, then we covered the bones in flesh; thereafter We produced it as another creature. So blessed be God, the best of creators (23: 12-14).

The teaching of Islam covers all fields of human activity: spiritual and material, individual and social, educational and cultural, economic and political, national and international. Some of the more specific questions are addressed below. In Islam, some remedies to overcome infertility are allowed and encouraged. It is essential if it involves the preservation of procreation and treatment of infertility in one partner of the married couple. There are different modalities available for the treatment of infertility for both the male and the female partners, depending upon the cause of the infertility. Some of these modalities have been practised for hundreds of years and never were of ethical concern: e.g., medical therapy, hormonal therapy, corrective and reconstructive surgery for male or female infertility. These treatments were not of major ethical concern because they did not separate the bonding of the sexual act from the process of reproduction. Medically assisted conception (MAC) enables a couple to have children without having sexual intercourse. This new type of treatment for infertility has created a great ethical debate all over the world, within different societies and among the followers of different religions. MAC involving a third party, who provides an egg, a sperm or a uterus, provoked even more debate, disagreement and controversy. Gender selection is interference in the deeds of the Creator and a Muslim would never want to choose a baby's gender. He or she would prefer to accept all the decisions and gifts of God, whatever they are.

> To Allah belongs the dominion of the heavens and earth. He
> creates what He wills, He bestows female upon whom He
> wills, and He bestows males upon whom He wills. For He is
> all knowing, all powerful (42: 49-50).

The Islamic perspective is that each child should relate to a known
father and mother. It is based on opinions accepted in the Islamic
world, and relies on the views of Fuqaha'a, physicians, ethicists,
lawyers and specialists. Marriage is a contract between the wife
and husband during the span of their marriage; no third party
should intrude into the marital functions of sex and procreation. A
third party is not acceptable, whether he or she provides a sperm,
an egg, an embryo or a uterus. If the marriage contract has come to
an end because of divorce or death of the husband, artificial
reproduction cannot be performed on the female partner, even if
sperm cells from the former husband are used.

In Islam the marriage of a man and a woman is not just a financial
and physical arrangement of living together, but a sacred contract,
a gift of God, aimed at enjoying each other physically and at
continuing the lineage.

> And God has created for you consorts from amongst
> yourselves, and out of your consorts He created children and
> grandchildren for you, and provided you out of His bounty.
> Will they then believe in vain things and be ungrateful to
> God's favour (16:72)?

> Among His signs is that He created consorts for you amongst
> yourselves, so that you may find peace with them, and He
> set love and compassion between you. Verily in this are signs
> for people who reflect (30:12).

The Prophet Muhammad has emphasised marriage by saying:
'Marriage is my tradition. He who rejects my tradition is not of
me'. In Islam, for a man and a woman to have a child, they must be

legally married. Thus, if a normally infertile married couple is able to procreate by in vitro fertilisation or artificial insemination, there is no obstacle to doing so. The condition is that no sperm other than her lawful husband's must be introduced into a woman's abdomen, and no sperm and ovum belonging to an unmarried couple should be combined in in-vitro fertilisation.

Married couples who cannot induce pregnancy in a normal way are allowed to have in vitro fertilisation as long as the fertilised ovum is placed in the womb of the woman from whom the egg was taken (i.e., not in the womb of a surrogate mother). The fertilisation has to be with the sperm of her lawful husband during their married life, not after divorce or after the death of the husband. This is the general conclusion of various Muslim jurists' meetings that discussed this subject.

The holy Quran has depicted a path, the Straight Path (Sirat-ul-Mustaqim), which when followed revolutionises the whole of life. It brings about a transformation in character and galvanises us into action. This action takes the form of purification of the self, and then unceasing effort to establish the laws of God on earth, resulting in a new order based on truth, justice, virtue and goodness. It is at once a faith and a way of life, a religion and a social order, a doctrine and a code of conduct, a set of values and principles and a social movement to realise them in history.

> Each one of you possesses his own formation within his mother's womb, first as a drop of matter for forty days, then as a blood clot for forty days, then as a blob for forty days, and then the angel is sent to breathe life into him (Saying of Prophet Muhammad).

Some prophets were childless and asked God to give them children.

> A mention of the mercy of thy Lord unto His servant Zachariah: When he cried unto his Lord a cry in secret, Saying: My Lord! Lo! the bones of me wax feeble and my head is shining with grey hair, and I have never been unblessed in prayer to Thee, My Lord. Lo! I fear my kinsfolk after me, since my wife is barren. Oh, give me from Thy presence a successor. Who shall inherit of me ad inherit (also) of the house of Yaqoob (Jacob). And make him, my Lord, acceptable (unto Thee). (It was said unto him) O Zachariah! Lo! We bring thee tidings of a son whose name is Yahya (John); we have given the same name to none before (him). He said My Lord! How can I have a son when my wife is barren and I have reached infirm old age? He said so (it will be). Thy Lord sayeth: It is easy for Me, even as I created thee before, when thou was naught (19:2-9).

There are many reasons that cloning can be justifiable for use, but the most convincing reason is that it allows couples with infertility problems to have children. Infertile women will be able to have children by having cloned embryos implanted in them. Also, at the same time for couples, it would eliminate the hassle of going through ordeals of mental and physically painful procedures with a small chance of having children.

The chairman of the OIC group said in his statement at the UN on 'International Convention Against Reproductive Cloning of Human Beings' that the human being is God's creation. Once a human being comes to life, it should not be destroyed or manipulated. The dignity of the human being should always be respected. He also mentioned that we strongly encourage other cloning techniques to produce DNA molecules, organs, plant tissues and cells other than human embryos, and believe that such techniques should be permitted.

STEM CELL RESEARCH

The human body consists of many kinds of cells. These cells are very diverse in their structure and function. For example, neurons that make up the brain are very different from cells that make up our liver, cells that allow our heart to pump blood look nothing like the cells that make up our skin. In spite of their vast differences, however, all cells in the human body contain the same DNA. DNA provides the information, in the form of genes, which is necessary to make all these various cell types. Put simply, liver cells are liver cells because only a small set of genes are turned on in these cells while the rest are shut off. In the same way, cells in the brain or skin have their own set of genes activated, and other sets turned off. However, because all cells contain the entire set of DNA, they possess the information needed to make any kind of cell, though most of this information is not being used.

How do cells become specialised to form the different organs in the body? Human development begins when a sperm cell fuses with an egg cell. This initial fertilised egg, although it is only a single cell, is able to form an entire human being. This cell starts to divide into additional cells, which at this early stage are all able to produce a complete organism. These cells are therefore called totipotent, meaning they have total potential to produce all cell types present in a living human. As development proceeds and an embryo forms, these cells become pluripotent, meaning they have potential to become many different kinds of cells but can no longer give rise to a complete embryo. Later in development, through a process called cell differentiation, these pluripotent cells eventually give rise to the different and more specialised kinds of cells in the body and the different organs begin to form. Such pluripotent cells are referred to as stem cells.

Stem cells are cells that have not gone through the process of cell differentiation and therefore have the potential to give rise to many different kinds of specialised cells. For instance a stem cell could be used to produce liver cells, brain cells, heart muscle cells, blood cells, etc. The current sources of stem cells include embryos (which, as explained above, consist of pluripotent cells) and foetal tissue. In addition, some recent evidence (illustrated graphically below) suggests that even adults have a small number of multipotent cells that can be isolated and can later differentiate into various cell types.

Figure 1

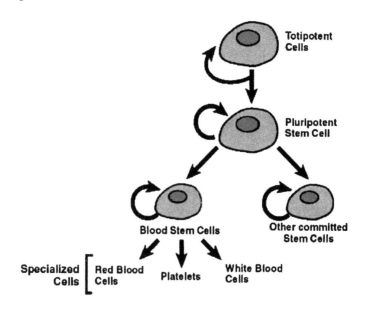

One source of stem cells is from embryos that were formed from a process called in-vitro fertilisation. This is a technique that has been used by doctors for some time, where eggs are removed from a woman after stimulation of the ovaries, and the isolated eggs are then fertilised by sperm cells in the laboratory. The fertilised eggs are allowed to divide for a few cycles and are then implanted into the woman's uterus, where a normal pregnancy can then take place. The purpose of this technique is to allow couples who cannot normally have children to be able to reproduce. The technique is not that efficient, however, and so doctors usually produce several embryos, hoping that at least one will be able to implant correctly in the uterus and start growing. The remaining embryos are either frozen for later use or are destroyed. Recently, scientists found that they can take these embryos at the stage before they are implanted into the uterus (within 1-5 days after fertilisation), and remove pluripotent cells from them. These cells can then be grown and divided on dishes in the laboratory, and then theoretically used to produce all kinds of tissues, from liver cells to heart muscle cells to brain cells.

Research on stem cells has much value both for scientific understanding of human development and for its potential to treat human disease. Many experiments on the effectiveness and safety of new drugs or treatments could be done on cell lines made from stem cells, instead of having to experiment on humans. In addition, stem cells might be used to produce liver cells that can then be formed into a functioning liver and transplanted into patients with liver failure. This would solve the current problem of organ shortage and could also solve the problem of immune rejection of organs. Stem cells might be used to create cells that produce insulin, which can then be transplanted into patients with type I diabetes. In short, stem cells have the potential to cure many diseases ranging from liver disease, diabetes, Alzheimer's and Parkinson's disease, heart disease and spinal cord injury, and the list can go on and on.

To make this potential of stem cells a reality, much research needs to be done in the next few years. For this research, scientists need an ample supply of stem cells. Controversy arises because the main sources of stem cells are embryos used for in-vitro fertilisation. By removing cells from these embryos, scientists are essentially destroying the embryo, which could have otherwise gone on to develop into a child. However, as explained above, these embryos were developed initially in the laboratory solely for the purpose of reproduction and, due to limitations of the in vitro fertilisation technique, these were produced in excess of what was required for this purpose. As a result, the remaining embryos would have either been frozen indefinitely or destroyed. Perhaps if research were limited to using only these already existing embryos, it would be more acceptable than if embryos were created and destroyed specifically for the sake of acquiring stem cells.

Are there any other alternatives? What about stem cells from adults? Some research has shown that even adult humans have a small number of cells that are multipotent, meaning they have the potential to become several different types of specialised cells. The best example of this is cells from the bone marrow. These cells have long been known to be able to produce the different types of blood cells, from white blood cells to red blood cells to platelets involved in blood clotting. Just this past year, a group of researchers showed that some rare bone marrow cells can also be triggered to form fat, cartilage, bone, and muscle. Additional research can theoretically be done on ways to make these multipotent cells become pluripotent; in other words to somehow trigger these cells to go in reverse and become less specialised, and then allow them to differentiate into many kinds of cells. In spite of this interesting research on adult stem cells, it appears that stem cells derived from adults will not be as versatile as stem cells from embryos. Adult stem cells may not be able to provide cells for all kinds of tissues, and in addition they are difficult to isolate because they are so rare in the body. Thus, adult stem cells do not hold as much promise as do stem cells from embryos.

Having recognised that in-vitro fertilisation is permissible in Islam, now the first question that we should ask is whether an embryo that is formed within a few days after an artificial fertilisation, and is not yet in the womb of its mother, should be considered a living being, with all the rights of a human being?

> O mankind! Revere your Lord who created you from a single person and created, of like nature, his mate, and from them twain scattered (like seeds) countless men and women. Revere God through whom you demand your mutual rights and (revere) the womb (that bore you), for God ever watches you (4:1).

According to the Shari'ah, we should make a distinction between actual life and potential life. We should also make a clear distinction between the fertilised ovum in the dish and the fertilised ovum in the womb of its mother. Indeed an embryo is valuable. It has the potential to grow into a human being, but it is not yet a human being. Similarly, there is a big difference in having something in a test tube or dish, or something in the body of a human being. As mentioned above, these embryos were developed initially in the laboratory solely for the sake of reproduction and, due to limitations of the in vitro fertilisation technique, they were produced in excess of what was required for this purpose. As a result, the remaining embryos would have either been frozen indefinitely or destroyed. If these embryos were treated as full human, it would have been forbidden to produce them in excess and to destroy them later. No one treats them as humans. Destroying such embryos is not, and cannot be, called abortion. Muslim jurists have made a clear distinction between the early stages of pregnancy (the first 40 days) and its later stages. It is mentioned that if someone attacks a pregnant woman and aborts her baby in the early stages of her pregnancy, that person's punishment will be less than that of the person who does that during full pregnancy. And if he kills the child after the birth, then he is liable to be punished for homicide.

The second question is whether, according to the Shari'ah, it is acceptable to destroy an embryo for the sake of research, even if this research can potentially cure many otherwise fatal diseases? Our answer is that the embryo in this stage is not human (Siddiqi, n.d.). It is not in its natural environment, the womb. If it is not placed in the womb, it will not survive and it will not become a human being. So there is nothing wrong in doing this research, especially if this research has a potential to cure diseases. However, it is important that we establish strict rules against the misuse of embryos. Research on embryos has the potential for misuse, for instance in regards to the donors of these cells, and we should anticipate what these misuses might be and establish safeguards against them. (For example, doctors might have an infertility patient go through extra cycles of ovulation just so they can obtain more embryos, or they might pay women to produce embryos, or embryos might be obtained without the consent of the donors). In making rules, the authorities should also clarify that there is a difference between the use of 'spare' embryos from in vitro fertilisation procedures, which would be destroyed regardless, as compared to the deliberate production of embryos for stem cell research. Each year thousands of embryos are wasted in fertility clinics around the world. Such embryos should not be wasted, they should be used for research.

It is also good to encourage research on the alternative: to use adult stem cells instead of embryonic or foetal stem cells. This would be much less controversial. However, it seems from the discussion of experts in the field that adult stem cells are not nearly as useful as embryonic stem cells in their ability to differentiate into different cell types, and would therefore not be as applicable in treating many diseases.

There is another important consideration that relates to the ultimate objective or purpose of any undertaking. Islamic teachings place a great deal of emphasis on *Neeyat* (intention). Allah's Apostle said that: 'The reward of deeds depends upon the intentions and every person will get the reward according to what he has intended'. Production of stem cells at the commercial level could easily be an industrial set-up with a stem cell producing factory for the purpose of exploiting others for commercial and monetary returns. This is obviously something that Islam will not approve. However, limited and defined supplies for curing serious diseases would be acceptable. In any such situation, a careful risk/benefit analysis becomes essential, including an attempt to determine the motive, which is not an easy task. This in only one of the major considerations that need to be brought into focus while examining the moral or ethical questions that relate to human reproductive biology.

Until more research is done on this subject and Muslim scholars deliberate in detail on various aspects of stem cell research, the following recommendations seem to be in order:

It is claimed by experts in the field that research on stem cells has great potential to relieve human disease and suffering. If this is the case then it is not only allowed but it is obligatory to pursue this research.

The use of embryonic stem cells should be limited and regularly monitored. From an Islamic point of view the appropriate practice would be to only allow isolation of stem cells from frozen embryos that were created for the purpose of in vitro fertilisation and would otherwise have been destroyed. Such usage would also require the informed consent of all parties involved. Safeguards against monetary compensation to embryo donors and against the creation of embryos in excess of what is required for in vitro fertilisation should be developed.

Perhaps research using stem cells derived from adults will eventually prove to be most promising. We should encourage further research on the use of adult stem cells, to the point where it will be unnecessary to use embryos for this purpose. Specifically, we should find better ways to isolate existing stem cells in the human body.

The modern age has seen such novelties as sperm banks, in vitro fertilisation, and surrogate mothers. Few people know how to take an ethical approach to these complex ethical issues. Surrogate motherhood, for example, is not acceptable because the new-born will not be aware of his/her mother as well as his lineage. Surrogate motherhood also creates social and psychological complications. By analogy, this would rule out almost all forms of surrogate motherhood, as the sperm that goes into producing the embryo is foreign to the host body in this case. The only exception to the last two cases is where a wife's ovaries are sterile but her womb is healthy, in which case (with the consent of all parties) the husband's sperm may be combined in-vitro with an ovum from a female donor (a process called 'egg donation') and placed in the wife's womb. Since she will nurture the baby for nine months until birth, she will be the natural and biological mother.

The artificial improvement of human beings will be practised as soon as the means become available. Many people will want to protect their children against genetic disease, against genetically preventable illnesses, or may even wish to enhance their intelligence, beauty, or other traits. The trouble is that once the means become available, other societies will also begin to have similar ideas. The memory of Nazi doctors sterilising Jews and killing defective children still lingers. The desire to better one's own breed and worsening the enemy's breed—however one happens to define that enemy—could become more irresistible as biotechnology hurdles are circumvented.

The important thing is to outline the basic approach and guiding principles that can be used to address the questions that come up from time to time. The following table summarises the Islamic view on some of the questions that are being debated based on the currently available information and the discussions that have taken place so far.

Table 1. Islamic views on issues related to genomics

Issue	Islamic point of view
Gender Selection	Gender selection is interference in the deeds of the Creator and Islam would never grant the choice of gender. Islam teaches one to be content with the Will of God.
Patenting of Human DNA	Research of a commercial nature leading to exploitation of others is not allowed.
Human Cloning	The cloning of humans, males or females, would be a disaster for the world. This would be the case whether the aim was to improve quality and select the offspring that is smarter, stronger, braver, healthier or more beautiful, or to increase the number in order to increase the population or make the state stronger. This would be a cause of evil. It is *Haram* and not allowed.
Embryonic Stem Cell	Issue is still being debated.
Surrogate Motherhood	Since marriage is a contract between the wife and husband during the span of their marriage, no third party should intrude into the marital functions of sex and procreation. Surrogate motherhood is not acceptable because the new-

	born will not be aware of his/her mother and lineage. 'None can be their mother except those who gave birth' (58:2). The only exception to the last two cases where a wife's ovaries are sterile but her womb is healthy, in which case (with the consent of all parties) the husband's sperm may be combined in vitro with an ovum from a female donor (a process called 'egg donation'), and placed in the wife's womb. Since she will nurture the baby for nine months until birth, she will be the natural and biological mother.
Gene Therapy	From a Muslim perspective human gene therapy should be restricted to therapeutic indications. Somatic cell gene therapy is encouraged, since it should lead to remedy and alleviation of human suffering. However, enhancement genetic engineering or eugenic genetic engineering would involve changing God's creation, which may lead to an imbalance of the whole universe and must therefore be prohibited. Gene therapy to manipulate hereditary traits such as intelligence, stupidity, stature, beauty or ugliness may unbalance human existence.
Infertility Therapeutic Cloning	In Islam, some treatments of infertility are allowed and encouraged. It is essential if it involves the preservation of procreation and treatment of infertility in one partner of the married couple.
Prenatal Diagnosis	If the decision not to transfer is performed to protect the mother's life or health or because of a foetal anomaly incompatible with life, it is acceptable.
Human Cloning	Based on current knowledge, the efficiency of embryonic development after nuclear transfer is so low, and the chance of abnormal offspring so high, that experimentation of this sort on human beings would be achieved at great risk to the offspring. Moreover, the deliberate generation of

	cloned human beings could infringe upon the dignity and integrity of human individuals. Cloning a human being is thus an unethical and reprehensible act.
Artificial Insemination with donor sperm	In Islam, Artificial Insemination by Donor is absolutely forbidden except if it involves the woman's husband.
Genetic Screening	For detection of genetic abnormalities and possible cure of birth defects, genetic screening would be acceptable.
Genetic Counselling	Acceptable

This is obviously an ongoing and open-ended debate in which new scientific discoveries or technical breakthroughs for manipulating human genetic material will have to be continually reviewed. What is needed is to have the kind of dialogue and discussion like the one carried out in this volume. Such an exchange also provides an opportunity to critically examine our individual perspectives with an open mind, intellectual integrity and objectivity.

COMSTECH has recently set up an International Committee on Bioethics to address the bioethical issues raised by the latest innovations in the field of human reproductive biology. Religious scholars and researchers from different member countries have been contacted for input and suggestions, especially on issues that need to be addressed from an Islamic point of view. International bodies like COMSTECH can play a pivotal role in addressing these issues by organising seminars and discussions among religious scholars and research scientists.

NOTE

[1] *The author is thankful to Ikram Abbasi for his help in the preparation of this manuscript*

BIBLIOGRAPHY

Kegley, J. (2000) Genetic Knowledge: Human Values and Responsibility, Lexington.

Kline, R.M. (2001) 'Whose blood is it, anyway?' Scientific American, 284, no. 4.

Nasim, A. 'Ethical Implications of Modern Researches in Genetics', paper presented at Seminar by the Islamic Educational, Scientific and Cultural Organization and the World Islamic Call Society, University of Qatar, 1993.

Nasim, A. 'Genetic Manipulations, Biotechnology and Ethical Issues: New Challenges for Muslim Scholars', paper presented at International Conference on Science in Islamic Polity in the Twenty-first Century, 1995.

Nasim, A. 'Ethical Issues of the Human Genome Project: An Islamic Perspective', paper presented at UNESCO Conference on Bioethics in Asia, 1997.

Nasim, A. 'Genetic Engineering: State-of-the-Art', monograph prepared for ISESCO, 1992.

Serour, G.I. and Omran, A. 'Genetics, Ethics and Human Values. Genome Mapping, Genetic Screening and Gene Therapy: Ethical Issues', paper presented at XXVIth CIOMS Conference, Geneva, 1992.

Serour, G.I. (ed.) (1997) 'Islamic Perspectives on Genetic Technology and Information Use', in Serour, G.I. 'Human Cloning, its Applications and Ethical Guidelines', paper presented at the Conference on The Cloning Dilemma, Dubai, April 1998.

Serour, G.I. (2000) 'Ethical Implications of Human Embryo Research', Islamic Educational, Scientific and Cultural Organization (ISESCO).

Siddiqi, M. (n.d.) 'An Islamic Perspective on Stem Cells Research'. Online. Available HTTP: <www.islamicity.com>.

Chapter 3

Impact of Modern Genetics: A Sikh Perspective

Gursatej Gandhi

INTRODUCTION

The Indian peninsular sub-continent, with an ancient culture dating back to the fifth century, is perhaps the most diverse in the world, both genetically and culturally. The high level of biodiversity, apparent from over 122,000 wild species of plants and animals, and the human cauldron of over 4,635 ethnic communities, reflect the geographical location of India at the junction of African, northern Eurasian and Oriental regions (Singh 1992;Gadgil et al 2000:100; Malhotra 2000:253). Major ethnic groups include Indo-Aryan (72%), Dravidian (25%), Mongoloid and others (3%).

This cultural heritage and biological diversity have been culprits in the relentless exploration and exploitation of India. Cultural diversity contributed to the tendency to isolate and subjugate subordinated communities, rather than absorb them, whenever different peoples at different times came in search of India's biological wealth, while biological diversity has nurtured exploration and exploitation of the country's ecological regimes. Of importance here is the structure of human populations, with variable levels of inbreeding, large families, large numbers of rare genetic mutations and disorders, and so forth.

The post-human genomic era and its spin-offs have rekindled interest in the genetic makeup of Indian biological wealth, in the search for ways to improve human life. Furthermore, as many as 1,500 languages and dialects reflect the linguistic diversity of India. In the Indian context, we regard people as unique individuals, who are intimately connected to the community by relationships to others in the present, past and future. In addition, the world's largest democracy is highly diverse in a cultural-religious sense and includes citizens from major religions like: Hinduism (80%), Islamic culture (14%), Christianity (2.4%), Sikhism (2.0%), Buddhism (0.7%), Jainism (0.5%) and others (0.4 %).

On the one hand, contemporary advancements in molecular biology and genetic engineering promise significant improvements in the quality of human life. On the other hand, however, the magnitude of human suffering flowing from poverty, belligerence and eco-degradation is as great as ever. As a country rife with natural calamities, infectious diseases and cultural taboos, India suffers from a multitude of problems: the tip of the iceberg is the fact that one-third of its one billion inhabitants live in poverty. The situation is abysmal. According to tradition, a doctor is revered as a demi-god, but India currently has only one doctor for every 2,508 people (Das 2002), creating a wide disparity in health care: it is available for those who can pay and rationed for those who cannot. Is it any wonder that in the context of India's enormous problems, modern genetic medicine and genetic engineering have not been major topics of public debate? To encourage discourse on these issues, this paper presents a synoptic perspective on the impact of modern genetics, held by many residents in Punjab, especially by Sikhs.

SIKHISM

The word "Sikh" means disciple. Sikhs believe in an omniscient, omnipotent and omnipresent God, and its religion is Sikhism. There are about 20 million Sikhs and most of them live in Punjab,

India. As many as 250,000 Sikhs reside in Canada, around 500,000 live in the US and about half-a-million have settled in the UK. In fact, Sikhism is the third largest religion in Great Britain (Barriar 2000; BBC online).

Sikhism is a young religion, barely 530 years old. It is synthetic in character. The founders, the ten Sikh *gurus* (teachers), adopted whatever was practical, good and useful for humanity, rejecting ritualism, formalism, and parochialism in order to improve the well-being as well as moral and spiritual discipline of humanity. The laws of God work in every sphere, i.e., the physical, moral and spiritual sphere. Sikhs believe that worldly phenomena result in bodily ailment, which is the physical law of causation. The law of *karma* is the moral law of causation moulded by our past and present actions. The spiritual law of love is the most significant: devotion of the Lord is love of the Lord, and this leads to self-realisation and salvation. Sikhism is a very synthetic religion: it accepts the law of *karma* (predestination) as enunciated by Hinduism, the Islamic doctrine of *hukam* (Arabic for judgement or legal decision), the Jewish and Christian doctrine of grace, the Buddhist concept of the four noble truths, the four cardinal virtues of Hinduism and the *tri-ratna* of Jainism, the spiritual ascent of Sufism and Confucian ideas about state and society (Kohli 1974).

Self- restraint in everyday life (rather than self-indulgence, self-denial or asceticism) is the golden rule for preparing the soul for salvation. The individual pulsates with vitality because of the soul. The soul is pure consciousness, the 'higher self' with no powers and ego; the 'lower self' has free will (faculties of mind) with the objective of obeying the will of God. Free will acts on the plane of ego, where providence never interferes. There is a systematic evolution of the soul as it passes through the mineral, vegetative and animal worlds. The Sikh scripture identifies 840,000 species with the human being as the climax of creation, for only by being born a human can realisation of God be achieved.

Each birth and death is considered hell. Before human birth, the soul passes through 840,000 hells for each act conducted. Sikhs neither desire heaven nor fear hell as these result from ego and actions in the world. There is no pressure to perform. Rather, remembering God in company, *Saad Sangath*, is imperative in Sikhism.

SIKH ETHICS

The main sources of Sikh ethics are the holy scripture, *The Adi Granth* (the first holy manuscript), and *Vaars* (verses) of Bhai Gurdas, the most famous exponent of Sikh tenets and the first interpreter of Sikh faith. The main tenets are truthful living, purity, justice, fearlessness, love, mercifulness, generosity, tolerance, sweet speech, humility and goodness. Sikh social, economic and political ethics include non-discrimination on the basis of caste or creed, as opposed to the "hidden apartheid" of caste-based discrimination, affecting 250 million people in Asia (Narula 2002); communal harmony; subsistence for physical and spiritual well-being; great reverence for women; the institution of marriage (a spiritual bond); prohibition of child marriage; acceptance of widow re-marriage; promotion of limited and compact families; opposition to exploitation and injustice; encouragement of community meals; and respect for all professions. The Sikh motto is 'service' and its slogan is 'excelsior'.

PUNJAB

Punjab, the land of five rivers, covers an area of 50,362 sq. km. and in 2001 had a population of 24,289,296, with a literacy rate of 75.63% among males and 63.55% among females. The 1999-2000 poverty ratios in urban areas was 5.75% and in rural areas 6.35%, representing a drop of 5.61% compared to the 1993-94 data, as a result of high agricultural growth (Economic Survey 2001-02; Satyanarayanan 2002). The Punjabi people (Sikhs as well as Hindus and minority religious groups) are relatively affluent and enterprising, and generally maintain an opulent life style. Agriculture is the main occupation of the Sikhs although they excel in other fields too. There is, however, a preference for sons over daughters: the male is regarded as the head of the family, there is male dominance in all matters regarding consent, and a male is required to light the funeral pyre.

SIKH BIOETHICS

In Hindu and Sikh traditions, especially in the Punjab, the distinction between religion and culture is minimal. Ethical decisions are grounded in both religious beliefs and culture values. The Punjabis take a duty- rather than a rights-based approach. In fact there is no equivalent word for 'rights', neither in Hindi nor in Punjabi. Furthermore, the ethical agent in decision-making is not the individual; rather a person is viewed as a combination of mind, soul and body in the context of family, culture and environment. Ethical matters, therefore, necessitate an understanding of the person's social as well as religious and spiritual contexts (Coward and Sidhu 2000: 1167).

God-fearing Sikhs calmly accept infertility, abnormal children in the family or aberrant reproductive organs, because they are consequences of destiny and past misdemeanours. In fact, They believe that these preordained outcomes tone down one's ego. So-called neo-Sikhs, however, strive for modernism, wealth and recognition in society—though the veneer of godliness, religious discourse and worship in *Gurudwaras* (Sikh Temples) remains. Issues concerning current scientific advancements are only of interest if they affect financial or societal gain. It is left to the intelligentsia (a small elite) to debate and study these issues. Only the older academics still view science with a religious overtone. A general trend with regard to the religious ethos is its individual convenience and its function as a fashionable ritual that is rather disconnected from science or a scientific attitude.

Generally, the older Punjabis still adhere to the traditional duty-based approach towards treatment options or medical interventions. The younger ones, though, are rapidly acclimatising to the rights-based approach, just like the second and third generation of Punjabis in the West, who have acculturated themselves to western bioethics (Coward and Sidhu 2000).

PREVENTIVE GENETIC MEASURES

In ancient Vedic texts (from 3000 B.C.), the foetus is regarded as a person with awareness (equating foetal life to adult life), while foetus killing is condemned as a cardinal sin (Azariah 1997). Among Sikhs, religious beliefs explicitly underline that the moment of conception is the rebirth of a fully-developed person, who has lived many previous lives. Each human being is born with a purpose and birth is never accidental. Each person has a store of memory traces from previous lives, which together with exercising free will in the present life, will influence rebirth in the next one. The life of the foetus is pristine. The Sikh scripture describes how the foetus prays for salvation, even when it is upside down in the womb. To be born as a human is a gift, for only through human birth can salvation be achieved by devotion to the Lord and service to humanity. Termination of a pregnancy by abortion, therefore, sends the soul back into the karmic cycle of rebirth.

The Sikh *gurus* strictly condemned and abhorred the practice of *sati*, and Sikhs have never been involved in female foeticide (for reasons of dowry and social stigma). Hence prenatal diagnosis for sex selection is traditionally condemned. Neo-Punjabis, in contrast, have taken to prenatal diagnosis for sex selection like a duck to water since the standardisation of ultrasonography for sex selection occurred during the late 1970s (Singh 1998: 398). They do so with a clear conscience, because they value economic stability, a norm of two children per family and social status.

The sex ratio in the 1991 census of Punjab was 1000 males to 874 females, the lowest in the country (Encyclopaedia Britannica India). A recent report in a local newspaper (Expert News Service 2002) noted that Punjab has the dubious distinction of having 10 districts (out of 15) with a declining sex ratio. A survey based on registers maintained in six nursing homes in Amritsar during the period 1999-2000 revealed a ratio of 1000 males to 829 females (unpublished data). It is significant to point out that more males have been recorded as being born in Sikh than in Hindu families, because this indicates that female foeticide does take place (despite the fact that no records of female foeticide exist). The headline of the article, which stated that 'every fifth Punjabi girl child is missing' (Expert News Service 2002), suggested that denial of traditional values is socially acceptable among Punjabis. The article further observes that since 1971 the sex ratio in the state has declined, not so much due technological advancement, but probably more because of the affluence and opulent life-style of Punjabis, who consequently emphasize the need for a male heir. The worst sex ratio has been recorded in the Malwa region, which is among the wealthier regions, while the most favourable ration has been recorded in Doaba, a predominantly agricultural sector that is rich but not opulent (Institute for Development and Communication spokesperson).

Legally, the Prenatal Diagnostic Technique Act of 1994 only allows screening for genetic disorders in government-approved institutes, yet female foeticide prevails anyway. Falling social moral values in all strata of society—whether illiterate, highly educated or professionally qualified—contribute to this malpractice, aided by medical practitioners, who indulge in it for financial gains despite the Consumer Protection Act of 1986 (Verma 1998: 215). Those in government hospitals, who charge nominal fees, however, have been exempted. Various state government agencies and medical associations are now questioning the declining sex ratio and the lack of implementation of the legislation (PCMSA 2002). The Sikh clergy, through its religious and Sikh temple organisations, have issued a decree condemning female foeticide, but it remains to be seen whether this will change Sikh behaviour (Sikh Clergy 2001).

The society *per se* has broadened its perspective in this context: those who can afford it can request prenatal diagnosis for sex selection or genetic disorders and abort a flawed foetus. Presently, the only facility for prenatal genetic diagnosis in the northwestern region is in Amritsar (Centre for Genetic Disorders, GNDU), although there is another one in Delhi. Limited public knowledge about genetic conditions has also led deeply religious and underprivileged Sikhs to continue regarding genetic disorders as part of their destiny. Genetic counselling, whenever and wherever provided, tends to be directive rather than suggestive, especially if provided by medical doctors, who are still regarded as demi-gods.

Pre-symptomatic, pre-conceptional and pre-implantation testing, as well as carrier screening, are considered individual ethical issues (Table 1). Lack of educational materials, media coverage (usually limited to positive scientific discourse), public lectures and debates have generally led to ignorance about human genetic disorders and treatments, except among those who are directly involved.

CLONING AND STEM CELL RESEARCH

The dilemma of cloning humans has barely affected the ordinary Sikh. If in advanced European nations 45% of the persons interviewed was neither interested in science nor informed about science and technology (Spit 2001), can the people in developing nations be blamed for their apathy? The literacy rate in Punjab is not synonymous with awareness about scientific achievements and endeavours. The general trend observed has been that the educated few either fully support or completely oppose cloning. The Sikh diaspora, in one of its online discussion forums, tried to engage in discourse on human cloning in the wake of condemning statements by the Vatican. However, these discussions failed to produce a consensus. Another forum recently decreed that Sikhism is neither for nor against cloning and stem cell research.

Personal interviews with literates outside the realm of science revealed their ignorance about cloning, while the nouveaux riches and those unable to conceive favored the cloning of humans without considering the consequences. The Department of Biotechnology has condemned human cloning but has also earmarked grants for embryonic stem cell research, albeit only from discarded IVF embryos. In fact, there are not too many ethical concerns at present, although scientists and officials agree that donor consent is essential. Institutes in Delhi, Hyderabad, Mumbai and Bangalore are already carrying out research on stem cells. Reliance Life Sciences in Mumbai is ranked third among the top ten institutes working on stem-cell research by the National Institute of Health of the US (Gupta 2001). The media has also only provided coverage on the benefits of stem-cell research. Only a few articles have debated the impact of human cloning on familial inter-relationships, property rights and emotional conditions, leaving out the ethical aspects.

Interactive discussions with scientists and geneticists reveal that most did not feel the need for nuclear cloning, while cloning for therapeutic measures was abhorred for ethical reasons. The post-graduate students of my department welcomed and approved the latter, but observed that human cloning should only be permissible for research purposes. Religious sentiments did not seem to influence their views. Interestingly, the discussion has recently veered in favor of organ donation (legalised as the Organ Transplantation Act, 1994), equating it to therapeutic cloning (Dureja 1994: 207).

GENETICALLY MODIFIED ORGANISMS (SUBSTITUTE CROPS)

Punjab is an agriculturally oriented territory and Punjabi farmers have grown accustomed to modern gadgetry and the cultivation of new varieties of crops. However, their families have generally moved to the urban areas, and so most of them now rent their land on a contractual basis. Currently, crops include wheat, rice, cotton, seasonal vegetables, sugarcane, maize, barley, and pulses.

In Vedic culture, cosmogony suggests that there is a link between human behaviour and dietary food systems (Azariah 1997). Agro-farming in India followed a 12-grain system to avoid famines and to insure against crop failure with chaff (for fuel and fodder) and ashes (dye for clothes) also being put to use. These plants have been regarded as having divine, curative and healing powers; they often served as herbal medicine. Harvesting and planting of food grains have been accompanied by ritualistic traditions. In Punjab, *Baisakhi* is celebrated with great fervour and various festivities mark the harvest season.

Of all the issues discussed here, the Indian population has paid most attention to genetically modified (GM) crops–through media coverage, public debates and collective protests—although primarily in the southern and western states and the metropolis rather than the Punjab. In the capital and in other states, campaigns against WTO, GM crops and TRIPS have been common. Some of the most prominent ones include the 'Bija Satyagraha' on March 5,1999, when 1500 groups nation-wide protested in Gandhian fashion against seed colonisation (Shiva 1999). A Delhi-based group filed a suit against Monsanto and the Indian government against cotton field trials and called for a five-year moratorium on GMOs till safety evaluations have been completed (Foundation for Science, Technology and Ecology 1999). China and 11 other nations formed an alliance to fight biopiracy (Stevenson 2002). Another group, Gene Compaign, has several hundred members and 35 core groups in various states, including Punjab, to protect farmers' rights and oppose patenting of indigenous crops (Sahai 2001).

However, some farmer groups are demanding the right to use GM crops in the wake of crop failure due to insect resistance (Agri Conclave 2002). Farmers in Punjab's cotton-growing belt are not aware of the GM crops, but were more than willing to try out new 'wonder seeds' since insecticides had proved totally ineffective against the cotton boll worm. But the farmers are ignorant about the risks of using GM seeds. Dr. S. S. Marwaha, director of Biotechnology at the Punjab State Council for Science and Technology observed: 'The decision to ban or go ahead with the genetically modified crop has to come from the centre. States have not been given any powers to take such decisions'. In Gujarat, where about 2000 hectares of GM cotton were planted this year, the centre instructed the state to burn it. The Genetic Engineering Approval Committee (GEAC) has prosecuted Navbharat Seeds, a local company that supplied the seeds. Reports also indicate that GM cotton is being grown in Andhra Pradesh and Punjab.

It has been argued that the first green revolution in the 1960s and 1970s depended on chemical outputs, while the second by Monsanto and other companies probably plans greater disruption with more than 18 GM crops already available. About 30 of the 300,000 plant species are edible, while only 20 are commonly used. Of these, six are cereals used as food and only ten species provide for 80% of the global food requirement (Azariah 1997). Hence, bioengineering seems like a necessity rather than an option. But the price to pay is that the pollen from GM crops can disperse over 60 metres by wind and consequently affect non-target species, causing cross-pollination hazards. GM pollen can result in allergenicity, replace the polyculture pattern of agro-farming and promote horizontal gene transfer, seed-dependency and genetic uniformity. In other words, bioengineering creates an imbalanced ecosystem and no one knows what kind of a legacy it will leave behind. The farmers will become slaves in the 'bio-serfdom' of the multinational companies (MNCs) and become victims of the 'third wave of colonialism'.

GM plants are not just (future) means for eradicating hunger. Food scarcity has often resulted from social and political factors. Indigenous knowledge and socio-religious cultures have effectively preserved biodiversity. Is this to be lost to the MNCs because of apathy among the experts, illiteracy among the agriculturists and the ostrich-like policy of the government? The holes in existing legislation can negate written agreements. This backhanded approach has resulted in field trials of GM cotton being carried out in southern states and in the Punjab.

OVERVIEW

Bioethics as the 'Love of Life' (Macer 1994) no longer has a place in the present-day scenario. Heritage and culture are either considered old fashioned or used by the media to portray 'the good old days'. The average Sikh (Punjabi) is more interested in amassing wealth, while the poor are struggling to survive. Religion was traditionally a source for developing human values and dignity, but it no longer serves this function. The societal stance, garbed in wealth (for with it, according to an old Punjabi saying, comes wisdom) categorically usurps religion and traditions to buy health care/medical interventions in order to create a successful human being. This points to future moments of anxiety, as the chasm between the have and the have-nots may exceed all limits and cause a revolution (akin to the French Revolution). In a caste-ridden set-up, the finding that the upper caste Indian male population is genetically closer to Europeans than the lower castes (which, like women, are regarded as more "Asian") can further promote genetic discrimination and lead to a 'genetic underclass'. The Science and Technology system as well as the 'higher' self of people needs to be refurbished. Guided by ethics, new genetic issues can be discussed and solved in order to realise the long-range benefits for the human condition.

The overall conclusion regarding modern genetics from a Sikh perspective is that the reaction of people depends on their level of education (rather than mere literacy), their attitudes towards science, their urban or rural roots, their socio-economic status and on whether their religious beliefs are moderate or fundamentalist.

BIBLIOGRAPHY

Ad Hoc Working Group on Biosafety. 'The Hijacking of Indian science by Monsanto', Cartagena, Columbia, February 1999.

Agri Conclave. 'Farmers for greater say on GM crops', *Hindu Business Line* (14 February, 2002).

Azariah, J., Azariah, H. and Macer, D. R.J. Macer (eds) (1997) 'Bioethics in India: Proceedings of the International Bioethics Workshop in Madras: Biomanagement of Biogeo-resources', University of Madras, Eubios Ethics Institute, January 1997. Online.   Available   HTTP: <http://www.biol.tsukuba.ac.jp/~macer/index.html>   (accessed January 1997).

Barriar, N.G., 'The Sikh Diaspora'. Ministry of External Affairs, Government   of   India.   Online.   Available   HTTP: http://meadev.nic.in/perspec/khalsa-spl99/kh9.html   BBC's Home page, 'Religion and ethics'. Online. Available URL: http://www.bbc.co.uk/religion/religions/sikhism/index.html

Coward,   H, Sidhu, T. (2000) 'Bioethics for Clinicians: Hinduism and Sikhism', *Canadian Medical Association Journal*, 163, no. 9: 1167-1170.

Das, A ., 'Anaesthesia experts won't swallow capsule'. *Indian Express*, 19 February, 2002.

Dureja, G.P. (1994) 'The transplantation of the human organs, Act 1994', *Journal of Anesthetic Clinical Pharmacology*, 11: 207-211. Encyclopaedia Britannica, Economic Survey of India (2000-01).

Express News Service, 'Every fifth Punjabi girl child is 'missing', *Amritsar Newsline* (5 March, 2002).

Foundation for Science, Technology and Ecology, 'India Complies with WTO ruling on TRIPS, *Bridges Weekly Trade News Agency Digest*, 3, no. 10, 15 March, 1999.

Gadgil, M., Joshi, N.V., Shambu Prasad, U.V., Manoharan, S., Patil, S. (1997), in D. Balasubramanian and N. Appaji Rao (eds) *The Indian Human Heritage*, Hyderabad: Hyderabad University Press: 100-129.

Gupta, S. 'The Stem Cell Saga', *The Week*, 16 September, 2001.ICAR Conference on GM crops, *Times News Network*, 6 November, 2001.

Kohli, S.S. (1974) *Sikh Ethics*, Delhi: Munshiram Manoharlal Publishers [85].

Malhotra, K.C. (1998) *Bioethical issues in Human Genetics in India*, in N. Fujiki and D.R.J. Macer (eds) *Bioethics in Asia*. Madras: Eubios Ethics Institute [253].

Punjab Civil Medical Services Association (PCMSA), 'Incentives Sought for Families with Girls Only', *The Tribune*, 9 March, 2002.

Narula, S., Devraj, R. 'Rights-India: Study on Caste's Origins in Race Undercuts Government Stance', Press release, World Conference against Racisim.

Sahai, S., 'Protecting Farmers' rights under WTO', *The Sunday Times*, 16 September, 2001.

Satyanarayanan, S., 'Poverty down to low of 26 percent', *The Tribune*, 27 February, 2002.

Shiva, V., 'GE protests begin in India. A new freedom movement against a new colonization', *Snowball Archive* (5 March , 1999).

Sikh Clergy, 'Takht Bans Female Foeticide-Offenders to be Excommunicated', *The Tribune*, 18 April, 2001.

Singh, J.R. (1998) 'Bioethics of sex preference', in N. Fujiki and D.R.J. Macer (eds) *Bioethics in Asia*, Madras: Eubios Ethics Institute.

Singh, S ., 'Officials Yet to Cotton on to Bt Cotton Spectre', *The Times of India*, 23 November, 2001.

Singh, K.S. (2001) *People of India: An introduction. Anthropological Survey of India*, Calcutta.

Stevenson, S., 'China, Brazil, India and Nine Other Countries Form Alliance against Biopiracy', Associated Press News Release (19 February, 2002).

Verma, I.C. (1998) 'Ethics and the Human Genome Studies and Genetic Services in India', in N. Fujiki and D.R.J. Macer (eds) *Bioethics in Asia*, Madras: Eubios Ethics Institute

Chapter 4

Hindu Bioethics, the Concept of Dharma and Female Infanticide in India

Santishree Pandit

INTRODUCTION

Hindu religion is multifaceted: it does not have a single founder and is not confined to a single book. Hence I use the concept of *dharma* in Shruti literature[1] and the Mahabharata[2] to discuss ethics regarding the treatment of women. There are two Hindu conceptions of the female: one as *Draupadi*, the strong one who controls all around her, the other as *Sita*, a docile yet self-respecting woman. But nowhere does the concept of dharma permit the use of medical methods to discriminate and kill female infants. This chapter explores the roots of this practice. Hindu tradition is diverse, but the practice of female infanticide in the state of Tamil Nadu is baffling. For it is a society where the Manusmritis has clearly rejected derogatory treatment of women. References to gender discrimination are also absent in Tamil Sangam literature.

Hinduism is not just a religion, but also a philosophical process as well as a way of life.[3] Hence there has been a celebration of diversity and cultural pluralism. Since it is not like other, monotheistic religions, multiple interpretations are possible. Although its view of gender is usually patriarchic, it highlights the importance of female dignity. This, one can see in the character of *Sita* when she has to return to her husband *Rama*,[4] but instead prefers go to her mother. Similarly, *Kannagi* in Sangam Tamil literature is the symbol of chastity but also of righteous power, expressed when her errant husband *Kovalan* becomes attached to the learned courtesan *Madhavi*. Madhavi is portrayed as the symbol of beauty with brains. She is not a cheap prostitute but a sophisticated beauty well accomplished in music, dance and poetry. The most radical representation of a liberated woman is *Draupadi*, who decided her own destiny and that of her five husbands, the Pandava brothers. She was a woman that kept the spirit of revenge high with the help of her cousin Krishna.

BALANCE WITH NATURE

> Let there be balance in space! Let there be balance in the sky! Let there be peace on earth! Let there be calmness in water! Let there be growth of plants! Let there be growth of trees! Let there be grace in all gods! Let there be bliss in the Brahman! Let there be peace! Let such peace be with everyone of us! (Sukla Yajurveda 36: 17).

Human societies everywhere are closely linked to their natural surroundings. These human societies are facing a problem that threatens the interdependence of Planet Earth and requires a reorientation of the discourses that have dominated the world. Can these hegemonic discourses be contested from alternative perspectives? I will attempt to construct a discourse on the basis of religious ideologies and consider issues related to biomedical testing and ethics from a very different perspective. The issue of civilisational differences has been one of the main debates following the Cold War, after the withdrawal and break-up of the Soviet Union. In the preceding bipolar world, relations and policies evolved on the basis of whether one was liberal democratic or communist. The USA and her allies saw 'red' forces everywhere. But now the demise of the Soviet Union has brought the issue of the 'Clash of Civilisations' into the forefront (Huntington 1994). Its main thesis is that the future battle lines will be drawn along the fault lines of civilisations. Huntington argues that the West is representative of Christian civilisation, with values and ideas that are unique but not universal, as opposed to Islamic civilisation. In his eyes Hindu civilization is not opposed to the West or in conflict with it. And he considers Buddhist civilisation as part of Hindu civilisation.

Doubts about the hegemonic discourse of the West and its failure to bring about a universalisation of values have led to a search for alternatives. Western civilisation has always believed in man's control over nature, which has resulted in the unravelling of the mysteries of nature and man's exploitation of nature. The Industrial Revolution and subsequent urbanisation made the European powers search for new pastures for trade and commerce. This led to the colonisation of Asia and Africa. Colonialism meant the exploitation of natural resources of the colonies in the South and their alienation—socially, economically as well as politically. This has also been a problem in Asia, though to a lesser extent. But the fear is that these repercussions will be worldwide. To deal with these developments, a need has come about to see all people and environment as a single family 'Vasudeiva Kutumbakam', the world as a single family.

The dominance of hegemonic discourse has been so pervasive that Galtung (1996) calls for a 'culture of peace' and regards Hindu and Buddhist civilisations as innately superior to Western Christian civilisation. On issues of peace, he promotes an inter-civilisational dialogue rather than a one-sided hegemonic interpretation as part of (post) colonial constructs of the 'White man's burden' and the 'civilising force of western values on the Orient'. This concept of the Orient as opposite, inferior, enigmatic and monolithic is also a construction of the West, especially that of colonialism and cultural imperialism (Said 1988). For Galtung, the philosophies of Hinduism and Buddhism offer 'a spirit of diversity, symbiosis and equity'. He also suggests that there is a need for a thorough transformation of violent Western culture and sees the present hegemonic discourse as a kind of Western exclusivism in which Oriental social thought and practices are marginalised.

HINDUISM AS NATURE-CENTRIC

This chapter uses the word 'Hindu' in the modern sense of the term, which came into parlance in the nineteenth century and depicts all the religious practices of the Indian sub-continent (Kaviraj 1997). It seeks to uncover the core of Hindu thought, indulging in Hindu fundamentalism for the sake of argument. To begin with, I emphasise that Hindu thought is nature-centric rather than anthropocentric: it regards man as part of the ecological system, not as separate from it. It brings out the symbiotic relationship between man and his environment, that is, the survival and well-being of human beings to a very large extent depends on the survival and well-being of nature.

This attempt to study the past from the present raises two issues regarding the interpretation of history. One, it is important to note that ancient Hindu texts did not deal exclusively with the environment. They were texts of religion, medicine, law and literature. However, any literature is a reflection of its culture, which contains predetermined notions about the environment. Two, the people of the Vedas and other texts were not suffering from man-made ecological chaos; they lived in harmony with an abundant nature. The construction of the past also has to be selective, for irrelevant concepts have to be ignored. For instance, *Bahuprajathav*, that is 'abundant progeny', was honoured in ancient India. Today its practical application would not only be absurd and out of place, but disastrous for India's ecology, economy and development.

THE CONCEPT OF DHARMA

Hindu jurisprudence (*Vyavahara Dharmasastra*) is embedded in Dharma as propounded in the Vedas, Puranas, Smritis and other traditional works. Dharma is an important Sanskrit expression and there is no corresponding word in any other language. It has a wide variety of meanings. For instance, the word Dharma is used to mean justice (Nyaya), what is right in given circumstances; moral, religious, or righteous conduct; being helpful to living beings; giving charity or alms; natural qualities or characteristics of living beings and things; and duty, law or custom having the force of law.

The Origin of Dharma

In the Mahabharata, Bhishma defines Dharma as that which contributes to the upliftment of living beings, that which ensures their welfare. Madhavacharya, the Minister to Hakka and Bukka, founder kings of the Vijayanagar Empire, concisely explains the meaning of Dharma as 'that which sustains and ensures progress and welfare of all in this world and eternal bliss in the other world. The Dharma is promulgated in the form of commands'. Dharma therefore embraces many types of righteous conduct, covering every aspect of life essential for the sustenance and welfare of individuals and society, including the rules that guide and enable those who believe in God to attain moksha (eternal bliss).

Dharma was founded as the solution to eternal problems originating from natural human instinct. The historical source of Manu[5] states that the force behind every action of a human behind is his desire (*kama*). Natural desires were found to be the desire to have sexual and emotional enjoyment and wealth, i.e. material pleasure (*artha*). Artha is explained by the Vatsayana sutra as connoting material wealth such as gold, cattle, corn and education or knowledge necessary to earn wealth.[6] The source of all evil actions of human beings was traced to the desire for material pleasure, which in turn gave rise to conflicts of interest among individuals. The desire (kama) of human beings could also be influenced by the other impulses inherent in human beings such as anger (*krodha*), passion (*moha*), greed (*lobha*), infatuation (*mada*) and enmity (*matsarya*). These six natural impulses represent the six enemies of human beings (*arishadvarga*), which, if allowed to act uncontrolled, could instigate them to entertain evil thoughts and pursue their own selfish desires, and thereby cause injury to others. Manu adopted this perspective to explain the causes of all civil and criminal injuries inflicted by the action of one against the other.

Dharma or rules of righteous conduct evolved as a way to prevent the problems arising from the natural instinct of human beings. After explaining that an ideal state of affairs would exist when people protected each other according to Dharma, Bhishma suggested that people deflecting from the path of Dharma are overpowered by sensual desires, passion and greed. Since stronger persons harass weaker ones, he proposed the three-fold ideal of Dharma, Artha and Kama (Trivarga) as a remedy. Later a fourth ideal, moksha—the desire to secure eternal happiness—was added. The King was entrusted with the responsibility of enforcing Dharma.

Artha and Kama as Subject to Dharma

The propounders of Dharma realised that the fulfilment of human desires was an essential aspect of life (Gita 16 – 24; Manu II 224 and IV 176).[7] But they believed that unless laws regulated desire, the latter was bound to have undesirable results. They agreed that for an orderly society to exist, peace, happiness, desires (Kama) for material enjoyment, and pleasure (Artha) should always conform to Dharma (Law) (Vatsayana Kamasutra 1.2.7-15; Gautama p. 221,

45 – 47, Apastamba p. 151, 14 – 19, Yajnavalkya 1 – 115 and Kautilya p. 12). Thus the proper means of acquiring Artha, i.e. material wealth and pleasures, must prevail over the desire to do so (Kama), and Dharma must control the desire (Kama) as well as the means of acquiring material pleasure (Artha). All the works on Dharma therefore prescribed rules of right conduct, observance of which was considered necessary for the welfare of individuals and society. In laying down Dharma, its propounders took an integrated view of life. Consequently, they prescribed rules of right conduct for almost every sphere of human activity, including religion, diet, interpersonal conflicts, education, asceticism, and so forth.

Basic Aspects of Dharma

While Dharma touches a wide variety of topics, various works declare the essence of Dharma:

> Truthfulness, to be free from anger, sharing one's wealth with others, forgiveness, procreation of children from one's wife alone, purity, absence of enmity, straightforwardness, maintaining persons dependant on oneself are the nine Dharmas of persons belonging to all the varnas (Shanti 60, 7 – 8; see also Sukla Yajurveda 1 – 122; Manu X – 63).

The principles set out above are fundamental and have manifested themselves through various provisions meant to sustain the life of individuals and society. For this reason, all the works on Dharma declare with one voice that it is Dharma that sustains the world. Every act or conduct in disobedience to the rules of Dharma was called Adharma and was declared to be injurious to society and individuals.

Manu (VIII, 15) forcefully expressed he necessity for practicing Dharma: 'Dharma protects those who protect it. Those who destroy

Dharma get destroyed. Therefore Dharma should not be destroyed so that we may not be destroyed as a consequence therefore.' This principle is of great significance because it incorporates the concept of rule of law. Orderly society can only exist if everyone acts according to Dharma or protects Dharma; orderly society would be an incarnation of Dharma and Dharma would, in turn, protect the rights of individuals. In short, Dharma would regulate the mutual obligations of individuals and society.

Vyavahara Dharma and Rajadharma

While explaining the origin of state (*Rajya*) and the creation of kingship, Bhishmacharya states that, in the past, there was an ideal stateless society in which everyone acted according to Dharma. But as powerful individuals, overwhelmed by their desires, began to encroach upon the life, liberty and property of other weaker individuals, the king gained the right to collect tax and the duty to protect innocent people and punish the wicked. In the opening verse of his Smriti,[8] Narada explains that no legal proceedings were required when people were habitually truthful. But as standards of behaviour declined, the system of legal proceedings for the enforcement of rights and punishment of wrongs was established, and the king was appointed to decide lawsuits. Positive civil and criminal law established the powers, duties and responsibilities of the king (*Rajadharma*), including the law regulating the courts and their powers, functions and procedures as part of Dharma.

Though the word Dharma covers rules concerning all matters, it can gain a more precise meaning depending upon the context in which it is used. Dharma in the context of legal and constitutional history refers to *Vyavaharadharma* (constitutional obligations) and *Rajadharma* (constitutional law) evolved by the society through the ages, which is binding for the king as well as the people. Here I focus exclusively on this sense of Dharma.

FEMALE INFANTICIDE AND SEX DETERMINATION TESTS

Deliberate discrimination against girls takes several forms, such as denial of nutrition, insufficient or delayed medical care, emotional deprivation and insufficient investment in their future (Basu 1989; Vaasanthi 1994; Iyengar 1999; George, Haas & Latham 1994; Martorell, Rivera & Kaplowitz et al. 1992). The worst and most recent form of gender discrimination is the abortion of female fetuses. The sex of the fetus is determined through biomedical tests and sonography. In this chapter I focus on female infanticide in Tamil Nadu, which involves the deliberate killing of female infants soon after birth, with the use of medicine that suffocates the child (Chunkath & Athreya 1997; Harris-White 1997: 89; Nielson, Liljestrand & Hedegaar et al, 1997). It is this kind of practice that Rajadharma, now Rashtradharma, opposed. How does one, then, link scientific discovery to its application in society and to religion? It is here that a conception of science based on bioethics relates to the Hindu view of life.

> Where women are honoured, the Gods are pleased, and where they are not, all sacred rites are fruitless (Manusmriti). And yet thousands of female foetuses are massacred every month under the most sophisticated pre-natal diagnostic techniques. What is ironic is that sex determination facilities have reached those villages of Punjab, UP and Gujarat where even potable water is not available (Das Gupta M, 1987; George, Abel & Miller 1992). And the practice, though banned by the government, still goes on uninhibited and on a large scale (Venkatachalam & Srinivasan 1993; Renganathan & Sivanandhan 1995; Mitra 1993).

It started in the mid-1970s, when aminocentesis was first introduced in India for its diagnostic value. Hailed as a remarkable medical achievement, this test was to help couples who were running a risk of giving birth to a genetically defective child. In this sense it was an achievement indeed, but little did we know about the implications. The procedure, which involves a test to detect genetic defects in the foetus, also revealed the sex of the child. And it was this latter aspect of the test that caught the attention of Indian doctors, who saw its immense potential in an Indian society that is so in love with the male child (Ramanamma & Bambawale1980: 107; Bumiller 1990).

Soon the business of sex determination (SD) was booming. Thousands of SD centres sprang up where doctors enabled couples to realise their cherished dream of having a son by selectively aborting female foetuses. Soon more sophisticated tests started gaining popularity. One study reveals that, through the use of aminocentesis tests, seventy-eight thousand female foetuses were destroyed in the country between 1978 and 1982. Another study indicates that SD clinics in Delhi conducted an average of 11,000 tests in 1988 (Patel V, 1989; Athreya & Chunkath 1997). These dramatic figures shook the government out of its slumber and forced it to ban such centres.

But a ban is futile until implemented properly. The government has failed miserably in this respect and the practice goes on unabated. Those who indulge in this menace have no fear of the law, because know that the chance of punishment is small. For this reason, India continues to be a society where female infanticide is common. The only difference between the past and today is that scientific developments allowed doctors to abort girls before birth.

No wonder that the country's social milieu remains unfavourable to women. Many people do not realise that India is the only country in the world where the female-male ratio has declined over the years: from 972 in 1901 to 935 in 1981, and then 930 in 1991.9

Unfortunately, India is also among the few countries where female mortality exceeds that of the males, even though the female is biologically stronger. In India, the female mortality rate in the age group of 0 to 5 years is about 55 percent higher than the male mortality rate (Department of Women and Child Development, Government of India 1997).

The problem with our society is that it keeps finding excuses to justify its faults (George 1992; 1993; 1995). Men get away with raping and then strangulating a girl; polyandry is justified under the garb of religion; and if crime against women rises, Indian people that the women must have provoked it.[10] Our problem lies in the fact that we don't look for solutions. Painfully indifferent as we are, we're not bothered if the number of abortions rises exponentially due to SD tests. We are not concerned if maternal mortality rate here is the second highest in the world. We are also not moved if on average 60 women die per 1000 abortions here. Some even suggest that scarcity will enhance women's value.

Today we can't imagine the psychological impact of female foeticide on young minds (Das Gupta & Mari Bhat 1996). After convincing them of the worthlessness of being a woman, how are we to teach them equality of sexes? Snuffing out a life just because it happens to be that of a female is against the norms of human decency. It is a reflection of baser motives. How would the world be when the one who engenders it ceases to be?

SUSTAINABLE DEVELOPMENT: AN INDO-CENTRIC VIEW

Sustainable development is not a technical problem, but a vision of the future that provides us with a roadmap. It helps us focus our attention on a set of values and ethical principles by which to guide our actions as individuals and in relation to institutional structures. Sustainability is a community's control of capital, in all of its natural and cultural forms, to ensure that present and future generations can attain a high degree of economic security and achieve democracy while maintaining the integrity of the ecological systems upon which all life and production depend.

Many of the problems we face today are not the result of incidental failures but of technological and scientific successes. Science can describe, with a high degree of precision, what is. To a lesser degree, it can help us to assess what can be. Science cannot tell us what should be, and that is the key issue of sustainability. Science is a form of know-how; it is a means without consideration of ends. There is a difference between knowing how to do something and knowing what to do. To paraphrase Einstein: 'We cannot solve the problems that we have created with the same thinking that created them'.

What Do We Know?

The problem of sustainability is not a problem of lack of knowledge. The problems of sustainability are primarily problems of power and political will, which hamper us in our task of avoiding harm and doing good in the short and long term. Immutable laws of nature seem to allow for the economic domination of nature at the expense of sustainable agriculture. The mantra of economic growth is based on the assumption that rising tides raise all boats, i.e., that increasing national wealth improves distribution and equity within a country. It proceeds from the ideal that comparative advantage and specialisation apply in an economy where capital is mobile, assumes that the market can deal with all issues, including equity. It seems to preach that competition is good and natural in all cases.

There is a need for a new kind of economics: ecological economics. This kind of economics encourages an economy that honours economic security, democracy and ecological integrity—an economy that goes beyond socialism and capitalism, working with indigenous peoples to help them to preserve their lives and cultures as well as their habitats. It strives to develop appropriate technologies and maintain an industrial ecology, and seeks ways to move from excesses to necessities. It asks what determines the sustainability of individual and institutional behaviour, and how this can be encouraged.

Sustainable agriculture also presupposes the maintenance of sustainable communities. The sustainability principle is cautionary: When in doubt, move slowly, think deeply and do not make irreversible changes. We must understand the politics of knowledge and the political economy of science. There are no knowledge products independent of institutional selling, financial support, place, pace and person. From the perspective of northern elites, sustainability refers to issues of poverty, inequity and injustice, and a joining of concerns, but among them the paradigm of science still prevails. The northern tradition of science has generally failed to value indigenous and experiential knowledge.

PROPOSAL FOR A NEW PARADIGM: UNCERTAINTY

In conclusion, I propose a new paradigm that advocates pragmatism and plurality. It stresses that tools and conceptual frameworks should be catered to the solution of the problem at hand rather than being limited by tools and conceptual frameworks of a particular discipline. It would accept uncertainty as a given, focus on data quality rather than data completeness, have explicit concern for future generations, sustainability and equity, and be concerned with heterogeneity and discontinuity.

History teaches us that we should expect the unexpected. We should therefore study history as part of the knowledge base for sustainability, as a constant reminder of the human incapacity to manage the planet. Knowledge is obviously better than ignorance. But wisdom is even better. We should proceed with caution and humility and try to avoid doing something that cannot be undone. Hindu philosophy emphasizes impermanence; change is a law of life. This also has been central to classical Indian Buddhism. Caution and uncertainty show the limits of human knowledge and action, hence there has to be a balance between nature, fauna and flora and human beings as well as between the two sexes (Chinchore 1992).

NOTES

[1] In Hinduism, the term shruti means 'that which is heard directly' and refers to scriptures that have been directly revealed to humans by the gods. Examples of shruti include the Upanishads and the Veda.

[2] Mahabharat is the title of an epic poem on the Mahabharat War, composed between 400 B.C. and 400 A.D, and rooted in the Rig Veda.

[3] See, for instance, the work of Sarvepalli Radhakrishnan, Sarvepalli, a scholar and statesman who was president of India from 1962 to 1967. Radhakrishnan's written works include Indian Philosophy, 2 vol. (1923-27), The Philosophy of the aUpanishads (1924), An Idealist View of Life (1932), Eastern Religions and Western Thought (1939), and East and West: Some Reflections (1955).

[4] Lord Rama is one of the most commonly adored gods of Hindus and is known as an ideal man and hero of the epic Ramayana.

[5] Manu, or the laws of Manu, were written down around 1500 B.C. (For an English translation, see G. Buhler, www.fordham.edu/halsall/india/manu-full.html.)

[6] Regarding the three aims of life, which are dharma, artha, and kama, Vatsayana says it is desire upon which all else rests. Wealth and virtue also rest upon desire. It is desire that stirs the citta; the citta which moves the mind; the mind which moves the soul. He does not consider moksha liberation.

[7] Regarding the three aims of life, which are dharma, artha, and kama, Vatsayana says it is desire upon which all else rests. Wealth and virtue also rest upon desire. It is desire that stirs the citta; the citta which moves the mind; the mind which moves the soul. He does not consider moksha liberation.

[8] The term smriti refers to 'memorised tradition'. Examples include the Puranas.

[9] Supportive evidence of widespread sex-specific abortions in the 1980s-90s can be obtained from sex ratios at birth (males per hundred) females which is highest in the North Western states in India (115 and 113 for Haryana and Punjab respectively) (See Women in India: A Statistical Profile, 1997). The sex ratio of hospital births in Punjab in 1988 was 122.

[10] Supportive evidence of widespread sex-specific abortions in the 1980s-90s can be obtained from sex ratios at birth (males per hundred) females which is highest in the North Western states in India (115 and 113 for Haryana and Punjab respectively) (See Women in India: A Statistical Profile, 1997). The sex ratio of Hospital births in Punjab in 1988 was 122.

BIBLIOGRAPHY

Athreya V. B., Chunkath S. R. 'Gender discrimination strikes: disquieting aspects of early neonatal deaths in Tamil Nadu', Frontline, 11 July, 1997.

Basu A.M. (1989) 'Is discrimination in food really necessary for explaining sex differentials in childhood mortality?', Population Studies, 43: 193-210.

Batliwala S. (1994) The meaning of women's empowerment: new concepts from action/ population policies reconsidered. Sen, G., Germain, A., Chen, L.C. (eds), Cambridge: Harvard University Press.

Bumiller, E. (1990) May You Be the Mother of A Hundred Sons, New York: Random House.

Chinchore, M. (1992) Dharmakirti and his Philosophy, New Delhi: ICPR.

Chunkath, S. R. and Athreya, V.B. 'Female infanticide in Tamil Nadu: some evidence', Economic and Political Weekly, 26 April, 1997.

Das Gupta, M. and Mari Bhat, P.N. 'Intensified gender bias in India: a consequence of fertility decline', paper presented at Annual Meeting of the Population Association of America, New Orleans, May 1996.

Das Gupta M. (1987) 'Selective discrimination against female children in Rural Punjab', Population & Development Review, 13: 77.

Department of Women and Child Development (1997) 'Women in India: A Statistical Profile', New Delhi: Government of India.

Galtung, Johan (1996) Peace by peaceful means: peace and conflict, development and civilization, London: Sage.

George, S.M., Haas, J.D. and Latham, M.C. 'Nutrition education can reduce gender inequity in growth of pre-school children in rural South India', paper presented at the American Institute of Nutrition Meeting, FASEB, Anaheim, April 1994.

George, S.M., Abel, R. and Miller, B.D. (1992) 'Female infanticide in South Indian villages', Economic and Political Weekly, 27: 1153.

George, S.M., Latham, M.C. and Abel, R. (1993) 'An evaluation of good growth monitoring in South Indian Villages', Lancet, 342: 348.

George, S.M. 'The government response to female infanticide in Tamil Nadu: from recognition back to denial?', paper presented at MIDS-ICSSR 25th Interdisciplinary Research Methodology Workshop for Southern States, Kottayam, August 1995.

George, S.M. (1995) 'The practices of female infanticide and female feticide: responses by Non-Government Organizations', in J.M.K. Sekhar and S.M. George (eds) Towards Prevention of female Infanticide, Tirupatur: Center for Rural Health and Social Education.

Harris-White, B. 'Development and death: adverse child sex-ratios in rural Tamil Nadu', Frontline, Madras, 4 April, 1997.

Huntington, Samuel P. (1996) The Clash of Civilizations and the Remaking of World Order, New York: Simon & Schuster.

Iyengar, P. 'Female infanticide: sex ratio in Tamil Nadu dips', Times of India, Bombay, 30 January, 1993.

Iyengar P. 'Girls in Salem are born to die', Times of India, Bombay, 24 August, 1999.

Jayalalitha, J. (1993) 'Fifteen-point programme for Child Welfare', Madras: Government of Tamil Nadu, Department of Social Welfare.

Kaviraj, S. (1997) Politics in India, Oxford: Oxford University Press.

Kielmann, A.A., Taylor, C.E. and de Sweemer, C. (1983) 'Child and Maternal Health Services in Rural India', in The Narangwal Experiment, Vol. 1, Baltimore: Johns Hopkins University Press.

Martorell, R., Rivera, J. and Kaplowitz, H. (1992) 'Long-term consequences of growth

retardation during early childhood', in M. Hernandez and J. Argente (eds), Human Growth: Basic and Clinical Aspects.

Mitra, A. 'Female foeticide. A primitive trend practiced the world over', Down to Earth, 31 October, 1993.

Nielson, B.B., Liljestrand, J. and Hedegaard, M. (1997) 'Reproductive pattern, perinatal mortality, and sex preference in rural Tamil Nadu, South India: A community based, cross-sectional study', BMJ, 314: 1521-24.

Patel, V. (1989) 'Sex determination and sex pre-selection tests in India: modern techniques for femicide', Bulletin of Concerned Asian Scholars, 21: 2.

Ramanamma, A. and Bambawale, U. (1980) 'The mania for sons: an analysis of social values is South Asia', Social Science and Medicine, 14B: 107.

Renganathan, A. and Antonysamy, S. (1995) 'Female infanticide in Salem district', report prepared by VRDP, Omalur and CEDA Trust, Dindigul.

Said, E.W. (1978) Orientalism, London: Pantheon Books.

Vaasanthi 'Born to Die: tragedy of the doomed daughter' Hindu, Madras, 20 November, 1994.

Venkatachalam, R. and Srinivasan, V. (1993) Female Infanticide, New Delhi: Har Anand.

Venkatramani, S.H. 'Female infanticide: born to die', India Today, 15 June, 1986.

Chapter 5

Human Cloning in a Thai Novel: Wimon Sainimnuan's *Amata* and Thai Cultural Attitudes Toward Biotechnology

Soraj Hongladarom

In 2000, a new novel appeared on the Thai literary scene. Its author, Wimon Sainimnuan, was a rather minor figure in the literary circle, having published only a few novels and collections of short stories, all of which did not receive much attention. Only a few readers knew and appreciated the work of this young author. However, the young author's new novel in 2000, entitled *Amata*, which is Pali for 'immortal', gained the author nation-wide fame when it was awarded the SEA Write Award, the country's most prestigious literary prize. Shortly afterwards, sale of the novel skyrocketed, its author rose from relative obscurity to become one of Thailand's celebrities. The novel was much talked about and discussed not only among elite Thai literati, but also among the general public.

The citation for the SEA Write Award in the second edition of the novel says:

> *Amata* is an imaginary novel about the future. It concerns the search for immortal life and is focused on the conflict between consumerism and religious belief of the East. The plot of the novel concerns cloning of human beings and organ transplantation, which leads to ethical and humanitarian problems. The outstanding point of this novel is that the author tackles the issues that could post problems in the future and takes these issues as the main plot. The conflict is expressed through two groups of characters. The tone is critical of the current condition of society, and its way

of telling the story has a strong emotional impact. The novel asks us to become aware of one of the common problems facing humanity and it challenges us to think further what is the real meaning of humanity and immortality' (Wimon 2000: i-ii).

There was much in the novel that differentiated it from other Thai novels. Most Thai novels have always dealt with such subjects as love, betrayal, competition among women for favour of her man, jealousy, and the lives of the rich and the famous. In short, most novels have been escapist, offering the readers a way to forget about the actual condition of the world. In fact, there have been a number of novels that deal with more serious issues. Many novels discussed the problem of social inequality and injustice and were instrumental in raising the consciousness of the Thai readers concerning the pressing social issues Thai society was facing. However, this new novel was different. Instead of treating the traditional subject matter of love and jealousy or the more recent subject of struggle for social justice, *Amata* deals with a very new topic, the emergence of biotechnology as a force in society. To my knowledge, *Amata* is the first novel in Thai language that takes this emergence as its topic.

Such a task is a daunting one. The Thai reading public has not been accustomed to reading fictional works dealing with biotechnology. The level of basic scientific understanding of the public still lags behind those of other comparable countries, and a very large proportion of Thais still believe in superstitions. One popular pastime for many Thais is interpreting what they take to be auspicious signs in natural matter for clues so that they can win in the national lottery. National newspapers often report the existence of such signs in plants, animals, or natural phenomena. The result is that the plants or animals in question immediately draw the attention of thousands of hopefuls who try in their various ways to interpret the plants or animals for their 'lucky' lottery numbers.

This is hardly a fertile place for a healthy interest in works of fiction dealing with biotechnology. Thus the awarding of *Amata* and its subsequent rise to fame is a very interesting phenomenon that deserves a close look.

What I want to do in this chapter is search for the underlying meanings of the rapid acceptance and fame of the novel. The novel is a clear case of the Thai cultural attitude toward modern biotechnology. I will analyse the novel to see how the typical Thai views the current advances in biotechnology, not only concerning human cloning, which is the explicit subject matter of the novel, but also other aspects of biotechnology that are debated in public, such as genetically modified organisms and the use of biotechnology in medicine. Here literature is seen as a document through which one can gaze into how people in the past viewed themselves, what they thought about and what they valued most. The method is not unlike that of a historian who views a piece of fiction from the past as a window to the minds of the people and the society where that piece came to be. Except that in this case the work in question is a contemporary one. But since literature can be regarded as an expression of cultural responses to changes in the social, political, scientific or technological environment, I believe there is at least a case for looking at this piece of Thai literature in order to see how Thais generally think about issues in contemporary biotechnology. I will also discuss how Thai culture and modern science and technology interact. Since Wimon's novel is imbued with the Buddhist values, which he set against those coming with the modern technologies, we can also see from the analysis of the novel how Theravada Buddhism, which is an integral part of Thai culture, is related to the issue at hand. Thus looking at the novel reveals several aspects of the interrelationship between Thai culture, Buddhism, and modern biotechnology.

I

The story line of the novel is simple enough. Prommin, 55, a global business tycoon owning a huge corporation, realises that he is getting old and needs to have some of his bodily tissues replaced in order to stay alive and continue managing his corporation and expanding his empire. This great technical feat is made possible by Professor Spencer, who works at Prommin's hospital and is head of the cloning team. Prommin has a 'son', Cheevan, 22, whom he has earlier cloned from himself, and whom he and his wife have raised as their own child. The novel begins at the time when Prommin is about to harvest Cheevan's body for tissues or organs for his own body. It also turns out that Prommin has cloned several copies of himself, but all died or were aborted, leaving only two 22-year-old copies, Cheevan and his 'half-brother' Arjun, whose 'mother' escaped from Prommin's hospital to avoid being harvested. (Note that the numbers in this novel are mostly double-digit with repeating numbers—perhaps symbolising the 'doubleness' and 'sameness' which characterize cloning.) When Cheevan learns about his fate, his mother arranges a meeting with Arjun. Arjun and Cheevan then conspire to fight against their 'father' and in the end, instead of replacing bodily organs on a piece by piece basis, Professor Spencer decides to exchange Prommin's brain for Arjun's, believing that he can put Prommin into Arjun's body. However, there is an ambiguity at the end of the novel. Arjun and Cheevan apparently believe that the seat of personal identity is not the brain, but the heart. So the two manage to deceive Prommin and Spencer into the brain-exchange surgery. And since the hearts are not exchanged, the identities of the two persons remain the same. There is a scene toward the end of the novel where 'Prommin' takes a podium in front of a large gathering declaring the success of the brain exchange surgery, whereas in fact it is Arjun who is talking.

Actually the novel itself is not a really good one in terms of literary value. The work shows many signs of having been incompletely conceived. Characters and methods of telling the story are not well developed. But the main point in the novel is not its literary value. What should be interesting in the novel is that it is the first time that a Thai novelist tackles a serious issue arising from the advent of advanced technology. Thus the novel is an important document which allows us a glimpse into how a typical Thai who has some basic knowledge of these advances thinks about the issue.

Characters in the novel, as I have said, are divided into two groups. Prommin, Prof. Spencer, and Prommin's jet-set daughter belong to the first one. For them the main purpose in life is to maximise profit, to expand the conglomerate and conquer the world—or, in the case of Spencer, to advance knowledge and technical know-how. Spencer belongs to the first group because he works with Prommin's company, and more importantly he is the head of the scientific team that has already performed cloning for Prommin and it is also Spencer who performs the brain exchange operation on Prommin and Arjun. It is clear that Spencer, a world renowned scientist, stands for the fact that science now serves the interests of big, globalized business rather than remaining true to the ideal of the disinterested pursuit of knowledge and truth. The third member of this group, Prommin's daughter, is an interesting case. Since she is a woman, she obviously cannot be Prommin's clone. Thus she represents a normal relation between father and child. Cheevan has been raised as Prommin's son, and if the incident did not happen he would have remained his son. However, the relation between Prommin and Cheevan cannot be the same as that between Prommin and his daughter, because Prommin himself believes that Cheevan is not actually his son, but a spare part storehouse to be harvested when he feels ready. His daughter, on the other hand, refers to her father as 'daddy', which in Thai language conveys the meaning that she is a sophisticated, foreign educated professional. She also works as her father's secretary and assumes a high position in her father's corporation. The fact that her 'brother' is about to be killed and harvested does not bother her in the least.

The second group consists of the clones Arjun, Cheevan, Cheevan's girlfriend and his 'mother' (who is obviously not a blood relation of him, but carried him in her womb). These represent a counterforce, a rebel group against the seemingly all-powerful force of globalisation and technical progress. As the one who carried Cheevan in her womb, Sasiprabha cannot bear to witness Prommin's killing of her own son. She is the one who first told Cheevan of the terrible truth and arranges for him to escape. However, she is powerless against her husband. Her voice is that of conscience, a feeble voice raised against the torrent of technical progress and selfish desire of her husband. The 'brothers' Cheevan and Arjun are needless to say the protagonists of the story. It is interesting to see that the novel has two protagonists who share roughly the same amount of importance in the story. We shall see that images and references to duality and perhaps duplicity pervade the entire novel. Cheevan and Arjun are strictly speaking not brothers; more correctly they are both clones of Prommin. Nonetheless their characters differ markedly, conveying the sense that clones are real human beings and their characters are formed through nurture. These two groups of characters neatly specify the current global conflict between the forces of globalisation and those opposing it.

The two groups of characters neatly represent the opposing sides in the debate on globalisation and the benefits of science and technology today. Prommin and Spencer believe that there is nothing that science and technology cannot do, no problem that science and technology cannot solve, and if there is any opposition, Prommin sarcastically says that those opposing what he regards as progress and development are bound to make use of it anyway. Before he goes on with his killing of Cheevan in order to harvest his organs, he consults his Vice-President, who is an expert in public relations and political lobbying. He told Prommin that there are still pockets of resistance, mostly from the NGOs and the religious groups. Prommin tells him that the price to pay for the first group to become more 'reasonable' is around a billion baht. As for the second group, he would like to emphasise that they should not interfere with worldly matters. They should go on meditating and practising their religious teachings, and leave the matter of curing diseases and prolonging life to him (Wimon 2000: 31-33). He says that before the religious groups say anything against human cloning, they should wipe the fat out of their mouths, for they keep on eating meat, thus keeping his company in business while they take a moral high ground:

> Tell them not to worry about sinners like us. Cloning and organ transplantation are our business. If it is a sin, then the sin is on us, not on them. We are happy to get the sin. It is like when they eat meat. They only eat it, but it is us that prepare the meat for them from the beginning. We take care of all the preceding stages.... Tell them also that, before they talk about morality or sins, they should wipe their fat-laden mouth first (Wimon 2000: 32; all the translations of the Thai text are mine).

According to Prommin, a law should be passed allowing unrestricted use of human cloning technology to help a lot of people who are suffering from various kinds of illness. Moreover, forbidding human cloning for therapeutic purposes has generated huge economic losses:

> Now the mortality rate of the population in our country is at 66 years old. But the illness rate is very alarming. I won't tell you that and will let Khun Samphop [the Minister of Public Health] have his own nightmare. I will only tell you that the

number of people suffering from diseases caused by infection and accidents, resulting in a need for organ transplantation, is as high as one million and one hundred thousand. However, we can only transplant the organs of less than half of these people. It must be a national tragedy that we have to let the other half who cannot receive organ transplantation die without any guilt. I take it as the guilt of our nation that we elect not to save their lives, even though we can do it. Why? Twenty-two years ago, I campaigned for the public to accept human cloning for organ transplantation, and requested that the government passed a law allowing that. Unfortunately, few people accepted it. Many were imprisoned by the bounds of morality... I feel sorry for those people who have to die; I am sorry for their lovers, relatives and friends, and I am sorry for myself for not being able to do anything even though we could have done it. All because of your morality, which blocked the proposed legislation (Wimon 2000: 43-45).

Prommin gives this speech in the context of his imminent killing of his clone Cheevan, and it is obvious that he is gathering public support for the action. Prommin continues:

In the near future, we might use cloned people as soldiers, policemen, workers in factories and farms, and many others. This will free us from the burden of work, so we will have more time for leisure activities... I would like to implore that the public accepts human cloning and organ transplantation. It is not a matter of life and death, and it is no different from killing animals for food or for sport that we are doing now. What is different is that the clones won't suffer pain like the animals we kill. Our acceptance would save countless, millions and millions of lives, which would be lost. I feel that the 22 years that this law has not been passed is a total loss. I do not want to lose any more time, so I want the public to support the government in their effort to pass this legislation...

Prommin then smiles lightly, his eyes sparkling:

> 'What is the most serious loss is that if the government passed this law 22 years ago, today I will present as gifts to each of you beautiful, young clones to take home' (Wimon 2000: 45-47).

> Prommin nods his head amid laughter and applause (idem).

In the novel we know that the real reason Prommin gives this speech is that he has a plan for harvesting clones not only for their bodily organs, but for many other purposes such as creating clones of beautiful girls to work in sex industry, and so on. As for those who oppose his argument, he has the following to say:

> However, I would like elaborate a little further. I may not have made myself clear enough. The first point is: Some people say that this proposed law will benefit me. I accept this point wholeheartedly. I am an entrepreneur, a merchant. Thus I naturally look for profit. Do other merchants such as those who sell fried bananas or *khanom krok* [Thai candy] not want profit? I am no different from these merchants. If there is a difference it's only that my enterprise is larger and is of a different kind. But I don't think the mindset of an entrepreneur is any different. But this is not different from the mindset of people in other professions too. Employees or civil servants may not be selling things as I do, but they also sell something, their labour, their intelligence... I only want to say that I look for profit, but please look at what I use the profit for. Of course part of the profit is for expanding and improving my business. This amount of money does not benefit me alone, but it creates jobs for millions of workers... I pay millions of baht in taxes every year.

Then:

Another point. My critics say that cloning and organ transplantation will benefit only the rich. This is only partly true, and is so only for a period of time at first. It is normal for a new business to have a high expenditure. This will make the price high because the investment needs to be recouped. And the goods can be produced only in a small number. But the price cannot be too high to be affordable, because then nobody would buy the product. But I am confident that in two years' time the price will go down because more goods will have been produced... This law will open up golden opportunities for everybody. How many millions of years have we human beings dreamed of immortality? They have searched for the elixir of life. Now I am making this a reality. So why don't you support it? Don't you want to live indefinitely? What do you live for if your life is full of sickness and hopelessness? Now you have the opportunity to have a perfect life and can enjoy it as long as you want (Wimon 2000: 122).

One thing should be clear. Prommin believes that human clones are not real human beings, but are in his words 'artificial humans'. Thus they do not lie within the realm of ethics. Ethics applies only to real humans, but since these clones are merely 'artificial' they do not need to be protected by ethical laws. Cloning sexy girls for the sex industry so that they do not require the same sort of rights as real sex workers would be a perfect, if utterly tasteless, example. Moreover, Prommin seems to believe that reproductive human cloning is the only way to produce tissues or even whole organs for therapeutic purposes. But of course one can have therapeutic cloning without producing a whole human being, if a small number of cells does not have the status of a 'whole human being'. In any case, it is possible, and much more economical, to produce totipotent stem cells which can develop into any kind of tissues or organs one pleases. Prommin himself recognises this fact. Asked whether his proposed legislation allowing cloning would be valid for reproduction or only for breeding cells for therapeutic purposes, he says he would like to clone himself, for it may be the case that he will exchange all parts of one of his clones for himself (idem). At any rate, Wimon would perhaps argue that the existence of therapeutic cloning does not change the situation. One can have therapeutic cloning for stem cells, so instead of producing walking, breathing human beings like Cheevan and Arjun, one can only produces stem cells. It would seem to Wimon that nothing changes. What is different is only that in Prommin's case the 'cells' in question are whole human beings, whereas in the therapeutic cloning case it is only tiny groups of cells. But what is to him more important is that this collection of cells — whether as totipotent stem cells or as breathing human beings — are harvested according to self-centred desire. Prommin presents the speech above to the Thai public in order to get their support for the cloning legislation. Deep down we know that he wants the law passed so that he can harvest Cheevan's organs. The self-centred desire is plain to see for everyone.

Furthermore, the ironic tone of Prommin's speech is unmistakable. While his argument may sound crass, simplistic and exaggerated (as is obviously the intention of the author), one has a sense that Prommin does have a point. Moreover, the point he is making is often heard from proponents of the technology as well as from representatives of corporations that promote their products to the public. Technology does have its benefits, and its coupling with the capitalist world system is just a necessity since this is the best means to bring out the fruits of technology to the widest possible public. The coupling of science and technology with capitalism and entrepreneurship is just the best way available in this day and age to enhance the effectiveness of the former in order to alleviate or eliminate whatever it is that afflicts human lives. His sarcasm regarding the leaders of the religious groups indeed echoes many in the real world today, who profess religious belief but seem to do so only by words and hardly by action. When Prommin makes fun of the Buddhist leaders, saying that monks and devout lay persons should wipe animal fat out of their mouths before preaching against killing clones, is clearly designed to instigate Thai Buddhists to think seriously about their religion and the relationship of Buddhism to modern society. When Prommin makes fun of Buddhist leaders, he is making fun of the readers of the novel also, since the majority of this novel's readers are obviously Buddhists.

We will save the question regarding the relation between Buddhism and modern biotechnology for the next section of this essay. Now, however, we should be clear about the basic intention or interpretation of this novel. What Wimon is trying to get his reader to grasp is that modern biotechnology is a monster bent on creating horror after horror. In Spencer's laboratory where the brain exchange operation is to take place, there are a large number of clones of all types of human beings to be used and harvested. All of them have to be suppressed by medication and do not have a speck of liveliness in themselves. Cheevan and Arjun, as we have seen, are only two survivors of countless clone victims who are either aborted spontaneously or deliberated killed for a variety of reasons. Chief among the horrors is the coupling of science and technology with big business. Prommin, the prime representative of global business, is served by Spencer, the epitome of modern science and technology. Spencer, we are told, admires Prommin so much that he is willing to work for him very loyally. This is due to Spencer's perception in Prommin of a certain quality that he finds would be ideal for him to work with, such as determination and an unreflecting dedication to the power of science and technology to solve any problems.

II

While Prommin rumbles on about the bright prospects of technology and globalisation, Cheevan and Arjun are looking for ways to save themselves and to avenge Prommin. The fight is on between the cloner and the cloned. Arjun is well-versed in Buddhist teachings, having studied in intensively after his mother took him away from Prommin's grasp. And it is Buddhist teachings that provide a powerful tool in the clones' struggle. According to Arjun, 'life is nothing but a series of memories, and one clings to life because one wants to taste new experiences' (Wimon 2000: 110). In fact there is nothing to life, and what one wants to remain when one does not want to die is nothing but an unconnected series of matter and consciousness. These are straightforward Buddhist teachings.

> We only imagine that death is precisely at the point where breathing stops. So we are afraid of the end point there. But the truth is that nothing dies, nothing is born. There are only those which we call birth or death. If you see this point, you won't be suffering' (idem).

The novel is full of these direct Buddhist teachings through Arjun's mouth. The teachings of Theravada Buddhism are put in direct opposition to whatever Prommin is pushing for. Arjun, a devout and very knowledgeable Buddhist, is devising ways to foil his original's plan, and his original, Prommin, believes that Buddhist teachers should 'wipe their mouths clean' before criticising anything worldly. The difference could not be greater. Prommin does not believe in Buddhism; he sees only material benefit as the supreme good. What he does is nothing other than satisfying his ego. He desires to live indefinitely and to keep expanding his empire. For him, as for Spencer, the seat of identity lies in the brain, for it is the brain that carries thoughts and desires. Thus, reason Prommin and Spencer, if Spencer puts Prommin's brain into one of his clones' body then the result would be Prommin himself in a brand new body, for the identity of the person goes with the brain. This would be the ultimate *therapeutic* cloning, for one does not have to replace one's tissues or organs on a piece by piece basis; one can replace the totality of one's material body for another while retaining one's personality, memories and desires.

Remember that we are now dealing with science fiction, and that the author of the novel is not an expert in biology or biotechnology. Nonetheless, since the author is a layman who takes interest in such matters, we could regard him as a representative of the public. The public does not consist of experts but, in a democracy, it has to decide what course society should take regarding these very rapid advances in science and technology. Hence there is a sense in which we can take what is going on in a novel for what is going on in the real world in which the novel is read. The novel can be a powerful social commentary. One is reminded of *Uncle Tom's Cabin*, a romance that contributed a good deal to the awareness of racial inequality in the middle nineteenth century in the US, a force that led to the American Civil War. In the same vein, by putting Buddhism on a loggerhead with modern biotechnology, Wimon comments on the contemporary situation in which biotechnology is employed as a servant of big business interests, pandering to egoistic, megalomaniac desire rather than serving the need of the majority of humanity.

That Buddhism is seen as the antithesis to the force of globalisation is itself a very interesting phenomenon. Arjun argues with Spencer and Prommin that it would be more beneficial to them not to replace organs on a piece by piece basis, but to exchange the brains, putting Arjun's brain into Prommin's body and vice versa. The result, Arjun would later convince the scientist and the megalomaniac, is that Prommin would get his new body, just like when one is bored with one's old home, having decided to have a new one, moves into it. Prommin and Spencer believe that, if the brain were put into a new body, this would be just like moving into a new home. Arjun believes that after Prommin's brain is put into his body, he would not become Prommin because he believes that the seat of identity is not located in the brain, but in the heart. Thus the reason why he is so eager to have Prommin's brain put into his body is that he would still be the same person, whereas Prommin would still be the same one he was before, since the hearts are not exchanged.

All this sounds very far-fetched and almost unbelievable. But the point is not that this scenario can or cannot happen. The point is that the story here is an allegory meant to tell us something about the current condition of science and technology and their opposition to Buddhism. It may or may not be correct for Arjun to say that the seat of personality and identity is in the heart, not the brain. However, the fact that Buddhism wins in the end—Arjun, under the guise of Prommin, finally takes over his original's enterprise whereas Prommin, after Arjun's brain was put into him, becomes forgotten since everybody else believes that this body is a useless one. The victory is bitter, cruel, and utterly complete. Prommin, who owns a global corporation and is an epitome of egotistical desire, now lies to waste in Spencer's laboratory, where Arjun, whom everyone in the company believes to be the new Prommin because everybody believes that the brain is the seat of identity, controls the company. We are asked to believe that, after the brain exchange operation, everybody stays the same, for it is in the heart that the real person, if there is ever one in the tenet of Theravada Buddhism, resides.

The conflict between Buddhism and modern science here is fraught with moral questions. Prommin and Spencer conspire to extend their egoistic lives indefinitely, but their attempts are frustrated because, according to Wimon, they do not realise that the seat of personhood is in the heart and not the brain. Perceiving an encroachment of advances in science and technology into the fabric of Thai lives and consciousness, Wimon turns toward Buddhism for a defence. Hence the advances of science and technology are here seen as a threat, not only to the moral fabric of a Buddhist society like Thailand, but also to its very identity. For Wimon the identity of Thai culture is inseparable from the belief in Buddhism, and if the belief system endemic of modern science and technology is allowed to go unchecked into Thai society, then Thais would lose an essential part of their identity. Trying to resist the encroachment of science and technology and to protect the Thai cultural identity, Wimon uses Buddhism as a shield. He tries to show that Buddhism offers a far superior system of belief in that it alone offers the means toward complete release from the cycle of suffering, the ultimate Buddhist goal and the ultimate truth, which modern science is in no position to offer. Since science and technology appear to cater only to desires and greed, centred on the belief in the existence of the individual ego, science cannot provide the real truth.

Resisting scientific and technological advances through Buddhism is thus a way to assert the cultural identity of the Thai people amidst the tide of globalization. Thai people should be proud, argues Wimon in the novel, that they have such a system of belief that is already superior to anything offered by modern science and technology. It is not surprising that the novel came out in 2000, three years after the economic collapse in July 1997, which triggered a worldwide downturn. Thais look at the event as a turning point in their history. A result of the collapse was that Thais began to question the direction and the policy their country had been pursuing until then. More specifically, they began to question the policy of completely merging the country into the current of globalization at every point. After the collapse, the King presented his famous birthday speech in December 1997, urging

Thais to become 'self sufficient', meaning not relying on foreign money but turning back to their roots and producing things for domestic consumption and not just for export. The speech found sympathetic ears, and it signaled a large number of discourses on the need for Thailand to reassert her identity if not her sovereignty in the wake of the country's request for help from the International Monetary Fund.

Showing that Buddhism has a lot more to offer than science and technology is part of this reassertion of identity that is going on in Thai society today. The resistance is not only against economic globalisation, but also against *cultural* globalization. Wimon sees science and technology as inseparable from selfish interests and the market system, which to him destroys the moral fabric of the society and which he perceives to be a direct threat to Buddhism as well. So the novel could be seen as a defense of Buddhism against modern science; or more accurately, the novel shows to the Thai readers that they still have an invaluable treasure in Buddhism and that it is no use to follow modern or western science and technology blindly. Arjun exchanges words with Spencer. He propounds the truths of Buddhism for the skeptical Spencer. Ultimate truth in Buddhism, says Arjun, is not obtainable by observation or ratiocination, but by the insight obtained solely through deep meditation. Spencer argues that science and its technologies benefit humankind; however, Arjun replies that these benefits are only material and physical and do not begin to address the most serious problems afflicting human beings: greed, anger and delusion.

III

Why put science and technology in such a bad light? And what does this tell us about Asian genomics? I don't think Wimon is so naïve as to believe that science and technology do not have any benefits at all. After all, Arjun and Cheevan themselves take some technologies for granted, and Arjun himself relies on the very technology that created him in his subversive act against his creator. Hence the reason why Wimon sounds so pessimistic against science and technology is that they are used against the basic Buddhist tenets of eliminating greed, anger and delusion. This, I believe, is what underlies the typical Buddhist and Thai attitude toward science and technology. The path toward *nirvana* starts with elimination of greed, anger and delusion and thus anything that contributes to this elimination would for the Buddhist be of positive ethical value. Hence it seems that the intrinsic nature of an act, such as human cloning, is neither positively nor negatively valued according to Buddhism; it is whether the act contributes to the Buddhist supreme good that decides whether the act is good or bad.

This does not mean that Buddhism teaches that there is no intrinsic value at all. Some acts will lead one astray from the path toward Enlightenment no matter what, such as killing, stealing, wrongful sexual conduct, and so on. However, since human reproductive cloning in itself does not necessarily consist of killing anybody (providing that there are no aborted embryos and there is no harm done to any organisms), it does not seem to be intrinsically bad. If this is so, then the main reason why Arjun is so opposed to human reproductive cloning is that it is done for the purpose of farming human bodies for their organs, with the ultimate aim of creating a business. To Buddhists' eyes, this is intolerable, for the act would certainly involve killing and would mean that human beings are created solely for the purposes of others. (Here we see an affinity between Buddhism and Kantian ethics in the West.)

So what this story tells us about Asian genomics is that: (1) the Thai attitude towards recent advances in science and technology is highly negative. The reason is that these technologies are perceived to be subservient to business interests and more poignantly to egoistic desires to prolong one's life indefinitely. However, an examination of basic Buddhist tenets reveals that: (2) Thai Buddhists do not view the processes and products of the advanced technologies as necessarily bad things. The technologies are bad only when they are applied with a frame of mind that leads one away from the path toward Enlightenment. That is, when they are applied for the purpose of fulfilling one's egoistic desires. Thus, if human reproductive cloning is performed with a frame of mind that furthers the movement toward Enlightenment, such as when it is performed with loving-kindness or compassion, then the act is not necessarily bad. Furthermore: (3) since Theravada Buddhism largely informs the Thai indigenous knowledge system, we see in *Amata* a concrete example of the interplay between the indigenous and the system of knowledge that originates from the West. What we see is that Buddhism is still the superior mode of knowledge in that it integrates the epistemological and ethical dimensions of knowledge systems. Knowledge is not to be divorced from ethical considerations. Prommin's dissection of a dog in order to learn where its soul resides is a typical example of how modern Western science is perceived as alienated from ethical considerations. And it is precisely for this reason that modern science has to be reined in by Buddhist teachings.

In my recent book, *Science in Thai Society and Culture* (2002), which is written in Thai, I argue that the way out of the problems arising from negative attitudes toward science and technology is that science and technology need to become part of people's lives. A way needs to be found in order that science and technology become integrated into the cultural fabric of Thai lives. I proposed many ways to do this, chief among which is that the direction of scientific research should be geared toward solving local problems and cater to local needs rather than toward serving global corporate interests. In short, science and technology should be 'localized'. Besides, not only do the objectives of research and development need to be geared toward local needs, but the activities that constitute science and technology themselves also need to be founded upon indigenous resources. I suggest that this will go a long way toward diminishing the feeling of alienation that the locals feel toward science and technology. Clearly, Wimon's attitude towards science and technology is highly alienated. This is perhaps not a healthy attitude to have in this day and age. Asians should find their own way of integrating science and technology into their cultural fabric without destroying the identity of their culture. For Thai people, this means that they should find a way such that Buddhism and science and technology can live together without destroying each other. How to actually accomplish that is a highly complex task, which cannot be discussed in any detail in this paper. Nonetheless, what we have learned from this paper, and from reading *Amata*, is that such a way cannot even begin to be found if science and technology are part of global business interests and do not answer to the needs of local lives.

BIBLIOGRAPHY

Hongladarom, S. (in Thai) (2002) *Science in Thai Society and Culture,* Bangkok: Institute for Academic Development .

Wimon, S. (in Thai) (2000) *Amata,* Bangkok: Siam Prathet Press.

Chapter 6

Implications of Japanese Religions in the Genomic Age: A Survey on Attitudes Towards Life and Death within Shinto, Buddhist and Christian groups

Noritoshi Tanida

INTRODUCTION

There are considerable cross-cultural differences in medical practices, especially in issues involving ethical problems such as reproductive medicine and the care of terminally ill patients. The difference been Western and Eastern countries is significant. Japan is a unique country where all kinds of medical technology have been adopted from Western culture, but the traditional way of thinking has persisted. Indeed, the matter of Japanese tradition and Western technology is often at the centre of discussions regarding life and death, as exemplified in the dispute over brain death and organ transplantation (Lock 1990: 99, Hardacre 1994: 585, Tanida 1996a: 201). Such a phenomenon is particularly marked in recent years, because Japanese attitudes toward death and dying have been changing. A typical example is the matter of euthanasia.

Although euthanasia was once a virtuous act (Gorai 1994), it has been a taboo since the end of World War II. Yet it is said that doctors have been practising euthanasia secretly (Bioethics Council of the Japanese Medical Association 1992: 1209). Recently, two such cases were disclosed: the Tokai University and Keihoku Hospital euthanasia cases. The Tokai University Hospital case in 1992 was the first euthanasia case where a physician was prosecuted and convicted of the murder of a patient in Japan. Here, the physician gave a potassium chloride injection to a dying comatose patient with multiple myeloma at the request of his family. In the Keihoku Hospital case in 1996, a physician gave a muscle relaxant to a dying comatose cancer patient without his or his family's request. The physician first proclaimed that his act was active euthanasia. However, after facing fierce condemnation by nurses, colleagues and media, he changed his claim to say that he intended to reduce convulsion rather than perform euthanasia. The police questioned him, but in the end he was not prosecuted because the patient died before the dosage of muscle relaxant became lethal. During the discussion over these incidents, some pretended that euthanasia did not exist or that no one asked for euthanasia in Japan (Tanida 1996b: 1103). On the other hand, according to the surveys, 40 to 70 per cent of lay people, 20 per cent of nurses and 15 to 30 per cent of doctors thought that, under certain circumstances, euthanasia was permissible (Tanida 2002a: 313).

Religion may influence medical practices, particularly in the case of terminally ill patients. Catholicism, for example, argues that extraordinary treatments may not be morally enforced on patients against their wish (Gillon 1986: 259), while Judaism maintains that once treatment is initiated, it may not be withdrawn (Schostak 1994: 93). Although the literature points to an affirmative attitude of Japanese Buddhism toward euthanasia (Becker 1990: 543; Perrett 1996: 309), Japanese religious leaders have generally remained silent during the discussions on euthanasia among secular people. Besides, previously, there was no survey of what Japanese religions think of euthanasia, end-of-life issues, or more broadly care of terminally ill patients. Religion is highly relevant to these issues. Therefore, the author conducted a questionnaire survey on the attitudes of Japanese religions toward end-of-life issues. Details of this survey have been published before (Tanida 2000a: 34, 2000b: 339). This article describes the views of Japanese religions toward end-of-life issues based on those results in comparison with results among secular people. Then, it discusses these findings' implication in the genomic age.

OVERVIEW OF JAPANESE RELIGIONS

Shinto

The word "Shinto" is a compound of two Chinese characters: 'shin' refers to 'god(s)' and 'to' means 'way'. Gods worshiped in Shinto are called 'Yao-Yorozu-no-Kami' or 'Eight-Hundred-Myriad-Gods'. There are so many gods in Japan, because people have respected and worshiped as gods anything or anybody with extraordinary power or talent. As a result, there are countless small Shinto shrines (dwellings of god) everywhere in Japan.

Shinto is a collective noun that designates religion or religious belief originating in indigenous faith in gods and spirits in Japan (Agency for Cultural Affairs 1998; Ono 1997). Shinto has no definitive founder, written sutra or established doctrine. Therefore, the definition of Shinto is often vague and often includes not only belief in gods and spirits, but also certain Japanese traditions and ways of thinking. Also, it is difficult to distinguish secular understanding of and religious belief in Shinto. Thus, Shinto cannot be expressed in one word, but its typical virtue may be love of purity. I suggest that the analysis of Shinto may lead to a deeper understanding of everyday life and behaviour of Japanese people.

The most important religious feature of Shinto is ancestor worship. Japanese people believe that death is separation of the soul and body, and the soul stays near this world. There is frequent commuting of the soul between the two worlds. And since people believe in rebirth, they often claim that a newborn baby is a reincarnation of a recently deceased relative. Because there are many souls, a collective noun became necessary to include all of them, i.e., the ancestral soul. Thus, the family worships the ancestor or ancestral soul, and the ancestor will protect descendants and work for their prosperity. Every small community of villages has its own rites and festivals (jinja) for the particular clan of the community. There are other rites and festivals that take place at home, which usually express gratitude for agricultural and fishery harvests. Special calendars are circulated every year by Shinto and Buddhist organisations, which designate the schedule of rites, festivals, and harvests. Thus, Shinto has been a mixture of indigenous belief in the soul, animism, Chinese religion and ideologies, and Buddhism. For example, in addition to ancestor worship, the deceased's remains or grave became sacred through the influence of Chinese culture (Kaji 1994). Now, the ceremony of reverence toward the family grave takes place in the Buddhist style. Attaching importance to living this life and the intact body derived from Confucianism (Kaji 1994). People's love of pleasure, fortune-telling, divine favour, and secret arts for immortality derived from Chinese Taoism (Kubo 1973: 572).

Shinto first acquired its own identity when Buddhism came from overseas. Like in Chinese culture, Buddhism was mixed together with existing religions, and Buddhist gods became gods in Shinto and Shinto gods became gods for Buddha. Thus, Japan has accepted all kinds of religious faith by way of incorporation into pre-existing belief, not by way of 'scrap and build'. This was possible because Shinto is not exclusive in its nature and has the potential to include anything. Even Christians modified the doctrine to allow the worship of the ancestor when faced with the firm beliefs of Japanese people.

Although it is difficult to divide Shinto precisely, current Shinto organisations can be divided into three denominations: Jinja-Shinto, Kyoha-Shinto and Shinkyoha (Agency for Cultural Affairs 1998). Religious faith of the Jinja-Shinto is described in 'the

Platform of Worship Life' (Yuki 1990). The preface notes that 'Shinto is the foundation of the universe, and seeks to foster the sacred spirit, bring peace to the world, respect the wishes of gods, esteem the teachings of ancestors and enhance the welfare of human beings through the sublimation of the self'. Its three objectives are: 1) to express thanks to the blessings of gods and kindness of ancestors and to practice worship with a clean and pure spirit; 2) to sacrifice oneself for society and act to build a good country on behalf of gods; and 3) to pray for prosperity and peace in the world under the Emperor.

The religious faith of Kyoha-Shinto consists of a variety of ideologies, including indigenous Shinto, Confucianism, Taoism, Buddhism, Shugendo (asceticism) and others. It is difficult to categorise these groups and organisations, but some scholars divide them into five categories (Agency for Cultural Affairs 1998): 1) mountain priests, 2) organiser- or founder-headed groups, 3) Misogi (ablution or purification), 4) Confucian and 5) Shinto atavism groups. Mountain priest schools worship sacred mountains and their believers engage in austere training in the mountains. Misogi schools emphasise the training of their body and spirit through ablution or purifying acts. Shinto atavism schools are influenced by the ideology of nationalists in the Edo Era (1603-1867), who advocated atavism back to the genesis of Japan. Until their appearance, Shinto had not been exclusive. Those nationalists particularly attacked Buddhism, and later had considerable influence on monotheistic policy from the Meiji Era (1868-1912) till the end of World War II.

Buddhism

Buddhism, or more exactly Chinese Buddhism, which is quite different from original Buddhism, was officially introduced into Japan in 538 (Agency for Cultural Affairs 1998). After a fierce conflict among rulers as to whether or not to accept Buddhism, Buddhism gained a firm position in Japan. Many temples were built and the principal temples remain in Nara, the capital at the time. In the following Heian Era (794-1192), Tendai and Shingon Buddhism were introduced from the Tang Dynasty in China. Their teachings are characterised by the idea that everyone has a potential to be Buddha. Jodo (Pure Land), Jodo-Shinshu and Nichiren Buddhism were founded in the Kamakura Era (1192-1333) and two Zen Buddhist organisations were introduced during the Song Dynasty. Jodo Buddhism teaches that one must realise <u>his or</u> her own powerlessness and nenbutsu (chanting Buddha) alone can lead people to Jodo (Pure Land) with the help of Buddha. Many people welcomed this teaching, particularly ordinary people and criminals, because good deeds, hard study and austerity were unnecessary. Jodo-Shinshu Buddhism established the idea of Tariki-Hongan or Salvation by Faith. The aim of Zen is to reach satori or enlightenment through meditation and spiritual concentration. Zen's satori cannot be expressed in words, only communication by spirit can transfer from the teacher to the disciple. Zen has strongly influenced the tea ceremony, flower arrangement, gardening and other typically Japanese cultural practices. Nichiren taught that chanting the name of the Hokke sutra was all that believers need do. His teaching was monotheistic and exclusive.

Christianity and Other Religions

Christianity was introduced to Japan in 1549. During the Edo Era, oppression against Christianity was extremely harsh. After the Meiji Restoration, Christianity was still prohibited by the government. But the government was forced to tolerate Christianity due to foreign pressure. Its inferior position under Shinto lasted till the end of World War II. Characteristic of Japanese Christianity is ancestor worship, which was officially allowed in 1983.

There are a number of religious schools that have founders but do not belong to any of the major religions. Some emerged independently from existing religions; others are amalgams of Shinto and Buddhism, Shinto and Buddhism and Christianity, and so on.

QUESTIONNAIRE

Questions regarding Euthanasia Cases

Clinical situations and questions regarding euthanasia are shown in the Appendix. The forms of euthanasia in this article are characterised on the basis of the act of the doctor (active or passive) and request by the patient (voluntary, non-voluntary and involuntary) (Kantor 1989), with the additional concept of indirect euthanasia (Emanuel 1994). Cases 1 to 3 dealt with terminal patients and Case 4 dealt with non-fatal illnesses. In each situation, the family gave its approval, because this is usually a prerequisite for the doctor's involvement in Japan. Respondents were asked whether they agreed with the doctor's decision to perform euthanasia. They chose one of five options: 'agree strongly', 'agree', 'neutral', 'disagree', 'disagree strongly'. The data indicate the percentage that answered 'agree strongly and agree', 'neutral' and 'disagree and disagree strongly'.

Religious Organisations

Although it overestimates the number of believers, the Ministry of Education provides a good overview of current religious activities in Japan (Agency for Cultural Affairs 1998). Table 1 describes the profiles of three principal religions—Shinto, Buddhism and Christianity—as well as other religions in Japan. In 1998, a questionnaire was mailed to 388 'inclusive religious groups' including 143 Shinto, 157 Buddhist, 58 Christian and 30 other groups, asking them to answer questions based on their and their leaders' religious faith. The persons who answered the questionnaire included 139 leaders and 23 theologians.

Secular People

The same survey was conducted among health care professionals in 1997 (Tanida 1998a: 138), pharmaceutical students in 2000, and medical students in 2001. Health care professionals, mostly nurses, included 62 males and 146 females with a mean age of 43 years. Pharmaceutical students included 178 females aged 19 and 20 years. Medical students included 53 males and 47 females with a mean age of 20 years.

Results regarding Passive Euthanasia (Table 2)

A total of 68 per cent of the religious groups agreed that voluntary passive euthanasia (Case 1) should be allowed. This figure rose to 75 per cent if the family requested it. There was no statistically significant difference among the four religious groups in their responses. When the results were examined for each religion, Zen groups were significantly less favourable to the doctor's act of non-voluntary passive euthanasia than other Buddhist groups. Protestant groups were more favourable than Catholics, although the difference was statistically marginal. Among secular people, the attitudes of health care professionals were similar as those of religious people. On the other hand, attitudes of pharmaceutical and medical students were different: students favoured voluntary rather than non-voluntary passive euthanasia.

Results regarding Active Euthanasia (Table 3)

In Case 2, a total of 19 per cent of religious groups agreed with voluntary active euthanasia. The corresponding figures increased to 63 per cent when a sedative was used until the patient's death (indirect euthanasia). There was significant difference in responses to active euthanasia among the four religious groups, which was due to a more favourable attitude of Shinto groups and a less favourable attitude of Christian groups. Notably, all Catholic groups disagreed with the doctor's act, whereas 40 per cent of Protestant groups did not oppose this act. Among secular people, attitudes were similar to those of Shinto and Buddhist groups. Students had the most favourable attitudes towards voluntary active euthanasia: 38 to 44 per cent agreed with this act.

Results regarding Non-Voluntary Active Euthanasia (Table 4)

In Case 3, a total of 12 to 16 per cent of religious groups agreed with non-voluntary active euthanasia. There were significant differences in the responses of the four religious groups. Shinto groups were more favourable to non-voluntary active euthanasia than other religions. Notably, Shinto groups did not require the use of potassium chloride and sedatives. Buddhist groups showed a slightly favourable attitude toward the use of sedatives. Christian groups were less favourable than other religions toward non-voluntary active euthanasia. Furthermore, Catholic groups were less favourable than Protestant ones. Among secular people, students were more favourable towards non-voluntary active euthanasia than others; their responses were similar to those of Shinto groups. Like the religious groups, 37 per cent of health care professionals accepted non-voluntary active euthanasia, if the doctor used a sedative, which seems to indicate that they did not distinguish between non-voluntary active euthanasia and so-called sedation at the terminal setting.

Results regarding Euthanasia in Non-Fatal Illness (Table 5)

In Case 4 with a quadriplegic patient, 14 per cent of the religious groups agreed with the doctor's decision to perform voluntary active euthanasia with a sedative. The corresponding figure was 40 per cent when the doctor opted for voluntary passive euthanasia. Responses to mercy killing were similar to those to voluntary active euthanasia. Christian groups were less favourable to active euthanasia and mercy killing than Shinto and Buddhist ones. When the results were examined in each religion, Kyoha-Shinto groups were less favourable to active euthanasia than Shinkyoha-Shinto groups. Catholics were less favourable to mercy killing than Protestants. Among secular people, students were more favourable to active euthanasia and mercy killing than religious groups, but their attitudes towards passive euthanasia were the same. The attitudes of health care professionals were similar to those of religious groups.

Respondents' Remarks

Nearly all Shinto groups advocated 'natural' death, due to their faith in the immortality of the soul. Some noted that medicine is a gift of the gods, but that the prolongation of life using artificial means is a disgraceful. Others noted that the patient should rely on the doctor or medicine, and believers in Shinto would accept any result regardless of the cause or intention. Among Buddhists, many noted that medical treatment is necessary for curable diseases; but they considered mere prolongation of life inappropriate. One Zen group noted that patients can make their own decision. One Nichiren group noted that emphasizing the sanctity of life is understandable, but that spiritual satisfaction is more important for the deceased and bereaved. The Catholic Central Committee expressed the Vatican's position on terminal care (Gillon 1986: 259). Nearly all Christian groups objected to active euthanasia and futile treatment, while respecting decisions by the patient. They also stressed the necessity of preliminary consultation. Remarks by the secular people were not different; they also tended to focus on the patient's wishes.

IMPLICATION OF RELIGIOUS PEOPLE'S ATTITUDES TOWARDS EUTHANASIA

The ethics of voluntary active euthanasia is one of the most controversial issues in clinical settings. Prohibitions against assisting in a patient's death have been cardinal in medical ethics since the implementation of Hippocratic medical morality (Emanuel 1994: 1890). Medical professionals are concerned that the act of active euthanasia undermines the core moral commitment of medicine and the trust between patients and medical professionals. However, circumstances surrounding euthanasia are gradually changing and there are now some exceptions. For example, in certain situations, physicians may practice voluntary active euthanasia in the Netherlands and Belgium. And physicians can legally prescribe a lethal dose of drugs to terminally ill patients who desire to terminate their own lives in the state of Oregon in the United States.

Japan has a long history of practising euthanasia (Gorai 1994). The Japan Medical Association published a report by her Bioethics Council saying 'there is no way other than allowance of euthanasia in very exceptional occasions as it is practised currently' (Bioethics Council of the Japanese Medical Association 1992: 1209). There are two court rulings that permit active euthanasia in Japan. The latest decision in 1995, by the Yokohama District Court, concurred with the 1962 Nagoya High Court decision and determined that there are four criteria for accepting euthanasia: (1) the patient suffers from unbearable physical pain; (2) the death of the patient is unavoidable and imminent; (3) all possible palliative care has been given and no alternatives to alleviate the patient's suffering exist; and (4) the patient explicitly requests physicians to help hasten his or her death. Since the criteria were declared, no euthanasia case has been reported. Regarding passive euthanasia and indirect euthanasia, the Japanese Academy of Science and Art has approved of these practices (Committee of Japanese Academy of Science and Art 1995: 70), whereas the Japanese media often equates passive euthanasia with killing patients (Anon 1997). Thus, there appear to be two extreme opinions regarding the discussion on euthanasia: allowance of active euthanasia on the one side, and denial of passive euthanasia on the other side; the two sides do not communicate with each other.

Japanese traditional and contemporary views of life and death derived mainly from Shinto and Japanese Buddhism. According to Shinto thinking, death is a separation of the soul and body. And the soul can be deified regardless of whether death is the result of euthanasia or suicide, as long as the dying process is natural, brave, virtuous or meaningful. It was mostly Buddhism that dealt with the value of life and death in Japan. The core of Buddhist philosophy regarding life and death is metempsychosis or transmigration of the soul (i.e., suffering) until nirvana or full comprehension. Therefore, euthanasia or suicide is by no means a way to avoid suffering in original Buddhism (Lecso 1986: 51; Becker 1990: 543; Perrett 1996: 309). It may be natural that Buddhist philosophy of metempsychosis and nirvana and the Shinto ideology regarding the soul influenced each other. For example, metempsychosis is not always a form of suffering in Japanese Buddhism. The corpse is mere existence without importance in original Buddhism, whereas Japanese Buddhism teaches that the corpse must be left untouched for a while before proceeding to have funeral (Kuge 1996: 27); Shinto teaching is the same. Euthanasia and suicide are not a continuation of suffering but a way to the Pure Land (heaven) from this Defiled World (Becker 1990: 543).

In accord with the idea of 'being natural', a majority of the Japanese religious groups favour passive euthanasia and indirect euthanasia at the terminal stage. Active euthanasia was greeted unfavourably among religious people in general. Nevertheless, their religious beliefs make members of Shinto groups more favourable to active euthanasia than Buddhist and Christian groups. Japanese tradition in favour of mercy killing (Becker 1990: 543; Gorai 1994; Perrett 1996: 309) may be the reason that Shinto and Buddhist groups respond more positively to this medical practice than Christians. The majority of Shinto and Buddhist groups, moreover, agree with the Catholic denial of extraordinary treatment at the end of the dying process (Gillon 1986: 259; Nairn 1997: 36). The reason for denial of the Catholic doctrine by a few Shinto and Buddhist groups was likely due to their religious faith in leaving medical decision-making to the doctor and family. This tendency is particularly strong in Shinto.

The attitudes of secular and religious people towards euthanasia displayed similarities as well as differences. More specifically, attitudes of pharmaceutical and medical students towards active euthanasia were similar to those of Shinto and Buddhist groups. But students responded more positively to voluntary active euthanasia than religious people and health care professionals, although more of them preferred voluntary to non-voluntary euthanasia than did religious people and health care professionals. Although indirect euthanasia appears to be accepted by health care professionals, other forms of euthanasia are greeted highly unfavourably among them. In general, health care professionals tended to prefer life-prolonging acts, whereas Shinto and Buddhist groups advocated 'being natural' when medical treatment for cure became futile at the terminal stage. Such a negative attitude toward euthanasia among health care professionals was ascertained by a recent study, which specifically focused on whether they complied with or refused patients' requests to directly hasten death (Asai 2001: 324; Tanida 2002a: 313). Over half of the doctors and nurses had been asked by patients to hasten death, of whom 6 per cent of the doctors had taken active steps to bring about death, but none of the nurses had done so. The results also showed that 22 per cent of doctors and 14 per cent of nurses answered that they would practice active euthanasia if it were legal. Such rates are significantly lower than those in an earlier Australian study (Kuhse 1993: 311).

What makes Japanese health care professionals less willing to assist in euthanasia or more reluctant to comply with a patient's wish to hasten death? It should be pointed out that a significantly greater number of Japanese disregarded the patient's desire as irrational as did Australians (Asai 2001: 324, Kuhse 1993: 311). Such an attitude probably in part derives from the Japanese tradition of not attaching importance to verbal expression (Tanida 1996a: 201). The illegality of euthanasia or the uncertainty regarding lower courts' decisions about active euthanasia (only the decision by the Supreme Court is regarded as written law in Japan) could not explain this, because only a small number of doctors would practice active euthanasia if it were legal. Presumably, health care professionals hold secular moral and ethical views that emphasize the sanctity of life. Furthermore, since the introduction of modern medicine from the United States, Japanese also firmly believe in the 'infinitive progress of medicine' (Callahan 1990: 1810), which has led to the 'prolongation of the dying process' in contemporary Japan.

The number of religious Japanese people was 32 per cent (26 per cent for Buddhism, 2 per cent for Shinto and 1 per cent for Christianity), while 63 per cent answered that they are atheists (Anon 1995). 54 per cent of families have a Shinto shrine in their house and 59 per cent a Buddhist family altar. Overall, 81 per cent of people visit the family grave to worship their ancestors and 56 per cent go to a Shinto shrine or Buddhist temple to celebrate New Year. 70 per cent believe in Buddhist cause/effect thinking and 50 per cent in the existence of the soul after death. Among the so-called atheists, 70 per cent believed in Buddhist cause/effect thinking and 46 per cent in the immortality of the soul. And 71 per cent of them believed in superstitious phenomena. 79 per cent of them visited the family grave and 54 per cent went to a shrine and temple to celebrate New Year. These phenomena indicate that religion is deeply rooted in the Japanese way of thinking. In fact, significantly more health professionals who believe in Buddhism would practice active euthanasia if it were legal than those who believe in Christianity (Asai 2001: 324). Thus, religion has a considerable impact on Japanese people, albeit unconsciously. Religion and medicine are distinct, but both devote themselves to caring for patients (O'Donnell 1970: 815). Although the Japanese religious world has been mostly isolated from the rest of society, the variety of religious opinions are likely to help people think about these important end-of-life issues in medicine. Thus, open discussion among religious and secular people is essential to expand and deepen understanding of these complex controversial end-of-life issues that every person faces.

IMPLICATION OF RELIGION IN THE GENOMIC AGE

Among secular people, prolonging life becomes a supreme aim of society. When patients are dying in the hospital, doctors and nurses try to prolong his or her life by cardiopulmonary resuscitation and other life-sustaining measures. A doctor who did not perform cardiopulmonary resuscitation on a dying cancer patient was fiercely condemned by ward nurses and expelled from the hospital in 1997 (Tanida 1998b: 166). According to a nationwide survey in 1996 (Anon 1996), only 12 per cent of doctors ever withdrew life-sustaining treatment in the terminal stage. In hospitals for the elderly, conscious or unconscious bedridden patients are forced to eat artificial nutrition, otherwise the doctor is condemned by the mass media as having killed the patient (Anon 1997). Health care professionals and the mass media in Japan are most strongly opposed to euthanasia.

The idea that the dying process should be prolonged is recent. As described earlier, such a pro-life attitude does not stem from Japanese tradition and culture. Buddhism emphasises the importance and respect for any life. They teach to make every effort to treat disease as long as the treatment is meaningful (Kuge 1996: 27). At the end of life, 'being natural' is the main Buddhist principle. In this regard, as in others, Shinto is quite flexible. However, the principal idea of love of completeness in Shinto is incompatible with prolonging the dying process. This pro-life attitude has probably been introduced from Western or Christian ideology, first as 'sanctity of life, then extended to 'prolonging the dying process'.

There may be several reasons for the current popularity of the pro-life view in Japan. These include: 1) the Japanese penchant for anything new and 2) characteristics of the Japanese health care system. By nature, Japanese love anything new and have been accepting all kinds of new medical technology from overseas. When Japanese learned of cardiopulmonary resuscitation technique, for example, it was naturally introduced as an everyday practice. As with other newly imported technologies, the appropriateness was not a major concern. Though it is a general attitude among physicians worldwide, Japanese physicians are particularly conditioned to help their patients recover. The Japanese health care system has also contributed significantly to spread of life-sustaining treatments. When physicians abandon life-sustaining treatments in the hospital, they will inevitably lose out in the care of terminally ill patients due to the Japanese fee-for-service system (Ikegami 1995: 1295). Thus, there is an economic incentive for Japanese physicians to prescribe unnecessary drugs and procedures.

These background factors may influence the introduction of genomic medicine. One such example is the story of gefitinib in

Japan. Gefitinib is a selective inhibitor of the epidermal growth factor receptor, which is derived from genomic research on tyrosine kinase of the cell. It appeared to be effective for patients with advanced non-small cell lung cancer, who do not respond to existing chemotherapy. With only limited data to show its effectiveness in shrinking tumor size, the Japanese government approved of its use in clinics on July 5, 2002. This rapid approval resulted in more than a hundred deaths, when patients reacted adversely to gefitinib. It should be noted that the United States government suspended approval of gefitinib, based on exactly the same data that persuaded the Japanese government to give its approval.

Japanese health care providers have repeatedly committed such mistakes (Tanida 2002b: 41). Now, with the introduction of genomic medicine, the same thing could happen. What role can religious people play in this genomic age? Dealing with life and death is the essence of religion. The attitudes of religious organisations have mostly been modest and sensible. It is unfortunate for Japanese lay people, who have not been able to listen to the wisdom of religious people with respect to these important issues. In this regard, several attempts in Shinto and Buddhist organisations are noteworthy. Some are speaking to the general population about their views toward life and death as well as about brain death and organ transplantation. Some Buddhist groups began to speak in public about their approach to medicine. Diverse attitudes among religious people are not disadvantageous here, because the general public would benefit from an exposure to different opinions on this important issue.

Appendix. Hypothetical Clinical Situations and Questions Related to Euthanasia

Case 1:

An elderly patient is bed-ridden in a nursing home because of disability. He suffered from repeated pneumonia and has caught pneumonia again. Antibiotics is considered to be effective to some extent. The patient has asked the doctor not to use antibiotics, because he wants to die quietly.

Question 1:

The doctor accepted his wish.

Question 2:

The patient has fallen into unconsciousness without verbalising his wishes. The family has asked the doctor not to use antibiotics. The doctor accepted the family's wish.

Case 2:

A patient with final-stage cancer suffers from severe pain and fatigue despite every measure. Her death is imminent. She has repeatedly asked the attending doctor for a peaceful death using drugs. Her family accepts her wish.

Question 3:

The doctor administered potassium chloride and the patient died.

Question 4:

The doctor administered a sedative to keep the patient unconscious till death.

Case 3:

A patient has fallen into irreversible coma without expressing his wishes. His death is inevitable and near because of his disease. Knowing of his situation, the family has repeatedly asked the attending doctor to hasten death, using drugs.

Question 5:

The doctor administered potassium chloride and the patient died.

Question 6:

The doctor administered a sedative, and the patient died.

Case 4:

A young patient has been quadriplegic for 6 years. He has suffered from pneumonia repeatedly. He does not look like the superb athlete he used to be. At present the patient's condition is stable. He has been fed on nasogastric tube nutrition. He is not depressed according to psychiatrists. He has repeatedly requested the doctor to apply euthanasia, using a high dose of sedative.

Question 7:

The doctor accepted his wish.

Question 8:

The patient has repeatedly asked the doctor to withdraw tube feeding. He has rejected water and electrolyte infusion as well. The doctor accepted his wish.

Question 9:

He has fallen into unconsciousness because of severe pneumonia without expressing his wishes. The family has asked the doctor for euthanasia. The doctor performed mercy killing with a high dose of sedative.

Note: At each question, respondents were asked to rate the degree of agreement with the doctor's decision or act. Their options were 'agree strongly', 'agree', 'neutral', 'disagree' and 'disagree strongly'. (Figures combine '(dis)agree strongly' and '(dis)agree'.

Table 1. Numbers of Organizations, Teachers and Believers Covered by the 388 Inclusive Religious Groups Registered by the Minister of Education in Japan December 31, 1997.

Religion	Organizations Believers	Teachers	Believers
Shinto (143)	86,785	65,484(5)	95,953,951
Jinja-Shinto (16)	80,249	26,975	91,674,061
Kyoha-Shinto (80)	5,687	35,020(5)	3,724,877
Shinkyoha-Shinto (47)	849	3,489	555,013
Buddhism (157)	84,336	216,919(38)	61,996,616
Tendai (20)	5,033	18,225(1)	2,659,958
Shingon (46)	14,987	61,664(25)	12,987,266
Jodo (23)	30,274	62,303(7)	19,571,212
Zen (22)	21,033	22,421(2)	3,270,740
Nichiren (38)	12,652	50,864(3)	23,306,275
Others (8)	357	1,442 1,442	210,165
Christianity (58)	7,751	10,641(2,103)	916,011
Catholic (14)	2,045	1,825(816)	455,557
Protestants (44)	5,706	8,816(1,287)	460,454
Others (30)	41,163	262,658(7)	6,874,650
Total (388)	220,035	555,702(2,153)	165,741,228
Total figures*	227,558	649,937(7,241)	207,758,774

* Total figures derived from all religious organizations in addition to the 'inclusive groups' in Japan.

Note: Organisations include shrines, temples and churches for propagation, most of which are qualified as individual groups. Teachers include priests, monks, and missionaries. Figures in parentheses immediately after religious group names are numbers of 'inclusive groups' in each religion. Figures in parentheses of the teachers are foreigners.

Table 2. Attitudes of Japanese Religious Groups and Secular People towards Passive Euthanasia.

Religious sects and Secular people	Voluntary passive euthanasia	Non-Voluntary passive euthanasia
Religious groups, total	68/18/14	75/19/6
Shinto, total	64/15/21	70/23/7
Jinja-Shinto	66/0/33	33/33/33
Kyoha-Shinto	56/19/25	38/25/38
Shinkyoha-Shinto	78/11/11	83/11/6
Buddhism, total	68/23/10	79/16/5
Tendai	88/13/0	100/0/0
Shingon	63/16/21	89/11/0
Jodo	73/27/0	82/18/0
Zen	58/33/8	33/42/25
Nichiren	64/27/9	91/9/0
Christianity, total	70/18/13	75/19/6
Catholic	63/13/25	50/38/13
Protestants	72/20/8	83/13/4
Others	79/7/14	79/14/7
Health care professionals	54/32/14	63/27/10
Pharmaceutical students	69/26/5	56/34/10
Medical students	70/23/7	50/42/8

Note: Figures designate percentages of respondents in each group by 'agree'/'neutral'/'disagree'.

Table 3. Attitudes of Japanese Religious Groups and Secular People towards Active Euthanasia and Indirect Euthanasia.

Religious sects and Secular people	Voluntary active euthanasia	Voluntary indirect euthanasia
Religious groups, total	19/27/53	63/24/13
Shinto, total	32/30/38	68/21/11
Jinja-Shinto	0/33/66	66/33/0
Kyoha-Shinto	38/25/38	63/25/13
Shinkyoha-Shinto	28/39/33	78/11/11
Buddhism, total	18/25/57	63/29/8
Tendai	38/0/63	88/13/0
Shingon	11/28/61	68/21/11
Jodo	27/9/64	45/27/27
Zen	0/42/58	67/33/0
Nichiren	30/30/40	45/55/0
Christianity, total	3/27/70	67/15/18
Catholic	0/0/100	63/13/25
Protestants	4/36/60	68/16/16
Others	15/23/62	38/31/31
Health care professionals	21/24/55	71/21/7
Pharmaceutical students	44/32/24	76/16/8
Medical students	38/38/24	58/28/14

Note: Figures designate percentages of respondents in each group by 'agree'/'neutral'/'disagree'.

Table 4. Attitudes of Japanese Religious Groups and Secular People towards Non-Voluntary Active Euthanasia.

Religious sects and Secular people	Non-voluntary active euthanasia with KCI	Non-voluntary active euthanasia with sedative
Religious groups, total	12/26/62	16/31/53
Shinto, total	21/29/50	23/35/42
Jinja-Shinto	0/0/100	0/0/100
Kyoha-Shinto	22/34/44	25/34/41
Shinkyoha-Shinto	24/24/53	24/41/35
Buddhism, total	10/28/62	16/34/49
Tendai	25/13/63	13/63/25
Shingon	5/21/74	16/16/68
Jodo	0/36/64	18/27/55
Zen	8/42/50	17/42/42
Nichiren	20/20/60	20/40/40
Christianity, total	3/15/82	9/18/73
Catholic	0/0/100	0/0/100
Protestants	4/20/76	12/24/64
Others	8/31/62	7/29/64
Health care professionals	13/21/66	37/36/27
Pharmaceutical students	21/43/36	27/43/30
Medical students	19/43/38	27/40/33

Note: Figures designate percentages of respondents in each group by 'agree'/'neutral'/'disagree'.

Table 5. Attitudes of Japanese Religious Groups and Secular People towards Active Euthanasia in Non-Fatal Illness.

Religious sects and Secular people	Voluntary active euthanasia	Voluntary passive euthanasia	Mercy killing
Religious groups, total	14/28/58	40/31/29	16/28/56
Shinto, total	19/34/47	40/38/23	25/33/42
Jinja-Shinto	0/67/33	33/33/33	0/0/100
Kyoha-Shinto	13/28/59	34/38/28	19/39/42
Shinkyoha-Shinto	33/39/28	50/39/11	39/28/33
Buddhism, total	16/31/52	43/30/28	16/31/52
Tendai	13/38/50	38/50/13	25/50/25
Shingon	16/26/58	32/26/42	21/21/58
Jodo	18/18/64	45/9/45	9/18/73
Zen	17/42/42	42/42/17	0/42/58
Nichiren	20/30/50	70/20/10	30/30/40
Christianity, total	3/15/82	42/21/36	9/15/76
Catholic	0/0/100	75/0/25	0/0/100
Protestants	4/20/76	32/28/40	12/20/68
Others	7/21/71	21/36/43	0/29/71
Health care professionals	18/34/48	38/34/28	16/33/51
Pharmaceutical students	35/24/41	36/29/35	23/40/37
Medical students	29/31/40	41/38/21	25/35/40

Note: Figures designate percentages of respondents in each group by 'agree'/'neutral'/'disagree'.

BIBLIOGRAPHY

Agency for Cultural Affairs (in Japanese) (1998) *The Annals of Religion 1998*, Tokyo: Gyosei.

Anonymous (in Japanese) 'Number of atheists increased among the elderly and those critical of religious organisations', *Asahi Shinbun*, 23 September, 1995.

Anonymous (in Japanese) '15% of doctors do not care about 4 conditions for active euthanasia', *Mainichi Shinbun*, 2 July 1996.

Anonymous (in Japanese) 'Killing the elderly', *Mainichi Shinbun*, 6 and 10 January, 1997.

Asai, A., Ohnishi, M., Nagata, S.K., Tanida, N. and Yamazaki, Y. (2001) 'Doctors' and nurses' attitudes towards and experiences of voluntary euthanasia: survey of members of the Japanese association of palliative medicine', *Journal of Medical Ethics*, 27: 324-330.

Becker, C.B. (1990) 'Buddhist views of suicide and euthanasia', *Philosophy East & West*, 40: 543-556.

Bioethics Council of the Japanese Medical Association (in Japanese) (1992) 'A report on how doctors should behave in terminal care', *Nihon Ishikai Zasshi*, 107: 1209-1217.

Callahan, D. (1990) 'Rationing medical progress. The way to affordable health care', *New England Journal of Medicine*, 322: 1810-1813.

Committee of Japanese Academy of Science and Art (in Japanese) (1995) 'Dying and Medicine', *Report on 'Death-with-dignity'*, 1061: 70-73.

Emanuel, E.J. (1994) 'Euthanasia. Historical, ethical, and empiric perspectives', *Archives of Internal Medicine*, 154: 1890-1901.

Gillon, R. (1986) 'Ordinary and extraordinary means', *British Medical Journal*, 292: 259-261.

Gorai, S. (in Japanese) (1994) *Japanese view on death*, Tokyo: Kadokawa-Shoten.

Hardacre, H. (1994) 'Response of Buddhism and Shinto to the issue of brain death and organ transplants'. *Cambridge Quarterly of Healthcare Ethics*, 3: 585-601.

Ikegami, N. and Campbell, J.C. (1995) 'Medical care in Japan', *New England Journal of Medicine*, 333: 1295-1299.

Kaji, N. (in Japanese) (1994) *Confucianism, The Silent Religion*, Tokyo: Chikuma-Shobo.

Kantor, J.E. (1989) *Medical Ethics for Physician-in-Training*. New York: Plenum.

Kubo, N. (in Japanese) (1973) 'Taoism', in E. Oguchi and I. Hori (eds) <u>Shukogaku-Jiten</u>, Tokyo: University of Tokyo Press.

Kuge, N., Ito, S., Fujimoto, K. and Arase, S. (in Japanese) (1996) 'How to Behave When Facing Death and Japanese Buddhist History', in K.

Mizutani (ed.) *Buddhism and Terminal Care*. Kyoto: Hozokan.

Kuhse, H. and Singer, P. (1993) 'Voluntary euthanasia and the nurse: an Australian survey', *International Journal of Nursing Studies*, 30: 311-322.

Lecso, P.A. (1986) 'Euthanasia: a Buddhist perspective', *Journal of Religion and Health*, 25: 51-57.

Lock, M. and Honde, C. (1990) 'Reaching consensus about death: heart transplants and cultural identity in Japan', in G. Weisz (ed.) *Social Science Perspectives on Medical Ethics*, Dordrecht: Kluwer.

Nairn, T.A. (1997) 'Reclaiming our moral tradition. Catholic teaching calls on us to accept the limits of medical technology', *Health Progress*, 78: 36-42.

O'Donnell, T.J. (1970) 'Medicine and religion. An overview', *Journal of the American Medical Association*, 211: 815-817.

Ono, S. (1997) *Shinto: The Kami Way*, Tokyo: Charles E. Tuttle.

Perrett, R.W. (1996) 'Buddhism, euthanasia and the sanctity of life', *Journal of Medical Ethics*, 22: 309-313.

Schostak, R.Z. (1994) 'Jewish ethical guidelines for resuscitation and artificial nutrition and hydration of the dying elderly', *Journal of Medical Ethics*, 20: 93-100.

Tanida, N. (1996a) 'Bioethics is subordinate to morality in Japan', *Bioethics*, 10: 201-211.

Tanida, N. (1996b) 'Public pretences about euthanasia in Japan', *Lancet*, 348: 1103.

Tanida, N. (1998a) 'Japanese attitudes toward euthanasia in hypothetical clinical situations', *Eubios Journal of Asian and International Bioethics*, 8: 138-141.

Tanida, N. (in Japanese) (1998b) 'Withholding or withdrawing life-sustaining treatment, life and self-determination', *Igakutetsugaku Igakurinri*, 16: 166-174.

Tanida, N. (2000a) 'Japanese religious organization's view on terminal care', *Eubios Journal of Asian and International Bioethics*, 10: 34-37.

Tanida, N. (2000b) 'The view of religions toward euthanasia and extraordinary treatments in Japan', *Journal of Religion and Health*, 39: 339-354.

Tanida, N., Asai, A., Ohnishi, M., Nagata, S.K., Fukui, T., Yamazaki, Y. and Kuhse, H. (2002a) 'Voluntary Active Euthanasia and the Nurse: A Comparison of Japan and Australia', *Nursing Ethics*, 9: 313-322.

Tanida, N. (2002b) 'Ethical consideration in clinical trials in Asia', *Drug Information Journal*, 36: 41-49.

Yuki, H., Ogida, M. and Sekioka, K. (in Japanese) (1990) *History of Religion*, Osaka: Sogensha.

Chapter 7

Genome, Artificial Evolution and Global Community

Hyakudai Sakamoto

INTRODUCTION

Recent advances in research on the human genome are provoking many problems in global policy regarding the future status of human beings and the whole life system on earth. At the same time, these advances are also raising serious bioethical and philosophical questions. First of all, how should we deal with the fact that we are going to have the technology to manipulate the entire system of the human genome and other non-human genomes? Although no science or technology can be complete, gene technology will soon fall into the hands of human beings, instead of God.

Secondly, which gene technologies will we actually realise and utilise in the early stages of the 21st century? Most probably, we will apply these technologies to health care and use them to treat bodily diseases such as cancer, hemophilia, ADA (adenosine deaminase) deficiency and so forth. And sooner or later, we will apply gene therapy to germ lines, which, in the long run, suggests the possibility of a future 'artificial evolution', replacing the 'natural evolution' of the past

Thirdly, how is this new concept of 'artificial evolution' justified ethically? I believe this kind of manmade evolution is the only way for human beings to survive in the future global environment. There cannot be any serious ethical objection against the idea of artificial evolution

Fourthly, what is the background philosophy for the concept of 'artificial evolution'? I will discuss the nature of modern European humanism in relation to individual dignity and fundamental human rights and I will conclude by suggesting that we should abolish an essential part of modern humanism and devise some alternative philosophies on the basis of an Asian perspective.

THE AGE OF BIOTECHNOLOGY

It is often said that we are living in an age of biotechnology. We should try to revise the philosophy of bioscience and bioethics in relation to the nature of human beings and human society, especially concerning recent trends in genetics and gene technology. In this chapter, I will focus on the problem of justification of recent trends in human genome research. In addition, I will also discuss genetic engineering from the viewpoint of the new idea of 'artificial evolution', which might urge us to re-examine and doubt the universal validity of the historical idea of humanism in the post-modern global community. Here the Asian way of thinking, together with Asian ideas about nature, might provide some insightful suggestions.

HEREDITY, HUMAN GENOME RESEARCH AND ARTIFICIAL EVOLUTION

The human being is subject to two unavoidable bodily and biological restraints: 'heredity' and 'evolution'. These two aspects of our biological human nature essentially oppose each other. Heredity is a bodily disposition to preserve one's own genetic make-up, and evolution is, on the contrary, a tendency to alter the hereditary genetic characteristics. We have survived because of the natural balance of these two mutually contradicting propensities of our bodily nature. Presumably this balancing has been done by way of irregular mutation and natural selection. We have, however, at the end of the 20th century, obtained the ability to control human evolution by means of 'recombinant DNA', i.e., by altering the genetic patterns of a human body artificially. We have acquired the third fire of Prometheus, so to speak.

Since a few years ago, gene therapy has been used to treat genetic diseases such as ADA deficiency, cancer, leukemia, and so forth throughout the world. Human genome research has rapidly advanced and all human genomes should be decoded in a few years. I also presume that, in a few years, human cloning will be practised somewhere in the world. The application of these contemporary technologies will certainly result in broad artificial changes in human genetic patterns. This may bring about the future transformation of the human species into another species. This will be a sort of evolution, but it is not a natural evolution, which is done by natural selection, but a man-made evolution, which is done by means of an artificial and planned selection of human beings. In the course of this new century, we will be able to control natural evolution to some extent. This new kind of evolution will be properly called 'artificial evolution' and is far beyond the notion of eugenics, which urges us to fundamentally revise the meaning of a better or happier life.

But any artificial procedure requires ends and purposes as well as methodologies and assessments. Now in which direction, to what goal, by what methodology should we lead humankind? And by what criterion should we assess this new kind of evolution?

ENVIRONMENTAL ETHICS AND FUNDAMENTAL HUMAN RIGHTS

One of the easiest answers to the question above is that we should apply gene manipulation technology in order to maximise human welfare and happiness and minimise human pain or unhappiness.

But what is happiness and what is pain? Here again, we may fall into the complex trap of utilitarianism. By now, however, we have developed another fundamental criterion for evaluating the future status of the human being, namely the criterion of an environmental viewpoint, i.e., 'survival by protecting the environment'.

Philosophically speaking, there are two types of ideas for protecting the environment. One idea is to protect nature in order to provide the best environment for future generations of human beings. Another idea is to protect nature for its own sake. These two ways of evaluating the environment clearly contradict each other in their logical consequences. The former is typically an anthropocentric way of thinking. The latter believes that we should not manipulate nature to pursue only the happiness of human beings. Here, 'nature' means natural environment, and at the same time, it would mean 'natural evolution'. This antagonism between the two forms of protecting nature raises serious doubts about the status of the concept of fundamental human rights: Is it within the scope of our fundamental human rights to change (improve or destroy) nature in order to foster human survival or increase our happiness? Now, most environmentalists would say 'No!' decisively. This rejection shares a common rationale with the rejection of gene therapy, cloning and gene manipulation in general in the sense that both rejections seem to try to avoid as much artificial manipulation of *nature*, on the one hand, and of *human nature*, on the other hand, as possible. I presume that every ELSI (Ethical, Legal, Social Issue) problem concerning gene manipulation fundamentally stems from this common source.

GENE MANIPULATION AND HUMAN RIGHTS

The Council of Europe launched global social-legal efforts to deal with this problem in 1982. The Council declared in its Recommendation 934 on Genetic Engineering that: 'Human Rights imply the right to inherit a genetic pattern that has not been artificially changed'. It added that: 'the explicit recognition of this right must not impede development of therapeutic application of genetic engineering (gene therapy)'. However, this recommendation suffered from a serious conceptual confusion. Can human rights be violated in the name of human happiness (e.g., by recombinant DNA)? What are the nature and substance of human rights and human happiness in relation to gene therapy?

In general, it is now common practice to distinguish *somatic* gene therapy from *germ-line* gene therapy, and to recommend the former and to prohibit the latter type of gene therapy. However, this distinction is only provisional, and not definite, because (1) somatic gene therapy *might* have some effects on the germ-line gene state and (2) the road from somatic therapy to germ-line therapy is a 'slippery slope'. Philosophical problems about gene therapy will, I believe, arise only in the case of 'germ-line gene therapy'.

Moreover, the supplementary item of the Recommendation tends towards paternalism or at least communitarianism. It implies that in order to promote the happiness of all human beings or human communities, human rights can be violated to a certain extent. (The one-child policy in China would be an apparent violation of fundamental human rights from a Western perspective. However, it would be acceptable from a communitarian viewpoint, because it will prevent overpopulation in China, or even in the world.)

PERSONAL VS. HEREDITARY IDENTITY: UNIVERSALITY OF HUMAN RIGHTS REVISITED

These questions have deep roots in the problem of personal identity vs. hereditary identity, and also in issues related to the universality of human rights. In the history of modern European ideas, the concept of human rights has always been discussed in relation to the concept of 'person', which is strictly distinguished from the concept of 'human being', so that human rights belong to an individual as a person but not as a human being. Here, I will refer to, among others, John Locke and Peter Singer as advocates of this theory to distinguish the concept of person from that of human being (Singer has recently applied the concept of 'person' to non-human animals.)

According to these thinkers, 'person' has the self-identity to which the dignity of an individual is attributed. This dignity has been often identified with 'reason', which is universally and *a priori* given to all human persons (as Kant argued). An analogue to this personal identity is bodily identity as a human being, which is properly represented as hereditary identity within modern biology and genetics. Therefore, it seems to me, legal theorists of the European Council readily assumed that preserving hereditary identity, i.e. genetic pattern, is a human right. However, this analogy is dubious. First of all, it seems that the universality of reason in a person, and therefore the universality of human rights, has been questioned through the development of modern society, as well as through the history of scientific knowledge. We now begin to believe that the substantial contents of human rights may change from time to time, from society to society and from culture to culture. Even in the same Euro-American society, the dignity of an individual, as the new idea of 'quality of life shows, is relative. Secondly, environmental thinking and new findings of the ecological sciences, together with new empirical and sometimes pessimistic philosophies, have raised considerable doubt about the exclusive status of human dignity. Why is only humankind given human rights? Why are not animals or trees given their rights, e.g. 'animal rights' or 'tree rights'?

Recently, people have turned their eyes to Oriental or Asian mentalities in which the idea of human dignity is relatively weak, and, therefore, the concept of 'fundamental human rights' does not work as in Euro-American societies. Are the concepts of 'person' and 'human rights' not fictitious constructs, which are applicable only in Western societies? For us to survive, substantial justification for human dignity should not come from the fiction of human rights, but from the scientific fact that we are now living in nature.

HARMONIOUS HOLISM AND ASIAN COMMUNITARIANISM

Here, I would like to consider the possibility of a harmonious holism and a new type of communitarianism. Presumably, the human genome should be protected and preserved, even if it might be partially harmful for the survival of human beings. But this is *not* so because its preservation is within the scope of human rights, as is ordinarily said, but it must be so only because its preservation is a harmonious activity of holistic nature. What, then, is harmonious holism?

Typical examples of harmonious holism can be found in East Asian traditions. Generally speaking, East Asian ways of thinking are said to be holistic and communitarian. The naturalism of Taoism represented by the concept of 'Tao', the communitarianism of Confucianism represented by the concept of 'Ren', and Japanese holistic harmonism represented by the concept of 'Hua' or 'Wa' all exemplify this way of thinking. These various thoughts and ways of thinking share the following basic characteristics:

(a) They assign a higher value to total and social order than to individual interests or individual rights and dignity, and this order is accomplished by the proper assignment of social roles and the fulfilment of corresponding responsibilities by individuals, groups or classes. This orderliness depends on the social system of each historical period.

(b) Social justice is interpreted in a very realistic way, as, for instance, social fine-tuning. There is no unique and absolute God, no categorical imperative, no free will, no autonomy to deduce justice and precepts to control people's behaviour, except to pursue social peace. Every ethical and moral code is essentially relative to times and regions. Eventually, there is only little room for the idea of 'fundamental human rights'.

(c) Fundamental naturalism is pervasive in all Asian philosophies. According to this sort of naturalism, our *prima facie*, non-natural and artificial human activities are ultimately included in nature as its small parts. Thus 'to be natural' and 'to be artificial' are not contradictory concepts at all, and the distinction is always blurred. Evolution used to be seen as natural in the past. But now 'artificial evolution' can also be thought of as natural in the Asian sense of the word 'nature'. In short, in Asian ways of thinking and living, there is no antagonism between nature and human being.

(d) They are inclined not to believe or pursue any 'invariance' or 'eternity'. Buddhist precepts, in particular, always emphasise that 'everything will change'. By contrast, Western culture has always sought 'invariance' and 'eternity', which remain identical through every change. Thus various kinds of 'conservation laws' have been established in the history of sciences, such as the 'law of energy conservation' and the 'parity conservation law'. In the same fashion, Western thinkers introduced the concept 'personal identity', which remains invariant through all possible changes as a human being. This idea of invariance is foreign to the traditional Asian ethos. This is the most significant difference between Eastern and Western ways of understanding human beings.

ETHICAL ENGINEERING: A CONCLUSION

Now, in the postmodern era, interpretations of 'human rights', 'happiness', 'life', and 'nature' vary across the expanding and globalising world. And still, we have to consider the aims of a future 'artificial evolution'. The best strategy is to cultivate the methodology of harmonious activity to reach a consensus, giving equal consideration to all senses of value. I call this methodology ethical engineering. In the notion of harmonious activity, I include the progress of science and technology only if it is not stained by excessive (non-harmonious) human-centrism. Thus, gene therapy and recombinant DNA are ethically compatible with the notion of preserving the genome. I think this process of social fine-tuning will be a piecemeal work of developing ethics to clarify the connotation of the concept of harmony and to seek a strategy for realising harmony in nature.

This way of thinking might lead to a new sort of communitarianism or, dare I say, perhaps even paternalism and eugenics, which have long been rejected in the Western world as involving the violation of human rights. We have to restrain ourselves from insisting on human rights too much. A philosophy of this new kind of communitarianism or paternalism will be backed up by many Asian traditional thoughts, for instance, by the Confucian ethical idea of putting a higher value on harmony and social benevolence than on human rights.

Now, in conclusion, it is clear that in dealing with ethical issues related to genome research, genetics, cloning, evolution and so on, it may not be a good strategy to refer only to the idea of 'fundamental human rights' or 'human dignity'. Instead, we should also refer to Asian types of communitarianism, which stress the welfare and harmony of community, local or international, social or familiar, physical or mental, human or non-human. When any antagonism occurs among communities at any level, we should just compromise without referring to any rigid principle. Only in this way can we hope to find the gateway to future prosperity and survival of humankind as well as of the whole life system on this globe.

Chapter 8

Biotechnology and Responsibility to Future Generations: A Confucian Perspective

Shui Chuen Lee

The contribution or significance of biotechnology to future generations lies in its power to change the genetic make-up of future living organisms, including human beings. Humans are not living in a void but in the midst of myriad living and non-living beings. Thus, future generations include not only future peoples, but also all species of living organisms, though our usual reference is to *homo sapiens* only. In this chapter I use the wider scope of the meaning of future generations and refer to human as well as non-human, sentient as well as non-sentient beings.

Person in the sense of autonomous individual reigns supreme in our moral debates about duties and rights. Thus, talk of responsibility to future generations is usually coined in terms of potential persons or future persons. Within the usual framework of moral deliberation, the conception of potential person seems unfitting and under heavy fire from all sides. One of the main objections is that such beings cannot make any claims on existing persons, for they are more or less shadowy figures in the dark. However problematic the existence of future persons may be, our responsibility to future generation is ineffable. The difficulty of relating our responsibility to future generations is due to the way we talk about ethics in terms of person, which is neither sufficient nor necessary for our moral experience. Taking future generations to include not only human beings but also all sorts of living organisms and the future world as a whole would make discussions about responsibility in terms of personhood much more problematic.

Our moral concern is obviously not limited to persons but applies to all sentient beings at the very least. For many cultures, contemporary environmental concerns include all kinds of living things and nature as a whole. Thus, we have to leave the domain of autonomy and relate our moral responsibility to future generations in other moral terms. Beneficence and doing-no-harm are more proper terms. Both are usually regarded as forming a continuum of our moral duty towards other beings: do-no-harm is regarded as posing a more stringent requirement for actions that affect the well-being of other beings. I shall argue that do-no-harm is a primordial expression of our moral experience and characterises our moral realm.

In the following, I will first argue that do-no-harm is a more adequate principle than autonomy for dealing with our moral experience, especially with reference to future generations. I will then elaborate, according to the Confucian line of thinking, a wider conception of harm than the person-centric one. The latter is in fact a twisted notion introduced by the autonomy model. This Confucian conception of doing-no-harm is then employed for the discussion of our responsibility to future generations with regards to our development and application of biotechnology.

RETRIEVING AN OLD PARADIGM: FROM AUTONOMY TO DO-NO-HARM

According to contemporary liberal individualism, the notion of autonomy is dominant in comparison with other important notions such as non-malfeasance, beneficence and justice. Autonomy and related ideas such as informed consent, truth telling, veracity and the limitation on paternalism are central themes with regard to bioethical issues. Bioethics is sometimes heralded as the triumph of autonomy (Wolpe 1998). However, historically, autonomy is not the concern of medical professions or ethics in general. It comes to prominence only after Kant's elaboration of his ethical theory, which identifies autonomy of the will as the origin of morality and combines it with the notion of a person. Though there is no doubt that autonomy constitutes one of our most important characteristics, both in terms of morality and personhood, it is not the sole and only concern of morality. For the West, the Hippocratic tradition has a clear priority over do-no-harm, which encompasses a much wider circle of moral concern for human beings. For Confucians, the moral mind is nothing other than a mind of commiseration that responds with alarm to the harms suffered by other beings, whether they are humans or animals.

In fact, autonomy covers only a small part of the whole spectrum of our moral experience, though that may be one of the most important parts of our moral life. However, even within the sphere of autonomy, it seems strange that any infringement on autonomy is simply regarded as immoral if it is not accounted for in terms of harm to its possessor, namely a person. For the immorality of an intrusion on one's autonomy remains an open question, at least theoretically, and it is not unreasonable to argue that such intrusion could be moral. For example, we feel strongly that we have a certain responsibility to prevent a morally competent friend from committing suicide. The respect of the autonomous person and the principle of informed consent are first of all principles shielding a person from harm (Beauchamp and Childress 2001). On the other hand, harm comes closer to the root of morality and is sufficient for the justification of a moral judgment or action. Harm by itself is aptly said to be morally relevant, whether the subject is an autonomous person or not. In fact, harm is a morally more encompassing term than autonomy because any infringement on a person's autonomy is also a kind of harm, while not every form of harm is an infringement on autonomy.

Furthermore, harm is a more flexible term, reflecting the richness and complexity of our moral experience; harm can be compared and can vary, while autonomy is either granted or non-existent. Harm allows us to talk of all sorts of actions and restrictions towards all sorts of living beings, be they persons or not, or be they sentient or not. It makes discussions about responsibility towards nature, towards sentient beings and future generations morally sensible. These kinds of moral discussions cannot be easily expressed in terms of autonomy. Hence, harm is a notion more cogent for moral talk, especially across the whole spectrum of living things.

THE CONFUCIAN CONCEPT OF HARM

Harm has been a key notion of moral discourse for much longer than the concept of autonomy. However, with the emergence of the concept of a person, the concept of harm was restricted to person-affecting situations.   Thus Derek Parfit argues that 'the moral obligation to do things to or refrain from doing things to individuals must be justified in person-affecting terms. That is, their morality turns in large part on the effect they have on persons' (Parfit 1984: 339; Harris 1992: 60). Although, as Harris (1992: 68) likes to say, death does not deprive a non-person of anything that it could value, the above strongly implies that only harm to a person is morally relevant. Yet it is unreasonable to talk of harm as only a person-affecting term, because there is obviously a lot of harm being done towards non-persons such as animals and 'pre-persons' like children and infants.

For Confucians, harm is a notion closely connected with morality and we have an almost absolute imperative to do no harm.

Mencius points out that it is our natural alarming response towards the suffering of others, such as a child at the brink of falling into a deep well, that shows the origin of our moral mind or the mind of commiseration (Habermas 1985: 77). It is unconditional and it compels us to act for the relief of suffering. The mind of commiseration is practical reason in the full Kantian sense. For it is a moral consciousness: it draws the moral differentiation and points out the direction or basic features of morality; it is an imperative and autonomous command; and consequently, it carves out the realm of morality. It thus constitutes, as in Kantian philosophy, the inner worth of a human being or person. However, it is more concerned with others in its original and natural setting: it reveals our deep moral concern for the sufferings of others. We have no less respect for the autonomy of the person, though this moral consciousness is primordially other-concerned. However, autonomy is not the only and sole value of the moral mind, nor is it regarded as its most important feature. The point of morality is our compassion towards the sufferings of others, though we ourselves are included and usually granted heavier weights than others. Reducing suffering and thus causing no harm is supreme for Confucianism. In fact, the Confucian conception of doing-no-harm encompasses a much wider circle of beings. It extends to all living beings whose natural development or growths are thwarted or who suffer unnatural death, and thus are regarded as being harmed. Further extension goes all the way to conceive nature and the whole universe as one body.

This feeling of commiseration provides not only a concern with all living beings; it unites human beings with all living beings. It commands us to feel others' sufferings as our own on the basis of equality. For Confucians, it reveals an ontological order of unity of all. Though being human has a privileged status in being able to actualise such unity consciously, all beings are ontologically one with each other. Thus Cheng Ming Tao, a Sung Confucian, suggested that the man of *jen* is one with the myriad things, the Heaven and Earth. All are proliferated through Tao and each is endowed with certain intrinsic value. It is precisely this practical or moral approach that establishes the reality of a moral metaphysics that Kant conceived, but did not fulfil, in his works. The moral command we receive through the manifestation of our moral consciousness is to succeed the Way of *Tao*, which means following *Tao* in its procreation and making up any defect that a living being may suffer (Lee 1999: 187-198). This moral concern commands us to help lessen the suffering of all living things and make do-no-harm a primordial moral imperative. This moral command extends even to keeping intact and properly preserving things of cultural value such as great arts, rare artefacts and other objects.

In this vein, the so-called principle of non-malfeasance is being treated as a direct derivative from the moral mind, which is the origin and constitutive element of morality. This principle has no less moral standing than any other, including the principle of autonomy. It is often more closely aligned to our moral consciousness and reflects a more communitarian sense of human beings as well as other living beings. According to Confucianism, it provides the ground for the supremacy of doing-no-harm over autonomy in cases of bioethics. In the following, I will first demonstrate how it delineates our responsibility to future generations in our development and applications of biotechnology, and how it accords with our moral intuitions. Then, I will discuss our responsibility towards other living beings in the context of issues related to genetically modified organisms (GMOs).

THE CASE OF STEM CELL EXPERIMENTATIONS

One of the most hotly debated bioethical issues today is the ways to obtain biological materials for stem cells experimentations. It is a good place to begin considering our responsibility to future generations, because the results of stem cell research are the foundation for our ability to influence our progeny for good or bad.

As a controversial issue, it has naturally produced two opposing camps. There are the conservatives who object to stem cell experimentations using anything other than those obtainable from a normal human being and from the umbilical cord after birth. The US government adopts a policy along this line and only supports old experiments and no new ones, which derive their stem cells from embryos (except those from tissues of aborted foetuses). It fears that any permission for getting stem cells from embryos will lead to more artificial abortions, which they regard as ultimately immoral. It also argues that the mother who agrees to abortion no longer has the right to represent and give consent to using the remains for experimentation. This conservative line of argument receives strong refutation both in that the consent for using aborted tissue is no different than cadaver transplantation, and in that abortion is a legal right for mothers, whereas the fear of artificial abortion is unfounded and easily manageable (Harris 1992: 89-117). Besides those countries that have not yet taken measures on this issue, the British government seems to adopt the most liberal public policy for obtaining stem cells for experiments. It not only allows embryos from abortion and extra embryos left over from IVF, but also permits—subject to restrictive regulation and evaluation procedures—the creation of embryos for such research (Chief Medical Office 2000). The main reason behind this policy is that embryos are regarded as living organisms without self-interests, while all types of embryos are of the same ontological status (Harris 1992: Chs 2 and 3).

Concerning this issue, Harris (1992: 48) points out that:

> When we bear in mind that, as Robert Edwards has argued, most of the secrets of the development of life are contained in

early embryos, and that we are extremely likely to be able to use what we learn from such embryos to save many lives and ameliorate many conditions which make life miserable, we would not only be crazy but wicked to cut ourselves off from these benefits unless there are the most compelling of moral reasons so to do. I have argued that there are no such compelling reasons.

Confucians would agree that this is precisely the main reason that we should continue the pursuit of genetics in general. However, this does not give such an enterprise the unconditional status to do anything. For some of its more extravagant endeavours we need convincing moral reasons, and for some others we just need to indicate whether they are necessary or not. For Confucians, scientific experimentation is but a means for relieving the pains and sufferings of humans as well as other types of living organisms. Scientific knowledge and technology are surely some of the effective ways for achieving this aim.

However, this adventure on the road of knowledge and technology should not be built upon unnecessary, humanly inflicted harm or suffering. Confucians do not agree that killing an embryo, which is a living organism by itself, involves no wrong or harm. While an embryo is but a small speck of cells, it is nonetheless a living being and has its own natural destiny to becoming an adult of its own species. In this respect, human embryos are no different from embryos of other species. It is no doubt so small that it is barely recognizable as an individual organism; however, its great potentiality commands even more of our awe and respectful handling than other cells. With respect to their potential, human embryos could be said to have a higher status than other species, analogous to the way a human being is higher in moral status than other species. Though it does not by this higher status achieve the absolute right to life, nor the right to be incubated in full, it has some outstanding status of its own. It could suffer by different treatments that we offer and requires at least some reasonable consideration for its deployment and destruction in experimentations.

It seems morally acceptable to use aborted foetuses and extra embryos for necessary stem cell experimentations that contribute significantly to future and presently living life-in-being, to use one of Harris's favourite terms (Harris 1992: 106). However, bizarre and irrational experiments with detrimental consequences, such as those resulting in deformed lives, should not be allowed. As for the other two types of creating embryos for stem cell experimentations, namely from donors' gametes and gametes from people with genetic diseases, we need more moral reasons. The creation of embryos from general donor gametes seems to be unnecessary except as a convenience for the researchers, because it is possible to obtain extra embryos from IVF. The creation of embryos from people with genetic diseases is a special case, because without this option, it would be very difficult if not impossible to find a proper treatment for their genetic diseases. It seems unreasonable to limit them and their progeny to natural cures when there is a way for discovering new ones. Confucians believe that the sacrifice of an embryo is morally acceptable in such occasions since it achieves more relief of pain than the harm done to such embryos.

GENETIC THERAPY AND ENHANCEMENT

Another important feature of biotechnology is the development of genetic therapy. It offers hope for treating not only those traditionally untreatable genetic diseases, but also for developing effective treatments of many diseases due to genetic malfunctioning or non-functioning. It also has the exciting as well as alarming potential for enhancing our genetic future. The former is called genetic therapy, the latter genetic enhancement. Both have important implications and hence involve a great of responsibility to future generations.

Genetic therapy aims to relieve human sufferings, just like medical services. There are generally two types of genetic therapy, the somatic and germ-line genetic therapies. The former has been widely accepted, because it focuses on direct cures for the individual patient and stops at that. The change in genetic composition of the patient will not be inherited. The latter is much debated and generally regarded as immoral. For this type of therapy has to change the genetic components of the patient and her progeny all at once and forever. Confucians usually have no qualms with this type of genetic therapy, because we believe that curing a disease means a reduction of pain and suffering. It is morally acceptable when the biotechnology for such treatment is mature enough to predict the results within a reasonable range and when it does not produce serious side effects. For such side effects would be transmitted to our indefinitely numerous progeny. Confucians respect the intactness of our human genome as long as it proves functional, but would not take it as sacred. Rather, Confucians take such genetic diseases as defects that require human intervention.

The enhancement issue is another story. There is no disease to deal with and no suffering, natural or humanly inflicted. The only reason for such a procedure is that it improves what we have now. The moral necessity is greatly diminished and it remains to be seen whether such enhancement is necessary. There are two broad lines of consideration for any such far-reaching procedures. Without good reasons, the benefit of doubt should be given to what has worked in the past. Second, good reasons should be given for any infringement on the natural course of nature. The main reason for genetic enhancement is to allow our progeny to be more competitive.

The need for enhancement in this respect is simply wanton. It usually means that those in a better politico-economical position will employ this genetic means to safeguard social or economical injustice, or at least inequality. It tends to offer legitimacy for egoistic gains over altruistic partnership among fellow people. Furthermore, it may result in the artificial creation of two types of *homo sapiens*: Those who start early and maintain a higher social, economic and political status will continue to stay ahead of others, while the progeny of those who cannot afford genetic enhancement from the beginning will always remain disadvantaged. Needless to say, this creates more divisions and antagonisms among people and results in more suffering than good. The only possible justification is that we may need to improve our genetic make-up to cope with a deteriorating future. However, it is not clear how genetic enhancement would equip us for such challenges.

THE FUTURE GENERATION: ENVIRONMENT AND GMOS

For Confucians, the future generation includes not only human beings but also all species in Heaven and on Earth—that is, the world and sometimes the whole universe, or what we can loosely call the environment. The thousands of species and our environment are practically as well as ontologically inseparable from human beings in the past, present and future. Confucians would take the whole as a close-knit family with intricate interrelationships, though each has her or his or its special concerns. Due to her moral capacity, the human being is regarded as the head of the family, who helps *Tao* as the promoter of humaneness rather than as dictator or predator of the rest. However, Confucians do not make the value of human beings absolute. We have to live in harmony with nature and with all species. Nature with its richness is not merely created for our use and should not be subject to human power and subjective wishes. Human beings and nature are partners; human beings are part of nature. Nature nourishes us and Confucians sometimes express their gratitude to nature by treating nature as their parents. It is obviously improper to exploit and harm nature for the selfish sake of human good. Hence, natural resources can be utilized, but only with due care and respect. This is our basic guideline in employing biotechnologies and creating GMOs.

In relieving some of our harsh living conditions, and for certain therapeutic treatments, we have been making GMOs all along. GMOs are surely products of our scientific success and contribute much to our happiness. On the other hand, GMOs will affect related wild species. By definition, GMOs are new brands of organisms that replace wild species in the long run for the sake of human beings. For some, it does not matter whether the so-called natural environment and its inhabitants suffer or not, since they regard the latter as not susceptible to harm in personal terms. This is a natural consequence of such points of view, which only treat the notion of harm in relation to persons. With such a conception, most inhabitants of the natural environment are not persons in any proper sense, and any drastic change cannot be attributed as doing harm to them. Where no person is harmed and many actual persons benefit, the creation and proliferation of GMOs is morally desirable. However, there is no reason to consider the destruction of natural species and habitat as doing no harm.

For Confucians, any species as well as any ethnic group has the right to thrive and not be demolished by any human means. Confucius regarded the extinction of a country, nation, or race as a great evil. This moral judgment could certainly be extended to natural species and habitats, except for those proven to be destructive to humans or other species. With due care, it seems possible to retain wild species when we try to grow new brands of organisms. With such qualifications, limited usage of GMOs, especially those related to cures of diseases and pains, is deemed morally acceptable by Confucians. Detrimental impacts of GMOs are not only causing more harm than good as a whole, but would be harmful in the person-affected sense too, for it would ultimately cause pain or suffering to human beings—albeit future persons in the long run.

The extinction of species, and thus loss of biological and genetic diversity, is a serious problem for human beings. Our responsibility to future generation demands that we try to leave the world a better and more enjoyable place than it is today.

BIBLIOGRAPHY

Beauchamp, T. and Childress, J. (2001; 5th edn) Principles of Biomedical Ethics, Oxford: Oxford University Press.

Chief Medical Office (2000) 'Stem Cell Research: Medical Progress with Responsibility—A Report from the Chief Medical Office's Expert Group Reviewing the Potential of Developments in Stem Cell Research and Cell Nuclear Replacement to Benefit Human Health', London: Crown Copyright. Online. Available HTTP: http://www.doh.gov.uk/cegc/stemcellreport.html.

Habermas, J. (1985) 'Psyche Thermidor and the Rebirth of Rebellious Subjectivity', in R.J. Bernstein (ed.) Habermas and Modernity, Cambridge: Polity Press.

Harris, J. (1992) Wonderwoman and Superman, Oxford: Oxford University Press.

Lee, S.C. (1999) 'A Confucian Perspective on Human Genetics', in O. Doering (ed.) Chinese Scientists and Responsibility Issues of Human Genetics in Chinese and International Contexts, Hamburg: Der Institute für Asienkunde.

Parfit, D. (1984) Reasons and Persons, Oxford: Oxford University Press.

Wolpe, P.R. (1998) 'The Triumph of Autonomy in American Bioethics: A Sociological View', in R. de Vries and Janardan (eds) Bioethics and Society: Constructing the Ethical Enterprise, Upper Saddle River: Prentice Hall.

Chapter 9

Respecting Nature and Using Human Intelligence: Elements of a Confucian Bioethics

Yu Kam Por

In recent years, there have been attempts to delineate a Confucian bioethics. Such attempts go further than commenting on specific bioethical issues from a Confucian perspective. They provide a general framework for responding to a variety of bioethical issues. But different writers have reconstructed Confucian bioethics in different ways. For example, Lee Shui-chuen regards Confucian bioethics as basically universalist in nature, whereas Fan Ruiping regards Confucian bioethics as a species of communitarian ethics.

Confucian bioethics, as understood and presented by Lee Shui-chuen, is primarily founded on 'the heart of compassion' (Lee 1999: Chapter 4). Such a bioethics is to a large extent valid to all humanity. Lee (2002: 190) notes that:

> For the Confucian, a person is first of all a member of the common moral community... Our unbearable moral feeling and concern for the suffering of others cannot but compel us to actions. It prescribes the direction: to prevent, remove, and do no harm. What is contrary to this direction constitutes immorality.

Fan Ruiping (1999: 21-22), on the other hand, regards the emphasis on family and relationships as the major characteristic of Confucian bioethics. Fan (1999: 21) argues that:

> The principle of *ren* requires one to apply one's love to all
> humans, but only after taking into account distinctions,
> orders, and the relative importance of social roles. One
> should begin with one's family in the context of a local
> Confucian community.

According to Fan (idem: 275), we should love all humans, but with
order, distinction, and differentiation.

Such attempts, though very different, are a restatement of
Confucian general ethics in order to apply it to bioethical matters.
My approach in this paper is somewhat different. I invoke a
Confucian perspective that is directly related to the subject matter
of bioethics, namely, that there should be a division of labour
between nature and human intelligence. There have been some
interesting thoughts relating to this theme within the Confucian
tradition, and it is my belief that the Confucian way of thinking
about this topic can enrich our discussion in bioethics and
contribute towards the development of a more adequate and well-
balanced theory of bioethics.

Sure enough, there have been different interpretations of
Confucian ethics. Even on the relation between man and nature,
there have been different or even opposing understandings of the
Confucian position. One view takes the Confucian position as
emphasising the unity of man and nature. The other view takes the
Confucian position as emphasising the division between man and
nature. In this paper I take the second view as having stronger
roots in classical Confucianism, and as more in line with the
humanistic spirit of Confucianism.

The Confucian position that I shall outline regards nature and
human beings as having different roles to play. While human
intelligence is too limited to be entrusted with the task of reshaping

nature according to a blueprint preconceived by humans, nature likewise is not perfect and should not be left to develop in its own way. Human intelligence should supplement the work of nature, but not replace it. Intervention in nature is justified in cases of remedy but not for the pursuit of maximal results. Such a view represents a middle position in the contemporary debate on bioethics. It aims at striking the right balance between respecting nature and making use of human intelligence.

DIVISION OF THE PROVINCE OF NATURE FROM THE PROVINCE OF HUMANITY

A basic insight of Confucianism is that the province of nature should be distinguished from the province of humanity. Both nature and humanity have their roles and limitations. Nature is not entirely trustworthy, because nature does not have a clear moral direction. But neither is humanity entirely trustworthy, because human beings are too limited in their ability and intelligence. They may not achieve their desired or expected goals even with the best intention and the most sincere attempt. One of the most outstanding Confucian scholars in the Han Dynasty, Gongsun Hong, characterises a true Confucian as someone who is able to 'distinguish clearly the provinces of nature and humanity and combine the best principles of ancient and modern times' (Watson 1993).

A true Confucian is someone who can tell what is the proper job of nature and what is the proper job of man, such that he would not take as his job what is properly nature's job, and he would not leave to nature what is properly man's job. On the other hand, a true Confucian is neither conservative nor fashionable. He learns from ancient people's wisdom, but is not limited by it. He will also make use of modern people's wisdom. So it is said that he combines the best principles of ancient and modern times.

The Confucian classics strongly support such a view on the distinction between the province of nature and the province of humanity has strong textual support in the Confucian classics. As the author of *The Book of Changes* observes: '[Nature] promotes all things without sharing the anxiety the sage has'. Here the way of nature is distinguished from the way of the sage. The sage has anxiety, but nature does not share the sage's anxiety. This implies that the course of nature may not be satisfactory in the eyes of the sage. What happens in nature may not go in the right moral direction as recognised by the sage.

In the *Doctrine of the Mean*, the Way of Nature is again contrasted with the Way of Man. The Way of Nature 'hits upon what is right without effort and apprehends without thinking'. The Way of Man, on the contrary, is deliberative, 'trying to choose the good and hold fast to it' (Chan 1963: 107), implying that moral deliberation is the essence of the Way of Man. Such moral deliberation is not involved in the Way of Nature. So the natural course of development of the Way of Nature is not always morally acceptable. This opens up the possibility that the moral mind should correct the natural course of development of the Way of Nature when it becomes morally undesirable. This implies that the Way of Nature is not always morally preferable.

In *Xunzi*, Knoblock (1999: 535) asserts that 'If you understand the division between Nature and Mankind, then you can properly be called a Perfect Man'. Nature and Mankind work differently. By each doing things in its own way, Nature and Mankind are regarded as supplementary to each other.

> Not to act, yet bring to completion; not to seek, yet to obtain—this indeed may be described as the work of Nature. In such a situation, the Perfect Man, however profound, does not apply any thought to the work of Nature; however great, he does not apply his abilities; and however shrewd, he does

not apply his acumen for inquiry into it. This indeed may be described as 'not competing with Nature in its work'. Heaven has its seasons; Earth its resources; and Man his government. This, of course, is why it is said that they 'can form a Triad' (idem).

This view on the distinction between nature and humanity is quite common in Confucianism in the classical period, and newly discovered archaeological materials corroborate it. In the Confucian texts from Guodian Tomb Number One, there are passages on the relation between Nature and Humanity. All of them hold the view that Nature and Humanity are distinct rather than unified. It is commonly believed that such texts are works of Confucians one or two generations after Confucius. In the following passages, for example, the distinction between Nature and Humanity is confirmed:

'There is Nature and there is Humanity. There is distinction between Nature and Humanity. Discern the distinction between Nature and Humanity, and then the right course of action can be known' (Li 2002: 86; my translation).

On the basis of the Nature-Humanity distinction, both Nature and Humanity have their proper functions. We should not expect Nature to do Humanity's proper job, namely, to be moral. Neither should we attempt to be able to fully understand the way Nature works and take up the task ourselves.

THE NATURE OF NATURE

But the interesting question is: What is the nature of Nature? Even if we accept that there is a distinction between the role of Nature and the role of Humanity, we still do not know what it means to respect Nature until we have a deep understanding of the nature of Nature. I think at least four things can be said about the nature of

Nature: (1) Nature is morally blind; (2) Nature is life-giving or pro-life; (3) Nature is complex and unfathomable; (4) Nature is pro-diversity. The Confucian universe is not entirely physical and purposeless. Nature is understood to have certain preferences and inclinations. Nature is pro-life and pro-diversity. But it does not have a mind as human beings have, as reflected in the quotation from *The Book of Changes*, which I referred to earlier: '[Nature] promotes all things without sharing the anxiety the sage has'. Nature does not consciously direct things to happen in the moral direction. So the course of Nature is not always acceptable according to the moral mind. As *The Doctrine of the Mean* states: 'Great as heaven and earth are, men still find some things in them with which to be dissatisfied' (Legge 1960: 392).

However, to say that Nature does not have a clear moral direction does not imply that Nature is morally neutral. The Way of Nature is regarded as life-giving and it tends toward promoting rather than destroying life—it gives rise to the life and development of myriad creatures, and this is regarded as a morally good thing. Here nature is seen as having the virtue of favouring life instead of being neutral or having no particular orientation. So Nature has a special preference for life. But how does Nature give rise to life and how exactly does life work? This is a complicated matter and quite beyond human ability to fully understand and control.

The course of development of Nature is described as *shen* or mysterious, because it is complicated and unfathomable. According to 'The Great Treatise' of *The Book of Changes*: 'That which is unfathomable in the operation of *yin* and *yang* is called *shen* [mystery]' (Chen 1963: 266). *The Doctrine of the Mean*, moreover, states that: 'The Way of Heaven and Earth may be completely declared in one sentence. They are without any doubleness, and so they produce things in a manner that is unfathomable' (Legge 1960: 420). This statement asserts the uniqueness and non-linear development of each life. No two lives are exactly the same. Even if two lives are genetically the same, a small variation of conditions may lead to very different subsequent development. As a result, lives in particular and Nature in general cannot be predictable. We cannot hope to have full control of it.

Nature is also non-neutral in the sense that it is pro-diversity. Heaven is considered as great enough to cover everything. The Earth is considered as great enough to carry everything. As an ancient saying goes: 'There is nothing that the Heaven does not cover and nothing that the Earth does not support' (Watson 1996: 67; Legge 1960: 427). And *The Doctrine of the Mean* suggests that: 'Ten thousand creatures can coexist without excluding one another'. What is said here is not that there is no limit to the size of population that nature can support, but rather that nature prefers heterogeneity to homogeneity.

THE ROLE OF HUMANITY

The role of humanity is characterised by the use of human intelligence as well as by the exercise of moral judgements. Nature has its accomplishments (and occasional failures) without thinking and trying. Human beings, however, cannot but make moral judgements, and they have to make decisions concerning which is the better line of development. The sage is the exemplar of the moral mind. Here it is said that Nature does not worry like the sage does. What the sage worries about is not her own good or bad fortune, but the pursuit of moral goals. According to the *Mencius*, the sage 'worries about the troubles of the people' (Lau 1984: 31) and 'worries about the affairs of the people' (idem: 107).

Hsü Fu-huan (1969: 20-21; my translation) claims that the emergence of the mentality of worry (*you-huan*) in Chinese history represents the awakening of humanity's moral consciousness and the emergence of the spirit of Confucianism:

The course of development of events in human affairs is closely related to one's action. Therefore one is responsible for the results brought forth by one's action. The feeling of worry is the state of mind a person has when he has a sense of responsibility and tries to use his own effort to overcome the difficulties he encounters but has not yet overcome.

According to Hsü Fu-huan's analysis, *you-huan* (worry or anxiety) is not a bad thing. It is actually a reflection of a person's concern about the states of affairs, a sense of responsibility, and trust in one's own ability and acknowledgement of the limitation of it. I would like to expand Hsü's explanation of *you-huan* into a five-part definition. Firstly, the person has to be aware that his action can affect results. If there is nothing that she can do, she may be sad, but she does not have to worry. It is only when she still believes that she may still do something, and is not sure how effective her action will be that she has to worry. Secondly, she must care about the results. If she believes that she can affect the results, but she does not care about them, then she would not worry. So *you-huan* implies the attitude of care. Thirdly, since she cares about the results and thinks that she should bring about one result rather than another, she has a sense of responsibility. If she thinks that she should make things happen one way rather than another, and she thinks she has an ability to make a difference, then he would regard it as her responsibility to do so. Fourthly, since she has a sense of responsibility, she will not feel morally comfortable if she does not do anything. She will try to do what she regards as right. She may not be successful, but she will at least try to see if she can make a difference. Lastly, since she has tried to do what he regards as right, and is concerned about the results, she is in the state of anxiety and worry.

Hsü Fu-huan's emphasis on the importance of the mentality of *you-huan* in the emergence of Confucianism (the tradition started by King Wen, King Wu and the Duke of Zhou and avowedly followed by Confucius) is supported by textual evidence. In *The Book of Changes*, a crucial stage in the development of Chinese civilisation, the rise of the Zhou [Chou] Dynasty, is associated with the mentality of *you-huan*. In 'The Great Treatise', the author writes that: 'The Changes came into use in the period of middle antiquity. Those who brought about the Changes had great anxiety and worry (*you-huan*)'. When was this period of middle antiquity? What happened at that time? In Chapter 11 of the same book explains that:

> The time at which the Changes came to the fore was that in which the House of Yin came to an end and the way of the house of Chou was rising, that is, the time when King Wen and the tyrant Chou Hsin were pitted against each other (Wilhelm 1989: 352).

Taking note that Nature does not share the anxiety the sage has and that anxiety (or worry) or *you-huan* is a mentality involving care and a sense of responsibility, we can infer that the Way of the Sage includes care and a sense of responsibility that may not be present in the Way of Nature. As a consequence, when the natural course of development worries the sage, the sage will not refrain from action, but will attempt to provide the necessary rectification.

Human beings can make moral judgements. They can tell what is bad and miserable. Without intervention, such misery will occur. But such misery can be avoided with some intervention. In that case, regulation or rectification of Nature is justified: 'It molds and encompasses all transformations of Heaven and Earth without mistake, and it stoops to bring things into completion without missing any' (Chan 1963: 265-266).

The natural course of development may cause worry. So responsible persons should not refrain from acting. But responsible persons should also be careful in their actions. They must avoid causing greater problems in his action to alleviate the problems he has identified. Confucius points out that a person who aims at behaving properly should have the following three qualities: (a) a passion for knowledge, which is close to wisdom; (b) persistence in practice, which is close to benevolence; and (c) awareness of one's own inadequacy, which is close to courage (idem: 105).

The use of human intelligence should moderate Nature, but it should also respect Nature. One must make use of human intelligence, but one should also know the limitations and inadequacies of human intelligence. The complexity and mystery of nature together with the intelligence of human beings allow human beings to have some degree of success in their manipulation of Nature, but they may also cause more problems than they can solve. If we look at the track record of human beings, we can find that human beings have not been very successful in their intervention with Nature. In the past, we never needed to worry about whether humankind as a whole had a future, but now we have to worry whether the earth will continue to be a place suitable for human life. If we are not successful in our intervention with the natural environment, then we should be even more cautious in our intervention with the genetics of animals and human beings, as they are even more complicated and have more far-reaching and irrevocable results. As Paul Ramsey (1970: 96) observes:

Mankind has not evidenced much wisdom in the control and redirection of his environment. It would seem unreasonable to believe that by adding to his environmental follies one or another of these grand design [for genetic engineering] ... man would then show sudden increase in wisdom... No man or collection of men is likely to have the wisdom to rule the future in any such way.

Another argument against intervening in Nature is that we should avoid decreasing the diversity of nature. Confucianism regards harmony as an important value, but harmony must not be confused with homogeneity. Actually, diversity, which is to be contrasted with homogeneity, is regarded as a basis of harmony.

If we manipulate the genes of plants, animals, or human beings, such that we get what we regard as the best plants, animals or human beings, then we run the risk of sacrificing natural diversity. Such a move is also regarded as an improper move, as it is a move towards homogeneity rather than harmony.

Two more points can be made about intervening with Nature. Firstly, the conservation of Nature is not the ultimate goal. Transformation is a greater virtue than conservation: 'The smaller energies [virtues] are like river currents; the greater energies are seen in mighty transformations' (Legge 1960: 427-428). To maintain things as they used to be is only regarded as a minor virtue. To help things transform in a progressive way is, however, regarded as a major virtue. Secondly, things should be regulated not by changing their nature, but by fully realising their nature (Legge 1960: 416). The essence of this point is that rectification should be in line with the nature of things, while adjustment should be made such that their potential can be fully realised.

GENERAL GUIDELINES AND PRACTICAL IMPLICATIONS

The duty to respect Nature and use human intelligence justify only limited intervention with Nature. This view acknowledges that Nature is complicated and human knowledge partial. It seeks to preserve diversity and address human moral concerns in a moderate way. This bioethical outlook requires that the use of human intelligence should be (1) minimal, not maximal use and (2) confined, not extended use. That is to say, the use of human intelligence should not aim at producing maximal results, but rather at developing remedies and reducing suffering. On the other hand, large scale, long lasting and irrevocable intervention should be avoided, because the outcomes of intervention are complex and unpredictable.

Consider the specific example of treating genetic diseases. There are over 3,000 kinds of human genetic diseases. Many such diseases have serious repercussions for the patients themselves. To refrain from doing anything to cure such genetic diseases is not a responsible attitude if we take the wellbeing of the people concerned seriously. Confucian bioethics can justify somatic gene therapy since the person concerned will benefited while the next generation will not be affected. In principle, it can also justify germ-line therapy, although this case calls for much greater precaution, because the changes may be long lasting and unpredictable. As Rollin (1995: 65) makes clear:

> Given the myriad foul-ups that providential nature has bestowed upon the human genome in the form of genetic diseases (the standard textbook of human genetic disease lists over three thousand such diseases in three thousand pages), which often cause horrendous suffering in children, it is hard to see why we should assume that Nature always know best. To be sure, we can always cause worse problems with our interventions, but what if we don't? (...) Cystic fibrosis, a genetic defect, is now being treated by use of inhalers that bring functional versions of the defective gene and its products to the lung. This way of supplying the products that are lacking due to inherent genetic defects is called gene therapy, or somatic gene therapy, in that the genetic defect inherent in the person's genome is not replaced or repaired, but rather the pernicious effects are

masked. The affected person still carries the defective gene and can pass it on to his or her progeny. Germ-line therapy, which has not yet been done, would remove, repair, or replace the defective gene at the embryonic level. Yet, in fact, if these therapies succeed, not only are they not wrong, they are breakthroughs to be lauded.

According to such a perspective, activities ranging from reproductive cloning to design of new humans are problematic, but activities ranging from genetic therapy to stem cell research and application can be more readily justified. The first group of activities is problematic with regards to the duty to humans, because it may have adverse consequences for the humans concerned and humankind as a whole. They are also problematic with regards to the duty to Nature because they attempt to replace the work of nature with the design of humans.

The second group of activities is more readily justified because they are quite acceptable with regards to the duty to humans since no humans are harmed, and they are quite acceptable with regards to the duty to Nature because such interventions are piecemeal and not irrevocable.

THE SIGNIFICANCE OF CONFUCIAN BIOETHICS

The Confucian bioethics that I propose in this paper seems to have something special to say about, and something significant to contribute to, our contemporary debates on bioethical issues. It provides a middle position with regards to intervention with Nature. It has a human-centred aspect as well as a non-human-centred aspect. It simultaneously affirms the duty to respect nature as well as the duty to use human intelligence. As a result, this moral outlook seems to be more balanced and reasonable.

There have been two typical positions regarding the intervention with Nature. One position regards the intervention with Nature as intrinsically wrong. The other position holds that there is nothing intrinsically wrong with the intervention with Nature. The first position is religiously inspired whereas the second one is secular and utilitarian in nature.

Take genetic engineering as an example. The first position holds that there is something intrinsically wrong with genetic engineering. It argues that genetic engineering blurs the line between different species of animals and the line between human beings and animals. From this perspective, genetic engineering is an example of mankind trying to play the role of God (Rollin 1995: 21; Reiss and Straughan 1996: 72). The second position holds that there is nothing intrinsically wrong with genetic engineering. There should be no boundary to knowledge and exploration. The important thing is to do it with precaution. It may not be the right time for us to intervene too much because we not have enough knowledge about the matter yet. It may be wrong to intervene if there are some harmful side effects. This means that it may not be wrong for us to engage in genetic engineering if we can find a way to avoid the harmful side effects. But such a bifurcation is not conducive to the discussion on genetic engineering (Rollin 1995: 10-11), because each side fails to see the point of the other side, and each side is reluctant to accept a reasonable solution of the dilemma (Osamu 1996: 86).

Compared with these two positions, the Confucian perspective can be regarded as a third way. It affirms that we should respect Nature as well as make use of human intelligence. Since the Confucian perspective respects Nature, it does not look at genetic engineering simply from a 'consequentialist' point of view. 'Messing with Nature' is something that we should avoid. However, Nature should not always be left as it is. There is a role for human beings to play. Sometimes the course of nature goes wrong. In such occasions we should use human intelligence to adjust the course of nature. The basic point is that human intelligence is not trustworthy enough to *replace* nature, but it is trustworthy enough to *supplement* nature.

In reflecting on and searching for a bioethical outlook that can serve as a more adequate and workable foundation for human action with regards to bioethical issues, different writers have pointed out the inadequacies of prevailing paradigms in bioethics. Ole Döring (2002) finds the need to look for a new consensus that reconfirms policies of caution and humaneness. Derrick Au (2002) points out that we need an 'ethics of the unknown' as well as an 'ethics of the unprotected'. The Confucian bioethics that I present in this paper meets such demands. Of course, to say that Confucian bioethics may have something to contribute is very different from saying that Confucian bioethics by itself can constitute an adequate theory of bioethics. I just want to make two points at this stage: (1) Confucian bioethics constitutes one possible alternative outlook; (2) Confucian bioethics may contain elements that are useful for constructing an adequate theory of bioethics.

What I have outlined in this paper are some guiding principles that constitute the fundamentals of a Confucian bioethics. Such guiding principles can serve as a framework for bioethical thinking. Utilitarianism regards one value, namely utility, as the sole criterion for ethical deliberation. Peter Singer (1979), in his *Applied Ethics*, regards equal consideration as the basis of moral judgements, including two aspects of consideration: wellbeing and autonomy. Beauchamp and Childress (1979) use four principles as the framework of bioethics: respect for autonomy, non-malfeasance, beneficence, and justice. A Confucian bioethics allows for various emphases, arguments, and conclusions.

We can take the different emphases in Confucian bioethics as a matter of cultural differences or as part of a global bioethics. My personal view is that all ethical theories have some element of truth. It is important to separate the truths from the errors. The ideal theory would accommodate all the elements of truth in different theories in a consistent way. Although the Confucian bioethics outlined above is far from complete, I hope that it contributes to our development of a general bioethics.

BIBLIOGRAPHY

Au, D.K.S. (2002) 'Manipulating Stem Cell and Withholding End-of-Life Care: Ethical Issues Compared', in Lee Shui-chuen (ed.) *Proceedings of Third International Conference of Bioethics*, Chungli, Taiwan: Graduate Institute of Philosophy, National Central University.

Beauchamp, T.L. and Childress, J.F. (1979) *Principles of Biomedical Ethics*, New York: Oxford University Press.

Chan, W. (1963) *A Source Book in Chinese Philosophy*, Princeton: Princeton University Press.

Döring, O. (2002) 'Deontological Versus Consequentialistic Arguments in Ethics: A German's View on Current Social Darwinism as Expressed in the Stem Cell Debate in Medical Ethics and How it Matters to China', in Lee Shui-chuen (ed.), *Proceedings of Third International Conference of Bioethics*, Chungli, Taiwan: Graduate Institute of Philosophy, National Central University.

Fan, R. (ed.) (1999) *Confucian Bioethics*, Dordrecht: Kluwer Academic Publishers.

Fung Y. (trans.) (1989) *Chuang-tzu*, Beijing: Foreign Languages Press.

Green, R.M. (2001) *The Human Embryo Research Debates: Bioethics in the Vortex of Controversy*, New York: Oxford University Press.

Holland, S., Labacqz, K. and Zoloth, L. (eds) (2001) *The Human Embryonic Stem Cell Debate: Science, Ethics, and Public Policy*: MIT Press.

Hsü F. (in Chinese) (1969) *The History of the Chinese Philosophy of Human Nature: The Pre-Ch'in Period* Taipei: Commercial Press.

Knoblock, J. (trans.) (1999), *Xunzi*, Hunan: Hunan People's Publishing House.

Lau, D.C. (trans.) (1984), *Mencius*, Hong Kong: The Chinese University Press.

Lee, S. (in Chinese) (1999) *Confucian Bioethics*, Taipei: Legein Publishing House.

Lee, S. (2002) 'The Reappraisal of the Foundations of Bioethics: A Confucian Perspective', in J. Tao (ed.), *Cross-cultural Perspectives on the (Im)Possibility of Global Bioethics*, Dordrecht: Kluwer Academic Publishers.

Legge, J. (trans.) (1960), *The Chinese Classics* (Vol. 1), Hong Kong: Hong Kong University Press.

Legge, J. (trans.) (1963) *The I Ching: The Book of Changes*, New York: Dover Publications.

Ling, L. (2002) *Guodian Chujian Jiaoduji* (Collation and Commentary of Bamboo Texts Discovered in Guodian), Beijing: Peking University Press.

Osamu, K. (1996) 'The Mean in Original Confucianism', in P. J. Ivanhoe (ed.), *Chinese Language, Thought, and Culture*, Chicago: Open Court.

Ramsey, P. (1970) *Fabricated Man: The Ethics of Genetic Control*, New Haven: Yale University Press.

Rawls, J. (1972) *A Theory of Justice*, Oxford: Oxford University Press.

Reiss, M.J. and R. Straughan (1996) *Improving Nature?: The Science and Ethics of Genetic Engineering*, Cambridge: Cambridge University Press.

Rollin, B.E. (1995) *The Frankenstein Syndrome: Ethical and Social Issues in the Genetic Engineering of Animals*, Cambridge: Cambridge University Press.

Singer, P. (1979) *Practical Ethics*, Cambridge: Cambridge University Press.

Tucker, M.E. and Berthrong, J. (eds) (1998), *Confucianism and Ecology*, Cambridge: Harvard University Center for the Study of World Religions.

Watson, B. (trans.) (1967) *Basic Writings of Mo Tzu, Hsün Tzu, and Han Fei Tzu*, New York: Columbia University Press.

Burton Watson (trans.; rev. edn) (1993) *Records of the Grand Historian*, Columbia: Columbia University Press.

Watson, B. (trans.) (1996) *Chuang Tzu: Basic Writings*, New York: Columbia University Press.

Wilhelm, R. (trans.) (1989) *I Ching or Book of Changes*, London: Arkana.

Chapter 10

Cross-cultural Approaches to the Philosophy of Life in the Contemporary World: From Bioethics to Life Studies

Masahiro Morioka

INTRODUCTION

The World Trade Center attack on 11 September 2001 was an epoch-making event because it clearly showed us the worst form of hostility caused by 'globalisation'. Of course, the current globalisation process has exploited and suppressed a number of developing countries in an unfair manner; hence, it is natural that people in these countries feel frustrated and express their hostility against, for example, the USA. However, it is wrong to kill innocent citizens in the USA, and it is even worse to kill the same number of innocent citizens in Afghanistan with air raids. As Mahatma Gandhi said, an eye for an eye leaves the whole world blind. What is needed is some different forms of action.

Bioethics is in the process of globalisation. Some scholars seem to think that this is a movement to spread 'American values' based on individualism, autonomy and freedom around the world. Anti-American emotions may have emerged in the field of bioethics in some places outside the USA, but just criticising American bioethics does not create anything. Any value system has its own faults. I will discuss this topic first, and then try to find a way of overcoming the conflict between 'values'. In the second half of this paper, I will discuss the idea of 'life studies' that I have advocated for years.

BIOETHICS AND CULTURAL BACKGROUNDS

The word 'bioethics' came to Japan in 1974 when V.R. Potter's book, *Bioethics*, was translated into Japanese. However, this word was not very popular until the late 1980s. In the 1980s, we had a severe debate on brain death and transplantation. Many people talked about the definition of human death and the meaning of life during this period. American- style bioethics was introduced in the late 1980s, and the Japanese Association for Bioethics was established in 1988. At that time, I was a graduate student majoring in philosophy. I read many bioethics papers, and translated some of them. My first impression was that it didn't seem to fit into my way of thinking about life. Many people around me were saying that they didn't agree with the idea that 'autonomy' and 'rights' must be the basis of bioethics. I was frustrated by the fact that American bioethics did not discuss environmental issues and nursing because I believed that these were also important subjects related to our attitudes towards life.

I published my first book, *An Invitation to the Study of Life: Beyond Bioethics*, in Japanese, in 1988. This was the first academic book that thoroughly criticised bioethics and environmental ethics. I insisted that contemporary medical issues and environmental issues should be discussed simultaneously in the same field because our attitude towards the environment must have some close connections to our attitude towards our own bodies and minds. I criticised the personhood argument and the narrow-mindedness of American bioethics.

It is worth noticing that just before we introduced bioethics from the USA, we had a nation-wide debate on brain death. Not only specialists but also journalists and lay people actively joined the debate. Japan was one of the few countries where a serious discussion on brain death lasted for a long period of time, more than 15 years. More than a hundred books on brain death appeared. There has been no such public discussion on brain death in North America up until the present. As a result, many Japanese scholars realised that American bioethics did not solve difficult problems they had encountered in the debate on brain death. In 1989, I published my second book, *Brain Dead Person*, in Japanese, stating that brain death should be interpreted as a form of 'human relationships' (Morioka 1989). I paid special attention to the emotions and relationships within the family of a brain dead person, because sometimes the family members at the bedside, touching the warm body of the patient, express the feeling that the brain-dead person still continues to exist as a human being. My conclusion was as follows:

> "Brain death" is not found in the brain of a "person whose brain ceased functioning," but in the realm of human relationships surrounding this person. What we should consider is "the realm of brain death," or "brain death as a field." In other words, the essence of "brain death" can be found in the relationships between people (idem: 9).

This book marked the beginning of the 'human relationship-oriented analysis' of brain death. Readers welcomed my perspective. This shows that Japanese academic bioethics attached great importance to 'human relationships' from the start and that modern individualism and human relationships were particularly important topics for Japanese bioethics in the 1980s (Morioka 1995).

I didn't emphasise cultural differences in bioethics in the above books, but Takeshi Umehara, a well-known critic, criticised the Western way of thinking lurking behind the concept of brain death in his provocative article, 'Opposition to the Idea of Brain Death: A Philosopher's Point of View', published in 1990. Umehara stated that the idea of brain death and transplantation goes back to Rene Descartes' dualism of mind and body, and that Japanese culture is based on a kind of animism which tells us that all beings in the world, including animals, trees, and mountains, have souls. He writes as follows:

> My view, based upon the studies of the council and upon my own disposition as a philosopher, is that the haughty "brain death theory" of Western science that derives from Descartes' separation of mind and matter ignores the awe of life and must be rejected. (...) Those who have no doubts about defining death as "brain death" have simply succumbed to the power of science and technology that has enabled the human race to build modern civilization and dominate all other life (Umehara 1994: 190).

Umehara's argument is based on the Japan/West dichotomy, a modified version of the East/West dichotomy, which is prevalent among ordinary people and scholars in Japan. This dichotomy tells us that Japan (or the East) is essentially different from (or sometimes even superior to) the West. For instance, Umehara concluded in the above paper that Japanese Buddhism influenced by animism is superior in nature to the Western Cartesian philosophy that created modern science and technology.

There had already been some articles and essays that contained this dichotomy in the 1980s. Umehara summed up this line of thought in his paper. I have thoroughly criticised his argument elsewhere (Morioka 1994); hence, I would like to point out just one thing here. According to opinion surveys 40-50 per cent of Japanese think of brain death as human death. Opposition to brain death is 20-40 per cent, lower than those who agree to the idea. Umehara fails to explain why the majority of the Japanese, being deeply influenced by animistic Buddhism, are in favour of brain death. From this perspective alone, Umehara's dichotomy seems to be very problematic.

BEYOND THE EAST/WEST DICHOTOMY

In the bioethics literature, there are many examples of this East/West dichotomy and its variations, but this is the trap we sometimes fall into when discussing the cultural dimensions of bioethics. Let us take a typical example: Hyakudai Sakamoto's paper, entitled 'Towards a New Global Bioethics', presented at TRT 7, Tsukuba, Japan, in 2002 (Sakamoto 2002: 31-34). Sakamoto has published similar papers, and this is the latest version. Sakamoto distinguishes 'Asian proper bioethics' from 'Western bioethics'. He writes as follows:

> Something is fundamentally different. First of all, in many countries in East and South East Asia, the sense of "human rights" is very weak and foreign, and they have no traditional background for the concept of human rights. (...) Asian people put higher value on the holistic happiness and welfare of the total group or community to which they belong rather than their individual interests (Sakamoto 2002: 32).

Then he goes on to say that Asian bioethics should be built on Asia's own 'ethos'. Its characteristics are as follows:

1. They put higher estimation on total and social well-orderedness than on the individual interests or individual rights and dignity
2. There is no unique and absolute God, no categorical imperative, no free will, no autonomy to deduce justice and precepts to control people's behavior except to pursue social peace... Eventually, there is no room for the idea of "fundamental human rights..."
3. There is no antagonism between nature and human being in the depth of Asian way of thinking, and way of living.
4. This idea of invariance is somewhat foreign to traditional Asian ethos (Sakamoto 2002: 32-33).

Sakamoto concludes that new global bioethics should be 'holistic' in contrast to European 'individualistic' bioethics, and that it requires 'some sort of communitarian way of thinking of a non-Western or Asian type'. And finally, he stresses the importance of harmonising the Asian ethos and the Western one.

One of the biggest problems with this kind of dichotomy is that it ignores a variety of values, ideas, and movements inside a culture or an area. For example, Sakamoto uses the words 'Asian ethos' even though there is no such thing as 'the' Asian ethos. He writes in his paper: 'The Japanese rejection of heart transplantation from the brain dead body was quite odd for Euro-American minds', but concerning this topic, Japan was the exception among East Asian countries. Other East Asian countries, such as Taiwan, Korea, and the Philippines, performed organ transplants from brain dead donors in the 1980s. Sex selection and surrogate motherhood are becoming popular in Korea, but are still prohibited in Japan. With regard to reproductive technologies, Korea and the USA seem to share the same ethos.

The same is true in the 'Western' countries. For example, Denmark and Germany went through a nation-wide debate on brain death in the late 1980s and 1990s. In Denmark, the ethics committee concluded in 1989 that brain death should not be human death. However, that report was rejected in the Diet in 1990. In Germany, a pregnant woman became brain dead in 1992, sparking a hot debate about whether she was dead or alive. In 1997, about 30 per cent of the Diet members supported a bill that did not define brain death as human death, but it was rejected. This outcome is very similar to the Japanese situation (Morioka 2001a). In Japan, 20-40 per cent of the Japanese constantly reject brain death. Siminoff and Bloch (1999) reported that even in the USA, 20-40 per cent of ordinary people felt hesitant to regard brain death as human death. In Europe and the USA, the number of donated organs has not increased much in recent years. This shows that many family members may refuse to give consent to organ donation from brain dead persons.

As is evident here, there are a variety of values and ideas in a culture or an area, and in addition, it becomes clear that 'Asia' and 'the West' share lots of ideas and values on life and death. The East/West dichotomy oversimplifies this internal variation and neglects the common cultural heritage that many people share in various areas around the world.

After opening the country to the world in 1868, the Japanese were very eager to absorb European ideas, such as 'human rights', 'freedom', and 'democracy'. Japanese history of the last 100 years could be illustrated as that of a harsh struggle between people who wanted to maintain hierarchical and paternalistic systems, on the one hand, and people who wanted to replace them with more individualistic ones based on human rights and freedom, on the other. In 1874, Taisuke Itagaki began a nation-wide political movement, 'the Freedom and People's Rights Movement (Jiyu Minken Undo)'. Many thinkers and activists joined Itagaki and were put in jail and killed, but this movement prepared the basis for Japanese democracy. (When Itagaki was stabbed, he is said to have shouted, 'Even if Itagaki dies, freedom never dies'!) When a group of severely discriminated people (Hisabetsu Buraku Min) demanded their civil rights in 1922, the words they uttered were 'freedom', 'liberation', and 'equality'.

The contemporary Japanese bioethics movement began in the early 1970s when disabled people claimed their 'right to live' and 'disabled children's right not to be killed by their parents', and when feminists claimed that their 'right' and 'freedom' to abortion must be maintained. It is striking that contemporary Japanese bioethics began with voices of minority groups demanding 'rights' and 'freedom'. Since I examined this topic elsewhere (Morioka, forthcoming), I will not write about it further here.

My point is that voices for 'freedom' and 'human rights' have already been integral parts of Japanese history and culture. They are part of the Japanese tradition. Hence, Sakamoto's argument that in Asia 'the sense of "human rights" is very weak and foreign, and that they have no traditional background for the concept of human rights' cannot be applied to Japan. His claim that 'Eventually, there is no room for the idea of fundamental human rights' is unfounded. Most of the younger Japanese philosophers and sociologists who are interested in bioethics take 'fundamental human rights' for granted, and then they are trying to fit bioethical ideas into contemporary Japanese culture and relate them to Japanese people's emotions. They stress the importance of 'human relationships' together with 'human rights'.

Even in the USA, so-called 'communitarian bioethics' has been discussed by Ezekiel J. Emanuel (1991) and Daniel Callahan (1996) in 1990s. American feminist bioethics has put a special emphasis on caring and relationships. It seems that current bioethics throughout the world seeks balanced development between 'individual freedom' and 'the value of community and relationships'.

Scholars at the City College of New York conducted a comparative study of US/Japan values in 1998. In their research, students in both countries responded to 'the values that they believed best characterise people in their country'. The results were interesting. The top 3 for the USA were 'Family', 'Education', and 'Friendship', and the top 3 for Japanese were 'Friendship', 'Peace/Getting Along', and 'Respect'. Both sets of responses look similar and sound communitarian (CCNY 1998).

Daniel Fu-Chang Tsai writes in his recent paper that Confucius' concept of person has two dimensions, namely, 'the vertical dimension', which is the autonomous, self-cultivating one, and 'the horizontal dimension', which is the relational, altruistic one (11). He says that 'some may argue that there is no vertical dimension at all in the Confucian personhood. This is incorrect'. He concludes as follows:

> When a person exercises autonomy, he is not choosing in a context-free, conceptual vacuum but considers himself a person-in-relation, with many roles to play and responsibilities to take, in accordance with different relationships... The tension might be difficult to resolve, but the traditional tendency of social orientation should surely be balanced by, and reconciled with, respecting the individual's rights and autonomy (Tsai 2001: 48,49).

Here we can see a well-balanced perspective on 'autonomy' and 'relationships'. This kind of mature thinking can be found everywhere on this planet and is not the patent of Confucius or East Asia.

We sometimes use the words 'Japanese bioethics', 'American bioethics', and 'Asian bioethics', but these wordings are apt to make us think that there is 'the' Japanese bioethics, 'the' American bioethics, and so on. This is not true. There are various bioethical ideas and actions in each region. Of course there are clear cultural differences between distant countries, but if we take a closer look at one area, we can find considerable gender differences, religious differences, economic differences, etc., and at the same time it is also true that we actually share many things across borders. Hence, we should say 'bioethics in Japan' instead of 'Japanese bioethics', 'Genomics in Asia' instead of 'Asian Genomics', and so on. Anyway, we have to abandon the East/West dichotomy and its variations.

LIFE STUDIES AS AN ALTERNATIVE TO BIOETHICS

As I mentioned before, when I first studied 'American' bioethics in 1980s, I was very frustrated because it seemed to me a somewhat narrow and shallow approach to the issues of life. Some of my friends had similar impressions. First, it discussed only medical issues. It did not deal with environmental issues. It is ironical that V.R. Potter who coined the word 'bioethics' in 1970 regarded this word as a kind of 'environmental ethics' rather than a medical ethics. For me, separating medical ethics from environmental ethics seems senseless because humans live on this planet surrounded by nature and our health and happiness cannot be separated from the environment. My first intuition was that medical ethics should not be separated from environmental ethics.

Second, 'American' bioethics did not ask questions such as 'What is the meaning of life?', 'How can we live in this society without regret?', and 'What is human?' Whenever we think deeply about difficult bioethical problems like selective abortion, euthanasia, manipulation of human genes, and organ transplantation, we come to the above philosophical questions in the end. In addition, psychological and sociological approaches should be introduced to research on these issues, but the word bio-'ethics' seemed to exclude these disciplines. I thought it would be more fruitful to discuss bioethics in an interdisciplinary forum.

Third, it took 'modern civilisation based on scientific technology and capitalism' for granted, and sought the methods of regulating the conflicts of interest among us. However, difficult bioethical dilemmas are created by the 'advancement' of scientific technology, and sometimes they are worsened by the mechanism of capitalism. In contemporary society, our desires are created by technologies and mass media and as a result, we lose the happiness that we enjoyed before. Of course it is impossible to totally abolish today's science and technology, but it is necessary to examine the essence of modern civilisation based on scientific technology and capitalism, and think about how to create an alternative civilisation and society. I believe criticism of modern civilisation should be one of the foundations of bioethical thinking.

For these reasons, I coined the term 'life studies' instead of 'bioethics' in 1988. The idea of life studies has gradually developed since then. In 1989, I published Brain Dead Person in which I discussed the topic from the viewpoint of life studies. I distinguished three concepts, namely, 'my brain death', 'brain death of intimate others', and 'brain death of strangers'. I made clear the differences of the meaning of death in these three cases, and demonstrated that these differences might be the cause of ordinary people's inconsistent attitudes towards brain dead persons in various settings. I also criticised the essence of modern medicine and scientific technology, and developed key ideas like 'partism of modern medicine' and 'efficiency and irreplaceability'. This book was the real first product of life studies.

Through research on brain death, I realised that there have been no empirical studies on the idea of life among ordinary people. Scholars sometimes talked about the Japanese idea of life and death, but their arguments were based on traditional Buddhist or Confucian literatures. It is not certain that today's ordinary people share these traditional ideas. I performed research using open questionnaires and gathered nearly thousand responses from ordinary people. I published part of the results in the paper 'The Concept of Inochi', in 1991 (Morioka 1991) and made various interesting discoveries. Many Japanese grasp the idea of 'human life' in relationship with that of 'nature'. The images of 'life', 'spirit', and 'nature' overlap with one another in their worldview. For many of them, environmental issues are conceived as problems of life. And here, too, their images of life vary. There is no such thing as 'the' Japanese idea of life. Interestingly, however, several patterns of grasping images of life were discovered. For example, there were many responses that suggested that life is interrelated on the one hand, and irreplaceable on the other. People seem to feel some dynamism between interrelatedness and irreplaceability. This research is still continuing and is one of the most important contributions to the field of life studies.

In 1995, an unbelievable event occurred. Members of the Japanese cult, Aum Shinrikyo, launched a sarin nerve gas attack in crowded subways in Tokyo, killing 12 people and injuring more than 5,000 people. At first, they were members of a small religious group seriously seeking the 'meaning of life'. However, they began to consider our society to be evil place, and planned to destroy the whole world in order to reconstruct a clean one. I was shocked by their action because I felt I shared many of their aims. This event made me think again the relationship between life studies and religion, and I published the book How to Live in a Post-religious Age in 1996 (Morioka 1996). In this book, I confessed that I am a man who cannot believe in any religions, nor believe in scientific materialism. I want to seek 'spirituality' and the 'meaning of life' outside of religions. I called this 'the third way between religion and science'.

Does this attitude lead to the denial of religion? No. My position is an agnostic one. I do not affirm or deny religions. I have had discussions with various religious people, and I found that we can talk about spirituality and the meaning of life without using religious language. If we respect each other's worldview and do not force one's own presuppositions on the others, we are able to have a deep discussion with each other concerning the issues of life, death and nature.

Life studies should be a project where people of faith and people without religion get together to communicate with and learn from each other. I conceive of life studies as a project where people with religion seek to think about life without using dogmatic words, and people without religion seek to think about spirituality and the meaning of life using ordinary language. I think this should be the basis of life studies.

Life studies also deals with human relationships with the environment. I wrote a series of essays from 1995-1998, and published them as a digital book, Life Torn Apart, in 2001 (Morioka 2001b). In these writings, I insisted that humans are imprinted with three natures, namely, 'the nature of connectedness (to all living things)', 'the nature of self-interest', and 'the nature of mutual support'. These natures are sometimes in harmony, but at other times they conflict with each other. In the latter case, mediation is impossible. In this sense, human life is torn apart and moves in two opposite directions, the direction of isolation and the direction of connectedness. Under this scheme, the problem of 'preservation' and 'conservation' in environmental ethics is clearly analysed, but we cannot expect simple answers to this heavy question. Contributions of life studies to environmental ethics and environmental philosophy will be enormous. This is a future challenge for us.

In the same year, I published another book, Life Studies Approaches to Bioethics: A New Perspective on Brain Death, Feminism, and Disability (Morioka 2001c). In this book, I demonstrated that incorporating feminist and disability studies would change bioethics into a more attractive field; like life studies, it would be filled with diverse ideas and focus on the process of empowerment. As I mentioned before, Japanese bioethics started in the early 1970s as 'feminist bioethics' and 'disabled people bioethics'. Their approach was closer to our 'life studies' in that they were seeking the 'meaning of life' and 'self-affirmation' in our discriminative society, and in that they severely criticised contemporary civilisation, scientific technology, and capitalism (Morioka, forthcoming). I examined 'men's sexuality', which sometimes indirectly forces women to abort a foetus when men are not willing to have a baby. This kind of 'symbolic violence', which is lurking in our society, should be emphasised in the field of life studies. I discussed the idea of 'the sense of fundamental security' as a key term for thinking about the negative psychological impact of new eugenics. I am currently writing a fundamental criticism of modern civilisation, which will be published as a book in the next year.

SCOPE OF LIFE STUDIES

I would like to present 'life studies' as a forum or project in which people who are frustrated with bioethics and other disciplines get together to discuss life, death, nature, scientific technology, and contemporary civilisation, although life studies itself is still in an early stage of development. The field of life studies consists of three categories: life studies as a forum, life studies as a project, and life studies on a personal level.

Life studies as a forum

First, we need a forum in which people with different backgrounds get together and discuss the issues of life interdisciplinarily. Of course, many conferences on bioethics plan to have interdisciplinary discussions, but the word bio-'ethics' makes people from some disciplines hesitant to join because it sounds like as if 'ethics' is the central theme. Life studies as a forum will take many forms, for example, conferences, small meetings, collections of essays, discussion groups, or a new research field such as cultural studies and disability studies. Even biologists, anthropologists, sociologists, and historian will be able to join more freely. The College of Applied Life Studies (CALS) at the University of Illinois, USA, which contains departments for community health, human sciences, and disability studies, is a good example of this forum (CALS homepage). In this category, the words 'life studies' are interpreted broadly.

Life studies as a project

Life studies as a project has a more limited scope. It aims at developing our knowledge about the meaning of life, death, and nature in relationship to modern civilisation, and it tries to find a way to live our own lives. We seek to attain a deeper understanding of the meaning of life, death, and our relationship with the natural environment. We also seek to attain the deep understanding of the essence of modern civilisation based on scientific technology and capitalism. And beyond that, we want to discover a way to resolve contemporary issues concerning life, death, nature, and bioethics without using religious language. Of course, both people of faith and people without religion are welcome, but this project must not have any special relationship with religious groups.

I wrote 'The Declaration of Life Studies: Six Proposals' in 2000. This shows the basic characteristics of life studies as a project. The outline of the six proposals is as follows:

1. Study as wisdom. Life studies is a kind of vivid development of our wisdom in which we contemplate the reality of life and death, struggle against our inner desires, and try to find a way of resolving contemporary issues concerning life.

2.   Criticism of modern civilisation. Life studies connects the criticism of modern civilization with issues concerning life, death, and nature. Life studies throws light on the essence of modern civilisation, and tries to show a way of overcoming the negative effects of scientific technology and capitalism.

3.   Meaning of life. One of life studies' aims is to think about how we should live in modern society without regret. Questions such as 'How should I live?' 'What is the meaning of life?' 'How should we change ourselves and social systems in order to attain the meaning of life?' are among the main questions of life studies.

4.   Relationship and irreplaceability. Life studies looks at every phenomenon and issue from the perspective of correlation between 'relationship and irreplaceability'.

5.   Reconsideration of desires, violence, freedom and spirituality. We try to find a way of overcoming our own desires and violence. We distinguish 'superficial freedom' that supports modern civilisation from 'rich freedom' that leads us to the real pleasures of life. We seek for 'post-religious spirituality' that is not based on a particular religion.

6.   Support from a distance. Life studies means a network in which everyone who is seeking the meaning of life supports others from a distance. We do not join a closed community where everyone has the same standards and values (Morioka 2000).

The ultimate goals of life studies would be: 1) to live and die our limited life 'without regret', and 2) to create a society in which everyone can live and die his/her limited life 'without regret'. In order to come closer to these goals, we have to think about the meaning of life and the essence of our civilisation seriously, and we have to communicate with each other to learn different ideas.

Looking from this perspective, one of the big problems is, of course, the gulf between economically wealthy countries and economically poor countries. In the latter countries, for example, many people are suffering from HIV/AIDS, but do not have access to medication. Behind this lies the 'structural exploitation' of developing countries by developed counties. But on the other hand, people in developed countries also suffer from acts of violence such as domestic violence, child sexual abuse, and stalking. They are not necessarily happy. Life studies have to tackle with these complicated structural problems in and between the North and the South.

Life studies on a personal level

Life studies include both thoughts and actions, thinking and living. As mentioned above, one of the ultimate goals of life studies is to live and die our limited life 'without regret'. In this sense, living our own life is an essential part of life studies. The dichotomy of theory and practice does not work here. 'Thinking' is a form of action, and we cannot act without a cognitive framework influenced by language. What is needed is wisdom that does not let our eyes turn away from oneself and one's own life. In this sense, life studies on a personal level should be a lonely act. This is the reason why 'support from a distance' is required. It is important to keep in mind that people joining life studies as a project must apply life studies on a personal level. We cannot separate the two.

I have written a number of works on life studies in Japanese, but this is only one of the possible variations of life studies. Everyone can develop his/her own life studies. In science, the words 'her science' or 'my science' are senseless. However, in life studies, the words 'her life studies' or 'my life studies' are meaningful descriptions of the concept. Morioka's approach is apt to be biased towards philosophy. There will be many more approaches to life studies on a personal level. Hence, Morioka's life studies never fully represent 'life studies as a project'.

The interrelated development of these three categories will be required for life studies and I would like to invite interested people throughout the world to contribute their thoughts on this topic (see Table 1).

CONCLUSION

The idea of life studies can be discovered in all periods or areas. What I am doing is to mould the idea to suit contemporary society. Unfortunately, 'American' academic bioethics in the 1980s seemed to lack the insights of life studies; I had to find them in other traditions, that is, feminism and the disability movement in Japan in the early 1970s. But this does not mean that some traditions are superior to other traditions in terms of life studies. Each tradition contains a number of valuable lessons that we should learn with a humble attitude.

Table 1 Scope of life studies

Life studies as a forum

↑↓ People with different background get together and discuss issues concerning life

Life studies as a project

↑↓ People explore the meaning of life, death and nature in relationship to modern civilization based on scientific technology and capitalism (without using religious language)

Life studies on a personal level

People live their own life without regret seeking the meaning of life

BIBLIOGRAPHY

Callahan, D. (1996) 'Communitarian Bioethics: A Pious Hope?' The Responsive Community, 6, no. 4:26-33.

City College of New York (1998). Online. Available HTTP: http://www.schoollink.org/projectmktplace/values_project.htm

College of Applied Life Studies, University of Illinois. Online. Available HTTP: <http://www.als.uiuc.edu/>.

Emanuel, E.J. (1991) The Ends of Human Life: Medical Ethics in a Liberal Polity, Cambridge: Harvard University Press.

Morioka, M. (forthcoming) 'Disability Movement and Inner Eugenic Thought: A Philosophical Aspect of Independent Living and Bioethics'. Online. Available HTTP: <http://www.lifestudies.org/disability01.html>.

Morioka, M. (2001a) 'Reconsidering Brain Death: A Lesson from Japan's 15 Years of Experience', Hastings Center Report, 31, no.4: 41-46. Online. Available HTTP: http://www.lifestudies.org/reconsidering.html.

Morioka, M. (in Japanese) (2001b) Life Torn Apart. Online. Available HTTP: <http://www.lifestudies.org/>.

Morioka, M. (in Japanese) (2001c) Life Studies Approaches to Bioethics: A New Perspective on Brain Death, Feminism, and Disability, Keiso Shobo. Online. Available HTTP: http://www.lifestudies.org/.

Morioka, M. (2000) 'The Declaration of Life Studies: Six Proposals (Rough Draft)'. Online. Available HTTP: http://www.lifestudies.org/lifestudies.html.

Morioka, M. (in Japanese) (1996) How to Live in a Post-religious Age, Hozokan. Online. Available HTTP: http://www.lifestudies.org/.

Morioka, M. (1995) 'Bioethics and Japanese Culture: Brain Death, Patients' Rights, and Cultural Factors', Eubios Journal of Asian and International Bioethics, 5: 87-90. Online. Available HTTP: http://www.lifestudies.org/japanese.html.

Morioka, M. (in Japanese) (1994) Reconsidering the Idea of Life, Chikuma: Shobo.

Morioka, M. (1991) 'The Concept of Inochi: A Philosophical Perspective on the Study of Life', Japan Review, 2: 83-115. Online. Available HTTP:
http://www.lifestudies.org/inochi.html.

Morioka, M. Brain Dead Person (in Japanese) (1989). First chapter online. Available HTTP:
http://www.lifestudies.org/braindeadperson00.html.

Sakamoto, H. 'Towards a New Global Bioethics', The Abstracts of Seventh Tsukuba International Bioethics Roundtable, 15-18 February, 2002.

Siminoff, L. and Bloch, A. (1999) 'American Attitudes and Beliefs about Brain Death: The Empirical Literature', in S. J. Youngner and R. M. Arnold (eds.) The Definition of Death: Contemporary Controversies, Baltimore: The Johns Hopkins University Press.

Tsai, D.F.C. (2001) 'How Should Doctors Approach Patients? A Confucian Reflection on Personhood', in Journal of Medical Ethics, 27: 44-50.

Umehara, T. (1994) 'Descartes, Brain Death and Organ Transplants: A Japanese View', New Perspectives Quarterly, 11. Online. Available HTTP:
http://www.npq.org/issues/v111/p25.html

Chapter 11

A philosophical Meditation on Genomics

Min Jiayin

INTRODUCTION

Genomics involves prenatal screening, artificial insemination, test-tube babies, using another's womb to have one's own baby, human embryo stem cell research, organ transplantation, euthanasia, human cloning and so on. In China, each of these topics has been widely discussed and debated. Most people in this country believe in Marxist materialism and atheism, and deem science and technology as the first productive force. Today, China pursues a strategy of relying on science and technology to achieve prosperity and is becoming a commodity society. Meanwhile the traditional Confucian culture attaches great importance to blood relationship and ethical values, treating the family as the basic unit of society, which has been a very strong conservative force. Chinese genomics has evolved in relation to these two cultural values.

Personally, I believe that the ethical debate on genomics is essentially an issue of human rights, i.e., a question of whether a person has full right to his own body, organ, life and life transmigration. Secondly, it is an issue whether mankind has a right to intervene in and change the reproduction process and mode, and even to create a new one. I hold a positive view on these two rights, but do not deny that we must reflect on their ethical implications and bear our social and moral responsibilities. Particularly in the economic sphere, genomics needs to remain within the bounds of the law, which must take its social consequences into account. Scientific research is value-neutral and, for science, there is no forbidden zone. These principles are also applied to genomical research, including research in the cloning of man. From the perspective of general evolution research, I am sure a new and superior form of life will evolve on the earth, and, based on systems philosophy, I am certain a revolutionary change will take place in the reproduction of human beings. Overall, I firmly support research on genomics and its social relevance.

Physics and chemistry dominated during the 20th century, while so far biology has dominated the 21st century. The initial years of this new century have already witnessed a series of bioengineering projects in the fields of biology and medicine, including prenatal screening, artificial insemination, test-tube babies, using another's womb to have one's own baby, human embryo stem cell research, organ transplantation, euthanasia, human cloning, and so on. Genetics has become a topic of heated discussion among scientists and in academic circles around the world. My study of major publications in the field of bioethics has led me to believe that correct conclusions can only be reached when issues are viewed from the general perspective of the evolution of the universe, mankind, society, science and technology

MANKIND NEEDS TO CONTINUE ITS EVOLUTION

General evolution theory argues that the evolution of the universe has been going on for at least 20 billion years since the Big Bang and that the evolution of the solar system has been going on for at least 4.7 billion years. Life on earth began about 3.6 billion years ago and the evolution of the ancient ape-man to intelligent and modern man can be traced back to half a million years ago. Human beings are the noblest, most complex and intelligent living species and at the same time the weakest species on this planet. Mankind is facing the menace of the ecological and natural catastrophe it has been creating.

From the cosmological angle, we find that our galaxy is just one of many galaxies and that our solar system is just a medium-sized star system, while our earth is just one of the nine planets of the solar system. However, on our planet, the evolution of life and human beings, resulting from highly complex processes, are indeed of tremendous significance. The information sent back by explorers of Mars in recent years told us that the hope of finding even the lowest form of life on that planet is dim. And it is even more improbable to find intelligent living creatures in the galaxy or the cosmos.

From the angle of natural and social science, the evolution of life on earth may be reduced to a process of systematic evolution: i.e., the self-organisational system, the self-reproduction system, self-study system, the autopoietic system and the self-creative system. I believe that a human being is not only an autopoietic system or a system of self-adaptation as put forth by the Santa Fe Institute pattern, but also a more advanced system of self-creation. Because humans use their brain as well as their hands, civilisation is continuously rising to a higher plane, while the intelligence of humans is also advancing very rapidly. But man as a biological species seems to have stopped evolving or even regressing in many aspects.

Generally speaking, the human physique is degenerating, especially among the young generation that is growing up in the comfortable modern city life. People's body hair has virtually disappeared, together with cold resistance. The contemporary human body requires clothes, blankets, houses and heating facilities to keep it warm. Heat resistance is also degenerating. Fans and electric fans are inadequate and air conditioners are becoming a household necessity. Mankind has long lost the ability of eating raw animal meat, grass roots and tree barks, while the intake of refined food is pushing up the incidence of diabetes and other 'illnesses of the wealthy'. True, life expectancy of human beings is longer than in the past, but that is largely due to the progress of medical science. What is even more worrisome is the fact that there are potentially more than 2,000 genetic diseases.

Meanwhile, the natural and social environment for the survival of mankind on the earth is deteriorating every day. Why are cardiovascular diseases the number one killers of mankind today? The reason is that a lack of physical exercise causes the weakening of the cardiovascular system, whereas stress, smoking, alcohol abuse, and obesity overburden the heart and blood system. Why has cancer become the number two killer? The primary cause has been increasing environmental pollution while the human physique has not grown more resistant to pollutants. Furthermore, the sudden emergence and rapid spread of AIDS, which destroys the immune system of the human body, makes people shudder at the prospects of humanity.

Besides, futurists have warned people that the greenhouse effect is irreversible and will definitely cause the spread of epidemic diseases. In short, if mankind wishes to survive, it must rely on scientific and technological progress, and follow the old Chinese saying that 'the wise never cease improving themselves'. It must try to reverse the deterioration of the human physique and promote the evolution of its physical capacity.

ARTIFICIAL CLONING IS A NECESSITY

In order to continue the evolution of the human body, mankind cannot merely rely on marriage and natural childbirth, because their randomness is obvious. According to a recent press report, Hitler's secretary revealed some historical facts on her deathbed. She said that she once asked Hitler why he did not want to have a child. The dictator replied that 'All geniuses in history have left only idiots behind'. Hitler showed some intelligence on this point. It is true that a marriage between non-relatives cannot guarantee the birth of children with no physical and/or mental deformities. And history has shown that mankind has not achieved marked evolutionary progress based on marriage and natural childbirth. On the contrary, the physical capacity of human beings has weakened. So mankind has to find a new way out, artificial reproduction.

Scientific and technological achievements have become the primary productive force in modern society. They have brought the 'material production system' from the production in the natural system to production in the artificial system in the last few centuries: manual production → manual-mechanic production → mechanic production → semi-automatic production → fully automatic production. They are developing a similar process in agricultural production. The milk, vegetables, eggs, fish and prawns that residents of Beijing consume today are produced mostly by the artificial-natural system (mechanised or semi-mechanised dairy farms, hothouses, poultry farms and aquatic farms). Modern science and technology have also brought the following production and spread of information: manual tools → machines → electrified means → automation. Examples include printing technology, typewriter, telegraph, telephone, film, broadcasting, television, computer, internet, and education by electronic means. Similarly management has progressed due to the above-mentioned information technology and information tools, especially in the collection and processing of information by large computers, and the forecasting and decision making by people working with computers.

Under these circumstances, how can modern science and technology be kept from participating in the 'reproduction system of human beings?' They cannot. They have produced innovations like prenatal screening, artificial delivery, artificial feeding, contraceptive tools and drugs, organ transplantation in extensive use. In view of this, it is no wonder that the knowledge of molecular genetics and the techniques of genetic engineering are applied to organs, tissues, cells and genes of the human body. This is only logical and in line with the law of development.

Genetic engineering involves prenatal screening, artificial insemination, test-tube babies, using another woman's womb to have one's child, artificial wombs, human embryo stem cell research, organ transplantation, euthanasia, human cloning and so on. What is the ultimate goal? In my view, the goal is to transcend the natural reproduction between the two sexes to reach sexual-artificial reproduction and ultimately fully artificial reproduction. This is in keeping with the development of modern science and technology and with the law of evolution governing human reproduction.

WOMEN EMANCIPATED FROM CHILDBIRTH

The most conspicuous inequality in human society is that between men and women, the deepest root cause of which lies in their unequal role in reproduction and the breeding of offspring. This arrangement is unequal whether it is caused by Nature or, as the Bible says, by God's will.

In sexual activities, a man's contribution is merely the ejection of sperm, whereas a woman's contribution is not limited to an egg but also includes the protracted torment of pregnancy and the risk of death. To every pregnant woman, the labour of childbirth means not only pain and loss of blood, but also a high risk of death. In 1997, childbirth resulted in the death of 63.6 women out of every 100,000 in labour in China. An EFE report on March 6, 2002, quoting statistics from Brussels, shows that about 600,000 women lose their lives in pregnancy or childbirth labour every year, while 40 times as many get seriously infected with complications. If we make a calculation based on this figure, as many as six billion women died during pregnancy or childbirth labour over the past 10,000 years. That amounts to the total population of the earth today. The toll of 3,036 taken by the terrorist attack in New York on 11 September, 2001 shocked the world and a great many people are still being tormented by the tragedy. Yet seemingly mankind does not feel sorry for 200 times as many deaths on the child delivery beds every year. What is even more absurd is the fact that some people are concerned about developing artificially-assisted reproduction and artificial reproduction (the technologies involving the creation of man-made wombs and human cloning).

The extra burden on women on the issue of childbirth far exceeds the examples mentioned above. Just imagine how many women merely play the role of machines of reproduction all their lives, how many women lose their health and looks in childbirth, and how many women have to give up education or work because of childbirth. Therefore, as long as human society favours only the natural way of the reproduction of human beings, which means a serious inequality in obligations and contributions between male and female, women's emancipation cannot be complete.

Therefore, I would like to put forth a new concept, 'women's liberation from childbirth', and two propositions: 'only when women are freed from childbirth, are they truthfully free' and 'only artificial reproduction technology can make women's liberation possible'. In this respect I pin my hopes on the experiments with the technology of 'artificial wombs'. The reason is that in comparison with human cloning, this technology is much simpler because it neither damages the existing custom of bigamy and the two-parent families, nor involve ethical, legal and social problems.

Actually, I read a news report in a tabloid called *Reference News* in the 1960s, when I was a college student, which said that a young Italian doctor succeeded in cultivating a human egg in an artificial womb for 36 days. Unfortunately the experiment had to be suspended due to interference from the Church. A follow-up report said that the Soviet Union then invited the doctor to that country, but I never heard about him again.

Forty years passed before I learned from the media that Dr Hongqing Liu, a Chinese-American working at Cornell University's Centre of Genetic Medicine and Impotence Research, and his assistants succeeded in making an artificial womb and letting an embryo grow in it for six days. But due to the restrictions imposed by American law on external fertilisation, the doctor had to stop his experiment. Since the law allows such experiments to last two weeks, however, Dr Liu plans to continue his experiment. Another report, entitled 'Is It the End of Natural Mothers?', announced that a large international symposium on artificial womb would be held at Oklahoma University on February 22-23, 2003. This news sheds another ray of hope for the liberation of women from childbirth. Let us hope that the dark clouds of prejudice and religious, ethical or social taboos will not overshadow this good news.

More than once I have read news reports from the press of Western countries, pointing out that an increasing number of white women are unwilling to get married and have children, which has resulted in the stagnation (or even decrease) of the total population. I have also read that Western nations are facing the danger of 'turning brown', because the number of coloured immigrants is increasing. Today, many young Chinese women are also reluctant to have children. A recent *Beijing Evening News* report says that a survey in Beijing, Shanghai and Guangzhou shows that the number of DINKs (families with double incomes and no kids) is growing fast.

Among the young adults of these three cities, 21 per cent favour 'marriage but no children', which is 15 percentage points higher than five years ago, and another 21.7 per cent say they have children involuntarily because of parental pressure. The survey also shows that more women than men do not like to have children and that the percentage rises with the level of income and education. The similarity in the statistics from the West and the East indicates that mankind seems to be bound to rely on artificial reproduction technology for its own propagation.

WHAT IS WRONG WITH EUGENICS?

Essentially, genomics and its relevant technologies serve as new eugenic means. Eugenics, founded by Sir Francis Galton, a cousin of Darwin's, should have won approval. But due to misunderstandings and inappropriate applications, it was looked upon as a bad discipline with negative long-term effects (at least in China).

There are two schools of eugenics, the positive and the negative. Traditionally, positive eugenics advocates improvement of the genetic properties of a species through selective reproduction, while negative eugenics advocates attainment of eugenics through a systematic expulsion of those individuals deemed inferior. Many states in the United States of the early 20th century passed legislation to impose compulsory sterilisation on criminals, idiots and mentally retarded persons on the basis of the negative eugenics. The country went on to adopt an immigration law that barred immigration from many countries and nations. That of course aroused widespread opposition and spoiled the reputation of eugenics. Hitler borrowed eugenics as his theoretical basis for launching a war of aggression and a campaign of ethnic annihilation. That thoroughly defamed eugenics. In China, however, a number of sociologists advocated eugenics before the founding of New China, and in the first 30 years or so after liberation eugenics was condemned as 'a reactionary tenet of Western bourgeoisie'. But in the last 20 years, eugenics has made a comeback.

In theory, it is definitely correct and necessary for mankind to seek eugenics. One rule of systematic science is the necessity of the optimisation of the system to achieve the best structure and function. Mankind throughout its history has never stopped improving the crops and livestock—through seed selection, breeding, hybridisation, etc. Then why should not mankind seek optimisation of itself? What comes in the way is the fact that the human kind is a super species that constructs ideologies, values self-respect and stands for human rights. We cannot practise passive optimisation but only positive optimisation. In other words, we should not deprive the disadvantaged of their right to reproduction, nor maltreat and have prejudice against the physiologically or psychologically handicapped. We should also not be hesitant to apply the available scientific and technological progress to improve the quality of human reproduction.

Genomics provides mankind with the most powerful eugenic means so far, especially when we have completed the gene chart of mankind and know the positions of the genes that cause genetic diseases. Take China, for instance: some 20 million babies are born in the country every year and among them about four million have a genetic deficiency or disease. Both the families of handicapped or diseased babies and society at large have to spend a great deal of energy and money on their treatment, and in most cases the hope of complete recovery is very dim. Then why not resolve this issue by relying on genetic engineering?

FROM LONG LIFE TO IMMORTALITY

It is only human to love life and fear death. I believe that throughout history no one has not wished for a long life or dreamed of immortality. With economic progress and better living conditions, especially with the progress of medical science, life expectancy in many countries grew from around 30 years to around 70 in the 20th century. But great as this achievement may be, it remains a far cry from immortality.

Looking back at history, human beings have realised almost every dream they had, but generally in a way beyond their imagination. For example, mankind in its early days must dreamed of having the capacity of running very fast with a heavy load like a horse. Today, this dream has come true, in the form of the motor car and train, which run even faster than a horse. Human beings must have dreamt of flying in the sky like bird and this dream has come true in the form of the aeroplane. Mankind must have dreamed of swimming freely in water and this dream has come true, in the form of a steam ship and submarine. So mankind should be confident that it can make inventions and discoveries to realise the dream of longevity and immortality.

In my personal view, man is seeking to realise the dream of longevity and immortality along three paths, namely, the transplantation of organs, the cloning of man and robots. However the overwhelming majority of human beings are not aware of the fact that mankind is in the course of discovering a way to achieve longevity and they panic at the prospect of immortality.

Let us first look at the technology of organ transplantation. Mankind came to understand the nature of life in the 19th century on the basis of insights from physics, chemistry and biology. Hence the proposition that 'the essence of life is metabolism of protein'.

People at the time realised that protein was a life material capable of self-cloning as the old dies and the newly cloned replaces it. Thinking along this line, we may come to realise that metabolism at an even higher plane, i.e., that of the organs of the human body (through self-cloning and substitution) should be of even more profound significance to life science. Unfortunately, no living creatures, including human beings, have the power of self-cloning of the organs. Organ transplantation in modern medical technology may be considered the realisation of the lengthening of life through 'external cloning'. The problem lies in the fact that it is very difficult to substitute the human organ with an organ taken from an animal and it is also difficult to cope with rejection. Now research into the stem cell of the human embryo may lead to the resolution of this problem. Should we really cultivate our own embryo stem cell to obtain cloned organs for transplantation, then, in a sense, mankind has resolved the issue of achieving immortality of the organs of the human body.

The successful cloning of a sheep in Britain in 1998 marked a new epoch in cloning technology, an epoch of cloning a complete body of a mammal through an artificial system. Should we continue along this path, a complete human being may be cloned. That would mean a new way of achieving immortality of the human body. But while superior to organ transplantation, this is immortality technology at the lowest plane because it is the cloning of the body. Quoting a Chinese proverb, it is only 'a walking mummy'. Man is a being at a higher plane, the being of psychological-self-consciousness and a social being (the totality of social relations). Only when the being of these two planes is cloned in the body of a human being, can it truly be considered human cloning. In other words, mankind would then realise immortality in the true sense of the word by relying on scientific and technological means. Unfortunately mankind is still very far from these two goals. But I am confident that mankind can do it.

The third way for mankind to achieve immortality is the production of robots. Modern science and technology can make intelligent robots and mankind is striving to reach this goal. The triumph of 'Deep Blue' over the international chess champion was an indication of the infinite potential of intelligent robots. I think that in the future the capacity of man versus that of intelligent robots in many ways will be like that of a sparrow versus that of a Boeing 747 plane. Suppose one day the psychological self-conscious being and the social being of Man can be incorporated into intelligent robots. Wouldn't that be another form of immortality?

IS IT NECESSARY TO SET UP A FORBIDDEN ZONE FOR HUMAN CLONING?

The most challenging and disputable issue in the field of genomics is the cloning of human beings. We may view this issue from both an active and a passive perspective. From the passive side, the cloning of human beings represents regress and stagnation, i.e., from sexual to asexual reproduction and from biological variation to mono-cell cloning. If we view the reproduction of biological individuals as a process of copying and translating biological genetic information, then human cloning produces an individual who is inferior to the original individual. So cloning has no positive significance for the existence, reproduction and evolution of mankind, except that it may satisfy some people's curiosity.

From the positive side, the application of cloning technology in livestock breeding may open up a new horizon in this industry. The cloning of rare animals on the verge of extinction, such as the giant panda, may make a valuable contribution to the conservation of the ecosystem. One day, when the technology of cloning animals of the highest order is mature, it could be applied to human cloning. First, a cloned man may be used as an object for research to find out whether the formation of a person's character and ability depends on nature or nurture. Second, human cloning eliminates the uncertainty of random variation in sexual reproduction and ensures progress in the reproduction of human beings. If cloning technology is applied in combination with gene monitoring, screening, correction and inlaying, a more refined individual may be reproduced.

If we look further ahead, our planet and even the solar system may one day become unsuitable for mankind. In order to continue to survive, mankind shall be forced to migrate to another planet with more suitable living environments for mankind. But to travel from the earth to another planet may take dozens or even hundreds of light years and even if a couple of young astronauts could make the trip under tremendously improved technology, they might have lost their reproductive capacity when they reach the new planet.

So the cloning of man has its positive side. If this technology is used in combination with other genetic engineering technologies, its positive significance may far exceed its negative side. I personally agree with the proposition that science has no forbidden zone and that science is value neutral. With a belief in those two principles, I disagree with the proposal for setting up a forbidden zone to prevent serious scientific research in the cloning of man. Besides, it is useless to set up a forbidden zone. Human society forbids rape, theft, robbery and murder not only morally but also by criminal penalties. Yet those crimes take place every day. Similarly, the governments of many countries have ruled out the cloning of man and we know that some scientists insist on continuing their research. Human cloning will become a fact sooner or later. When one day it becomes a fact, I hope our governments and people will be prepared for it.

ON THE 'ZERO-PARENT FAMILY'

As a student of philosophy, I hate to discuss sex, marriage and family. Despite their apparent simplicity, these issues are extremely complex. The basic fact is that the human being is a creature of indiscriminate intercourse with a strong sexual desire and reproductive power, which has allowed it to become the most intelligent animal. Mankind was forced into the self-binding shackle of patriarchy owing to certain social conditions and needs some 5,000 years ago. This put mankind in a most embarrassing position. Mankind has to abide by the marriage-family mode but seeks to break with it in every possible way. It would be very difficult for many people—for archbishops, kings, presidents, teachers, scholars, religious believers, husbands and wives—to avoid being hypocritical on the issue of sex and marriage.

The result is a kaleidoscopic picture created by indiscriminate intercourse in the human society over the past 5,000 years. Many people give up education, careers, bright prospects and even lives for love. Love, marriage and family have always been (and will continue to be) important themes of literature, arts, films and television. By the 20th century, this patriarchal pair-marriage mode, which is not compatible with human nature and by no means sacred and eternal, suffered from numerous attacks and violations. Freud's psychoanalysis argues that this marriage mode causes the depression of human nature as well as physical and mental illnesses. The invention and popular use of the condom and contraceptive drugs and induced abortion have made it possible to separate sex from reproduction. In the face of this reality, perhaps no one has sufficient reason to insist that the patriarchal pair-marriage family mode is pure, sacred and eternal.

In that case, genetic engineering technology could help catalyse some new sexual patterns. The application of the technology of artificial wombs and cloning is no more than an evolution from manually aided reproduction to artificial reproduction by which human sexual life is thoroughly divorced from sexual reproduction. This is a step forward from 'the single-parent family to zero-parent family' pattern, thus freeing mankind from the contradictions, depression, hypocrisy and disorder that have haunted mankind in the past 5,000 years. When reproduction is divorced from sexual activities, each will play its own destined role.

PROBLEMS OF ETHICS AND LAW RELATED TO GENOMICS

Despite my statements above, I do not promote hasty experiments with human cloning. It is not because such experiments involve ethical and legal problems, but because the technology is not mature yet. The general medical practice is to gain experience and constantly improve the techniques in experimenting with animals until the technology is mature before it is done on a human being. When the technology is mature, I will have no objection to experiments with human cloning for scientific purposes, especially for medical purposes.

I am opposed to the practice of using ethics and law as a pretext to obstruct the progress of genetic engineering. The reason is very simple: ethics and law should not be used to block scientific progress and they can never succeed. Generally speaking, ethics and law set rules for people's social behaviour. Ethics is formed by habits and customs and people's moral considerations, whereas law is made by human beings for maintaining social order. In view of evolution, a common phenomenon is that it is not people's social behaviour that changes with the change of ethics and law. On the contrary, it is ethics and law that change along with people's social behaviour.

In ancient China, girls were supposed to limit their movements within the inner courtyard. That was ethically correct. In modern China, however, it is ethically correct for girls to go out to school, to work and to travel across the world. Confucian ethics stipulates that: 'Men and women should not have bodily contact in daily interaction'. Today young men and women commonly embrace and kiss in the streets of Beijing. A century ago, it was legitimate for a man to have many wives in China. Today it is a crime if a man marries a second woman before divorcing the first. The Chinese media commonly used the phrase 'illegally living together' 20 years ago, whereas today the phrase does not include the word 'illegally'. People today debate the ethical feasibility of DNA check-up and correction in human insemination; within half a century, or at most a century, it might be a crime if such checks and corrections do not occur.

Genomics has been a hot topic among Chinese academics in recent years. Many express the view that the application of genetic engineering may give rise to a series of ethical, legal and social problems. Personally, I would say that there is no reason to panic. Just resolve problems as they arise.

Let us take one of the most disputable issues regarding human cloning. A common question is: 'Who is the cloned version of A, his son or his brother?' This is a typical example of applying an old ethical concept to a new thing. Couldn't we just call the number one cloned version of A A.C1 and the second version A.C2? Another challenge is: What if the cloned person is imperfect? The solution: the person who does the cloning operation should be held responsible and may buy an insurance policy for his proiect. A third challenge is: How to deal with the issue of inheritance? That can be resolved easily by a will.

My general view is that science is the product of man's mental exploration and that nothing can block the advance of science and technology. The dialectics of scientific progress lies only in the self-negation and self-denial by science itself. Scientific research on the 'perpetually moving machine' and ether theory went on for centuries, for instance, and was ultimately refuted by science itself. Experiments in alchemy were carried out for a millennium of years and finally discarded by chemistry itself. Mankind at first pinned its hope on the airship, but after countless experiments decided to build the aircraft. This is also the case in the research and development of genomic technologies.

I would like to propose that we should create a relaxed ethical-legal environment for research on genomics, with just a few conditions:
- Man should have the right to be his own God in altering his own DNA and choose his own path and speed of evolution.
- The individual should have the right to determine his own life, organs and way of reproduction. This is a basic human right.
- Any scientific experiment with a person's life, organ or cell must have the prior consent of that individual.
- The researcher must assume the social responsibilities for the results of the experiment he carries out and be held responsible for its ultimate consequence.
- Strictly forbid the cloning by hybridisation between human beings and beasts.

As for the application of research results to fields beyond scientific research, particularly to commercial purposes, I propose prompt legislation in this regard, such as a law for euthanasia and a law for manual-assisted reproduction and some day a law for cloning. This is because the application of a result of scientific research usually has both positive and negative effects, and any indiscriminate application for the sole purpose of making profits is bound to damage the interests of society and the majority of people. Therefore, proper legislation can promote the positive side and suppress the negative side of a result of scientific research when it is applied to practical use.

CHINESE CULTURE AND GENOMICS

Against the backdrop of Chinese culture and the predominant values of the Chinese people, there are both favourable and unfavourable conditions for genomic research. On the favourable side, in Chinese history, the people of the Dynasty of Xia believed in the 'mandate of Heaven' and those of the Dynasty of Shang believed in gods and ghosts. But when the Dynasty of Zhou began to rule over China in the 11th century B. C., the 'mandate of Heaven' and 'gods and ghosts' gave way to a belief in human ethics. In China today, the national ideology is Marxist philosophy and the overwhelming majority of the Chinese people, including scientists accept the world outlook of materialism. Thorough materialists are fearless. They are immune to the religious belief that God creates everything and free from theological bindings and intervention. They believe in the dialectics of the development of the universe and accept Darwin's theory of biological evolution and general evolution theory.

On the negative side, however, the Confucian mentality of 'Confucius never talks about disorder, power, the weird and god' seriously hinders the imagination and creativeness of the Chinese people. Confucianism takes man as the ethical subject, thus resting Chinese culture on ethics as its foundation and seeking social stability by fettering the minds of the people to prevent creative struggles for reform and revolution. Taoism, another major influence on mainstream Chinese culture advocates obeying the law of Nature, never mentioning the 'conquest' and 'remoulding' of nature. After the high-handed dictatorships under the Yuan,

Ming and Qing dynasties, which lasted for 600 years, China as a nation lost its creativeness and became content with copying and stealing the fruits of the research of foreign nations. This has been another grave weakness of Chinese culture.

Today, Chinese scientists involved in life science have reached a fairly high level and benefit from good conditions in terms of equipment and funding. But we have not contributed significantly to genetic engineering research. The reason lies in the fact that the favourable conditions have not been fully tapped whereas the unfavourable conditions remain serious obstacles. The conservative mentality of giving prior consideration to ethic values has remained predominant. Let us look at these facts:

1. Chinese authorities and some Chinese scholars remain steadfast in their opposition to the cloning of man. Their attitude is: 'We do not approve, support or permit it'.

2. China promulgated a law on August 1, 2001, forbidding 'child bearing with another woman's womb' and the purchase or sale of the sperms of celebrities and eggs of famous models.

3. The Chinese convention is that 'parents rear children for old age' and 'sons and daughters are bound by duty to support old parents until their death'. So the attempt to pass a law on brain death was aborted.

4. In 1986, at the request of her youngest daughter, Dr. Pu Liansheng in Hanzhong City, Shaanxi Province applied euthanasia to end the suffering of a seriously ill and very old woman. This was the first case of euthanasia in China. Later, the other two daughters of the dead woman sued the doctor, accusing him of murder. The doctor was jailed for three months

and, although he was ultimately found not guilty, he lost his job, wage and chance of being assigned an apartment.

5. In 2001, nine uremic patients who could no longer tolerate the suffering in Xi'an City, Shaanxi Province jointly wrote a letter to the media, appealing for legislation to make euthanasia legitimate. Nothing has happened.

6. In 2002, a 72-year-old veteran soldier Wang Wenzhen made a will endorsing euthanasia to be applied to him in the future when he was seriously ill. When he went to the notary public to have his will notarised, his request was turned down.

In contrast, despite the fact that leaders of the British and American governments in their public announcement oppose the cloning of man, essential breakthroughs seem to have occurred in these two countries. The Massachusetts Advanced Cell Technologies of the United States recently announced that they had succeeded in cloning the first early human embryo in the world. In February of 2002, American specialists used external fertilisation DNA screening and succeeded in helping a couple suffering from Alzheimer's disease give birth to a healthy baby. Great Britain gave green light to human cloning in the medical field in February 2002, approving the cloning of human embryo for research purposes and the foundation of the world's first embryonic cell bank. So for China, which is accustomed to the cultural clone and the scientific and technological clone, it may have to clone the achievements of others in genetic engineering if it refuses to change its traditional values.

BIBLIOGRAPHY

Aisile, R. (1993) *Shengbei yu jian*, Beijing: Zhongguo Shehui Kexue Chubanshe.

Guangling, X. (2001) 'Gaya jiashuo – zhongxin de diqiu xitongguan', *Ziran Bianzhengfa Tongxun*, 1.

Jianhui, L. (2001) 'Rengong shengming: tansuo xin de shengming xingshi', *Xitong Bianzhengxue Xuebao*, 3.

Jiayin, M. (ed.) (1995) *Yanggang yu yinrou de bianzou*, Beijing: Zhongguo Shehui Kexue Chubanshe.

Jiayin, M. (1999) *Jinhua de duoyuanlun*, Beijing: Zhongguo Shehui Kexue Chubanshe.

Junfang, G. (ed.) (2002) 'Kelong Shiyan tashang buguilu' *Kexue Shijie*, 2.

Lasiluo, E. (1988) *Jinhua – Guangyi zonghe lilun*, Beijing: Shehui Kexue Wenxian Chubanshe.

Lifujin, J. (2000) *Shengwu jishu shiji*, Shanghai: Shanghai Keji Jiaoyu Chubanshe.

Mingxian, S. (2001) 'Keji yu lunli', *Shanghai Shifan Daxue Xuebao*, 1.

Qinsheng, Y. (ed.) (2000) 'Yuzhou yu renlei de weilai', *Kexue Shijie*, 12.

Qinsheng, Y. (ed.) (2002) 'Yuzhou yu renlei de weilai', *Kexue Shijie*, 2.

Quoqing, C. (1998) 'Rujia yiliguan lungang', *Xibei Daxue Xuebao*, 1.

Renzong, Q. (1998) 'Lun 'ren' de gainian', *Zhexue Yanjiu*, 9.

Renzong, Q. (2000) '21 shiji shengming lunlixue zhanwang', *Zhexue Yanjiu*, 1.

Renzong, Q. '21 shiji renlei jiyinzu yanjiu yu kexue lunli', *Keji Ribao*, 5 January 2001.

Shaoping, G. (2001) 'Jiyin gongcheng lunli de kexin wenti', *Zhexue Dongtai*, 1.

Sumin, L. (2001) 'Kexue yanjiu de 'jinqu' yu 'lüse tongdao', *Zhongguo Yixue Lunlixue*, 5.

Wei, X. (2001) 'Shengming lunlixue de ji ge remen huati', *Zhongguo Yixue Lunlixue*, 2.

Xinjian, S. (2000) 'Shengming kexue fazhan guiji ji zhexue yiyi', *Wuhan Jiaotong Daxue Xuebao*, 2.

Yanguang, W. (2001) 'Renlei jiyinzu jihua', *Yixue yu Zhexue*, 5.

Yuan, W. 'Dingkezu zhichilü Beijing zui gao', *Beijing Wanbao*, 4 March 2002.

Zhengwei, H. 'Zai ganggang jiesu de lianheguo tebie huiyi shang Zhongguo dui shengshixing kelongren shu bu', *Beijing Wanbao*, 4 March 2002.

Zhuanjun, L. (1995) 'Zhongguo xing lunli wenhua de fazhan quxiang', *Zhongguo Yixue Lunlixue*, 1.

Chapter 12

Bioethics and Medical Genetics in Japan[1]

Norio Fujiki

In 1987, my experience in genetic counselling services at the Kyoto Prefectural University of Medicine led to the International Bioethics Seminars in Fukui (Fujiki et al. 1985; Bernard, Kajikawa & Fujiki 1998; Fujiki, Boulyjenkov & Bankowski 1990; Fujiki & Macer 1992; 1994 1998; Okamoto, Fujiki & Macer 1996; Fujiki, Sudo & Macer 2001; Fujiki et al 1983; Shirai & Fujiki 182). In this paper, I discuss our experience with genetic counselling services and analyze opinion surveys conducted in Japan and other Asian Countries. I will do this by referring to the UNESCO Universal Declaration on the Human Genome and Human Rights (Appendix I) and the Ethical, Legal and Social Issues (ELSI) Guidelines on Medical Genetics Services.

TRENDS IN GENETIC COUNSELLING SERVICES

Since 1960, I have performed approximately 4,000 cases of genetic counselling. In 1993, I moved to TOYOBO's Tsuruga Laboratory[2] and started using new methods of DNA testing in order to improve our method of diagnosis (Fujiki 1996). During the last seventeen years (1984-2001), our follow-up studies have increasingly made use of DNA analysis. Most clients are women over twenty, facing choices of pregnancy (approximately one-third) and marriage. One quarter of the clients is also patient, and sometimes the spouse, another family member, or consanguineous couples decide to seek counselling. A common issue concerns the question of whether to have children or not. This question relates to the chances that the child is affected by mental retardation, and other concerns regarding malformation, psychosis, neuromuscular and skeletal disorders, deaf-mutism and harelip. One problem is that some prospective parents fear their child will be afflicted by acquired diseases that are actually hereditary.

Genetic classification indicates that 7.7 per cent of diseases are genetically dominant, 9.6 per cent recessive, and 2.5 per cent X-chromosome-linked recessive (excluding metabolic diseases, which occur at a rate of 3.4 per cent)[3]. In addition to single-gene diseases, we deal with cases of chromosomal anomaly (10.7 per cent) and multifactorial diseases such as mental retardation, psychoses, malformations and common polygenic diseases like diabetes, hypertension, heart disease and cancer (38.7 per cent). There are also questions related to consanguinity, blood-type incompatibility and drug effects, constituting 24.9 per cent of the 3,344 cases (see Figure 1).

OPINION SURVEYS ON MEDICAL GENETICS IN JAPAN AND ASIA

Bioethical standards in genetic counselling concern various concepts of medical care, including the quality of doctor-patient or counsellor-client relations, patient autonomy in decision-making, confidentiality, telling the truth and informed consent. To gain a better understanding of these ethical issues, we conducted a follow-up study. First, we followed 370 cases in Kyoto. For reasons of privacy, we sent them questionnaires by mail, with a response rate of one-third. The study showed us the great impact of new biotechnologies on the quality of human life (Fujiki 1983). In Nagoya and Fukui, in 1975 and 1981 respectively, we conducted follow-up surveys ten years after counselling. In both cases the response rate was about 50 percent, which, compared to the Kyoto data, is fairly good. The results of the two cases differed a little with regard to the appreciation of genetic counselling. In the relatively urbanized areas, individuals did not overestimate genetic risk, whereas in the more rural areas, such as in Fukui, they did (see figure 2).

Figures 4 and 5 show the opinion surveys on prenatal diagnosis and selective abortion among the general public and among health personnel held in 1975 and in 1981 (Shirai and Fujiki 1982). The results suggest that Japanese attitudes towards the bioethical aspects of abortion are similar to those of people in Western countries (Fujiki 1988; 1990). However, explicit differences regarding the determinants of attitudes toward abortion and sex selection are found between Japan and other countries surveyed in Asia (see Figure 9). The surveys indicate that this is probably due to religious and social factors. In fact, there were points of agreement and disagreement. Respondents agreed on the need for carrying out selective abortion of a foetus with Down syndrome; they disagreed on the ethics of withholding treatment from severely handicapped infants.

In India, Thailand and Japan we conducted surveys on the relationship between congenital defects, abortion and prenatal diagnosis (Figures 6-9). Half of the respondents in all three countries confirmed that they knew there are congenital diseases. In India, 42 per cent of the respondents had learned about prenatal diagnosis in school and 12 per cent from magazines and newspapers; in Thailand less than 10 per cent in school and 32 per cent from magazines and newspapers; and in Japan 10 per cent in school and 40 per cent from magazines and newspapers. Two-thirds of the respondents in India knew the meaning of the term prenatal diagnosis; the figure was 51 per cent in Japan and 41 per cent in Thailand. In the three countries, 70 per cent of the respondents supported abortion if the test result was positive for congenital defect. After having explained the concept of probability for carrier detection, only 55 per cent of Thai respondents said they would be shocked by positive test results, compared to 46 per cent in Japan (see Figure 7).

Differences were found between attitudes in India and other countries for cases in which a high chance of serious defect in the baby was suspected. In these cases, the application of prenatal diagnosis for sex selection was totally disapproved of in Japan (44 per cent), followed by Thailand (65 per cent) and India (63 per cent), and mostly approved in Beijing (80 per cent) (see fig.7). One of the most profound dilemmas of modern medicine concerns the question of whether ordinary medical care can justifiably be withheld from newborn infants with severe congenital defects. It is difficult to find ways of applying the rapidly developing biotechnology for the treatment of human genetic diseases without affecting the dignity of the patients involved. Moreover, the recent growth in awareness of changes in the quality of life and the cultural and historical differences in the perception of birth and death has generated heated debate about the introduction of new genetic technologies in the biomedical sector.

Japanese domestic opinion surveys indicate that limited knowledge of the handicapped and heredity might lead to misunderstandings and prejudice towards the handicapped, even among medical students, clients and nurses (see Figure 10). We conducted an opinion survey among students about prenatal diagnosis, selective abortion and the new biomedical possibilities created by developments in biotechnology (see Figure 11). Illustrating these bioethical issues by referring to the early detection of human thalassemia, the ecological and ethical consequences of the human supremacy over animals, as well as the issue of withholding treatment from severely handicapped infants, we tried to form a view of Japanese attitudes towards the applications of new biotechnology (see Figures 5 and 12).

In 1993, we conducted an international opinion survey with the support of WHO, UNESCO, IUBS (International Union of Biological Sciences)[4], the Council for International Organizations of Medical Sciences (CIOMS) and Japan's ELSI (Ethical Legal and Social Issues) committee on human genome research. The survey compared attitudes in many countries with regards to their different religious and cultural backgrounds. The opinion poll covered various issues in relation to genetics, such as genetic heredity and the handicapped, biotechnology and genetics, medical genetics and also attitudes to the environment and genetics (also, see Wertz and Fletcher 1989; Wertz, Bulyzhenkov, Fletcher and Berg 1987). In order to develop a cross-cultural ethics, we examined people's reasoning so as to facilitate the formulation of international bioethics. The surveys indicate that most of the respondents were prejudiced, and ethical and emotional views were common to their countries of origin. Other issues were controversial among the respondents in the same society, especially selective abortion. Since much prejudice derives from a lack of knowledge, it is the duty of the clinical geneticist, as a special advisor, to cooperate with the mass media in providing information that is accurate and easy to understand by the general public (see Figures 6-9).

Research in India, China, Thailand and Japan produced data that indicate considerably different attitudes towards the first stage of the human life cycle. In India, 32 per cent of the respondents agreed entirely that an abnormal foetus has a right to survive, with 47 per cent of them saying life should be preserved and 49 per cent disagreeing. The most frequently chosen reason for the latter was that the sick infant cannot be happy in this world (60 per cent), followed by the opinion that a handicapped child has low values as a human being 40 per cent (see Figure 7) (Verma and Fujiki 1992, 1994). In Thailand, 24 per cent of the respondents agreed entirely that an abnormal foetus has a right to medical service, with the most common reason for this that life should be preserved and respected (46 per cent) (see Figure 7), followed by the reason that there are many handicapped people who can live happily with the support of other people (45 per cent). However, 37 per cent disagreed, with the most frequent reason that such a child would be unhappy (45 per cent), followed by the view that their life is not valuable (26 per cent) (Ratanakul 1992, 1994). In Beijing, 33 per cent of the respondents agreed that an abnormal foetus has a right to survive, with main reason for this being that life should be respected (59 per cent). On the other hand, the number of supporters for the selective abortion of an abnormal foetus equaled the high number of Indian respondents (72 per cent), though the support for sex selection was much lower (60 per cent) (see fig. 7).

We can compare these data with the survey results in Japan, where 50 per cent agreed entirely that an abnormal foetus has a right to survive, with the most common reason for this that life should be preserved and respected (50 per cent), followed by the opinion that we have no right to select foetal life (29 per cent). However, 40 per cent of these respondents disagreed: 30 per cent because the child would be unhappy, others because of the family burden due to economic and psychological conflicts (30 per cent). In recent surveys conducted in Japan, there appears to be much better understanding of handicapped people. Also, if the social situation is improved for the handicapped, then many more people agree with the view that an abnormal infant has a right to survive.

The value of handicapped people is most highly regarded in Japan and least in India, probably because of the difference in financial burden in each country (Verma and Takabe 1994). This difference was expressed in the respective attitudes towards withholding treatment to severely handicapped infants. It also exemplifies the limitations of the application of new genetic technologies in areas where the financial burden is already high. Among respondents, some were aware of both the merits and dangers of genetic risk, but could not decide what to do. Some did not understand the term at all. Therefore we should make scientific knowledge more accessible at popular science seminars, such as the forums held in the Fukui Prefectural Life Academy (Fujiki 1996). Of course, we cannot offer ready-made solutions for all problems and each should respond according to their own knowledge, following their own interpretation of biotechnology and their own ethical, legal and social criteria. It is important to think about the long-term implications of such problems because anyone faced with serious bioethical problems needs access to precise information and critical judgment.

OUTLOOK TO THE FUTURE

As shown in the WHO strategy adopted to eradicate thalassemia, clinical provisions of human genetic knowledge, such as early diagnosis, neonatal screening, prenatal diagnosis followed by selective abortion, carrier detection as well as genetic counselling (together with such preventive measures as prohibition of inbreeding, eugenic family planning and treatment) have been very effective. Recent developments in human genome research have been applied to our practice of genetic counselling, using predictive measures made possible by SNPs techniques[5]. As a result, however, new bioethical problems have arisen, such as the justification of presymptomatic diagnosis and the possibility of discrimination caused by genetic susceptibility for common diseases by using predictive markers.

We have conducted domestic opinion surveys on heredity and handicapped people among students and the general public in different areas of Japan. Our surveys indicate the existence of misunderstandings and prejudices about handicapped people, also when it was quite clear that these handicaps were hereditary and incurable. Differences in responses seemed to derive from the amounts of information available to the respondents, and the interest they had for specific social problems. However, the data show that positive views of the handicapped increase every year, and handicapped children are increasingly seen as having human dignity. Due to education, the opinion spread that a deleterious gene in itself is no ground for discrimination.

Since 1962, our international opinion surveys have extended to various Asian countries (such as India, Thailand and Japan), with the support of the WHO, the UNESCO, IBC (International Bioethics Committee), the Japanese ELSI committee on Human Genome Research, and the Ministry of Education. The research covered various issues related to heredity and handicapped persons, medical genetic services and human rights. These research programmes included discussions between physicians and social scientists. We must emphasize the importance of education, in order to obtain agreement on bioethical guidelines in different countries as well as the importance of support by international organizations like UNESCO, WHO and HUGO for facilitating discussions in each country. One result was the UNESCO IBC Declaration on the Human Genome and Human Rights.

We encountered many misunderstandings and prejudices, and initiated bioethical debate among the general public and in our international bioethics seminars in Fukui. We have also learned that in order to educate the general public and to remove national, economic, social and religious barriers between countries and individuals, we must pay more attention to education on human genetics and bioethics and continue research in these areas. We need to educate the public on the significance of new biotechnology and human genetics, as well as on the bioethical considerations for human life and human dignity. We must discuss morality very carefully and make our decisions based on a common understanding of both newly developed technologies and traditional evaluations. Finally, we must emphasize that more time is required for the development of the medical curriculum in human genetics and bioethics at medical schools in order to educate the general public.

NOTES

[1] The research on which this article is based was supported by research grants from the Ministry of Health and Welfare, Ministry of Education, Culture and Science, Japan, and the National Institute of General Medical Sciences of the United States and the World Health Organization for the past 35 years.

[2] Toyobo, a company involved in biochemical analysis, was established in 1992. It engages in gene analysis services for clinical diagnosis, genetic traits and the identification of, for instance, various infectious diseases, leukemia, testing for bone marrow transplantation, Y chromosome-neurodigenerative and neuromuscular diseases.

[3] In the case of a dominant hereditary disease, the offspring of an affected parent has 50 percent risk of inheriting the gene for it; in case of a recessive hereditary disease the chance is 25 percent.

[4] The IUBS, founded in 1919, is part of the International Council of Scientific Unions (ICSU) based in Paris. It is a registered non-governmental organization (NGO) at UNESCO and other United Nations Organizations.

[5] Usually the genetic differences between people are limited to differences in one base and are called single nucleotide polymorphisms (SNPs). They refer to the locations in which one letter of the genetic code varies from that of another person

APPENDIX I

UNESCO UNIVERSAL DECLARATION ON THE HUMAN GENOME AND HUMAN RIGHTS

UNESCO unanimously approved this declaration on 11 November 1997 at the General Assembly, after drafts from the International Bioethics Committee and changes by a meeting of Government Experts on 25 July 1997. It proclaims the following principles (Lenoir 1997):

Human Dignity and the Human Genome

1. The human genome underlies the fundamental unity of all members of the human family, as well as the recognition of their inherent dignity and diversity. In a symbolic sense, it is the heritage of humanity.

2. All people have a right to dignity, regardless of their genetic characteristics.

3. That dignity makes it imperative not to reduce individuals to their genetic characteristics and to respect their uniqueness and diversity.

4. The human genome, which by its nature evolves, is subject to mutations. It contains potentialities that are expressed differently according to each individual's natural and social environment, including the individual's state of health, living conditions, nutrition and education.

5. Humans in their natural state shall not give rise to financial gains.

Rights of the Persons Involved

6. Research, treatment or diagnosis affecting an individual's genome shall be undertaken only after rigorous and prior assessment of the potential risks and benefits pertaining thereto, and in accordance with any other requirement of national law.

7. In all cases, the prior, free and informed consent of the person involved shall be obtained. If the latter is not in a position to provide consent, authorization shall be obtained in the manner prescribed by law, guided by the person's best interest.

8. The right of each individual to decide whether or not to be informed of the results of genetic examination and the resulting consequences should be respected.

9. In the case of research, protocols shall, in addition, be submitted for prior review in accordance with relevant national and international research standards or guidelines.

10. If, according to the law, a person does not have the capacity to give consent, research affecting his or her genome may only be carried out for his or her direct health benefit, subject to the authorization and the protective conditions prescribed by law. Research which does not have an expected direct health benefit may only be undertaken by way of exception, with the utmost restraint, exposing the person only to a minimal risk and minimal burden, and if the research is intended to contribute to the health benefit of other persons in the same age category or with the same genetic condition, subject to the conditions prescribed by

law and provided such research is compatible with the protection of the individual's human rights.

11. No one shall be subjected to discrimination based on genetic characteristics that are intended to infringe, or have the effect of infringing, human rights, fundamental freedoms and human dignity.

12. Genetic data associated with an identifiable person and stored or processed for the purposes of research or any other purpose must be held confidential in the conditions set by law.

13. Every individual shall have the right, according to international and national law, to just reparation for any damage sustained as a direct and determining result of an intervention affecting his or her genome.

14. In order to protect human rights and fundamental freedoms, limitations to the principles of consent and confidentiality may only be prescribed by law, for compelling reasons within the bounds of public international law and the international law of human rights.

Research on the Human Genome

15. No research or applications concerning the human genome (in

16. particular in the fields of biology, genetics and medicine) should prevail over respect for the human rights, fundamental freedoms and human dignity of individuals or, where applicable, of groups of people.

17. Practices that are contrary to human dignity, such as reproductive cloning of human beings, shall not be permitted. States and competent international organizations are invited to co-operate in identifying such practices and in taking, at the national or international level, the necessary measures to ensure that the principles set out in this Declaration are respected.

18. Benefits from advances in biology, genetics and medicine concerning the human genome shall be made available to all, with due regard to the dignity and human rights of each individual.

19. Freedom of research, which is necessary for the progress of knowledge, is part of freedom of thought. The applications of research (including applications in biology, genetics and medicine) concerning the human genome, shall seek to offer relief from suffering and improve the health of individuals and humankind as a whole.

Conditions for the Exercise of Scientific Activity

20. The responsibilities inherent in the activities of researchers (including meticulousness, caution, intellectual honesty and integrity in carrying out their research as well as in the presentation and utilization of their findings) should be the subject of particular attention in relation to research on the human genome, because of its ethical and social implications. Public and private scientific policymakers also have particular responsibilities in this respect.

21. States should take appropriate measures for fostering the intellectual conditions favourable to freedom in the conduct of research on the human genome and for considering the

ethical, legal, social and economic implications of such research on the basis of the principles set out in this Declaration.

22. States should take appropriate steps to provide the framework for the free exercise of research on the human genome, with due regard for the principles set out in this Declaration, in order to safeguard respect for human rights, fundamental freedoms and human dignity and to protect public health. They should seek to ensure that research results are not used for non-peaceful purposes.

23. States should recognize the value of promoting, at various levels as appropriate, the establishment of independent, multidisciplinary and pluralist ethics committees to assess the ethical, legal and social issues raised by research on the human genome and its applications.

Solidarity and International Cooperation

24. States should respect and promote solidarity towards individuals, families and population groups who are particularly vulnerable to, or affected by, disease or disability of a genetic character. They should foster research on the identification, prevention and treatment of genetically-based and genetically-influenced diseases, which affect large numbers of the world's population.

Implementation of the Declaration

25. States shall adopt normative measures that they consider appropriate for meeting the purpose of this Declaration.

26. The principles set forth in this Declaration shall serve as basis for the normative measures adopted by States. They shall also guide those in charge of institutions and any other persons responsible for the application of such measures.

27. States shall be duty bound to promote (through education, training and information) respect for the aforementioned principles based on human dignity and freedom, and to ensure both nationally and internationally that they are recognized and effectively applied.

28. The International Bioethics committee of UNESCO shall ensure the implementation of this Declaration. For this purpose, it may make recommendations or give advice. Nothing in this Declaration may be used by any State, group or person for ends contrary to the rights and freedoms set forth herein.

The 2001 summary of the document's major points highlights:

1. Equal access to available services.
2. Non-directive counselling.
3. Voluntary rather than mandatory services (except for newborn screening that benefits the newborn).
4. Full disclosure of clinically relevant information.
5. Confidentiality, except when information could avert serious genetic harm to family.
6. Privacy from employers, insurers, etc.
7. Prenatal diagnosis only to ascertain the health of the foetus.
8. Availability of and respect for choices, including abortion choices.

9. Children should be tested only when it may provide a medical benefit to the child. The Guidelines apply equally to adopted children.
10. Research follows ethical protocols, includes informed consent and is subject to ethical review. These guidelines include pre-implantation diagnosis and other assisted reproductive technologies at the research stage.
11. National review for gene therapy protocols (see Table 6).

FIGURES

Figure 1. Disease categories of genetic counsellin1g in Kyoto, Nagoya and Fukui (1961-94): 2470 cases, 3344 accumulated cases

Hereditary Disease (Excluding Metabolic Error) 744 (22.2%)

Autosomal Dominant		259 (7.7%)		Autosomal Recessive		320 (9.6%)	
Marie Ataxia	35	Brachydactyly	6	Deafmute	178	Microcephaly	4
Polydactyly	23	Hyperkeratosis	4	Albino	29	Laurence-Moon-Biedl	3
Recklinghausen	37	Charcott-Marie-Tooth	4	Retinitis Pigmentosa	25	Kugelberg-Wellander	3
Achondroplasia	19	Alzheimer	4	Limb-Girdle PMD	14	Fukuyama PMD	2
Cataract	10	Dysionia	5	Werdnig-Hoffman	8	Retinal Dysplasia	2
Navus Pigmenti	9	Marfan	3	Epidermolysis Bullosa	7	Myoclonus	2
Parkinsonism	8	Leber Disease	3	Xeroderma Pigmentosum	6	Others	37
Van der Hoeve	7	Spastic Paraplegia	9	X-linked Recessive 165 (4.9%)			
Hereditary Tremor	8	Retinal Aberration	2	Colourblind	114	Ichytiosis	3
Myotonic Dystrophy	9	Leukoplakia	2	Duchenne PMD	32	Others	16
Tuberous Sclerosis	8	Others	39				
Deafmute	5						

Metabolic Error 113 (3.4%)

AD 11 (0.3%)			Autosomal Recessive 85 (2.5%)			
Thalassemia		4	Phenylketonuria	14	Adrenogenital Syndrome	4
Alloalbuminemia		2	Baib Excretor	5	GM, Gangliosidosis	4
Dubin-Johnson		2	Tay-Sachs Disease	5	Metachromatic	3
Others		3	Cretinism	5	Leucine Sensitive	3
XR 17 (0.5%)			Hurler Syndrome	5	Methemoglobinemia	2
Hemophilia		6	Galactosemia	4	Von Girke Disease	2
Lowe Syndrome		2	Wilson Disease	4	Others	25
G6PD Deficiency		2				
Lesch-Nyhan		2				
Others		5				

Chromosomal Anomaly 357 (10.7%)

21 Trisomy	217	Long Y	14	X0	7	XYY	2
Balanced Translocation	26	18 Trisomy	9	Cat Cry Syndrome	6	13o	2
Translocated Down	15	21 Trisomy Mosaic	8	X0 Mosaic	4	Others	40
		XXY	7				

Polygenic or Unclear 1294 (38.71%)

Constitution (Including Psychosis & Mental Retardation)	648
Malformation	436
Perinatal Defect	210

Miscellaneous 834 (24.9%)

Consanguinity	510	Acquired Anomaly	81	X-Ray Effect	17	
Incompatibility	149	Drug Effect	40	Others	37	

Figure 2. Follow-up study of genetic counseling

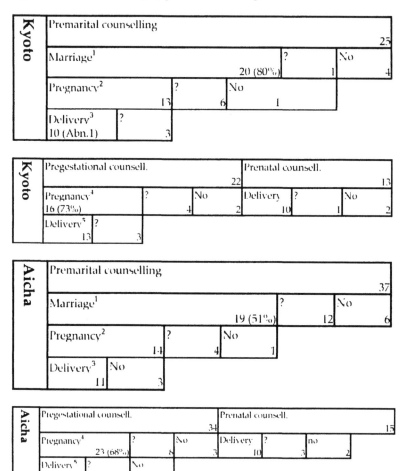

Fukui.	Premarital counselling							57
	Marriage*1				44 (77%)	? 4	No	9
	Pregnancy*2			38	? 1	No 2		
	Delivery*3 35 (Abn.1)	? 3						

Fukui.	Pregestational counsell.			26	Prenatal counsell.			7
	Pregnancy⁴	20 (77%)	? 4	No 2	Del. 4	? 3		
	Delivery⁵ 15	? 3	No 2					

[1] Number of women that decided to get married after premarital counselling (1).

[2] Number of 1 that decided to become pregnant (2).

[3] Number of 2 that decided to deliver (3).

[4] Number of women that decided to become pregnant after pregestational counselling (4).

[5] Number of 4 that decided to deliver.

Figure 3. Consensus Survey on the Handicapped and Heredity

Psychological Effect of Carrier:

	1961	1970	1981
Shocking %	31	35	50
Highly shocking %	65	62	48
Natural %	4	3	2

Marriage of a Handicapped Relative?:

	1961	1970	1981
No %	7	6	9
Depends on the case %	32	29	46
Needs counselling %	42	53	33
Yes, but no children %	7	6	5
Other %	12	6	7

Figure 4. Selected results of opinion survey on genetic medicine

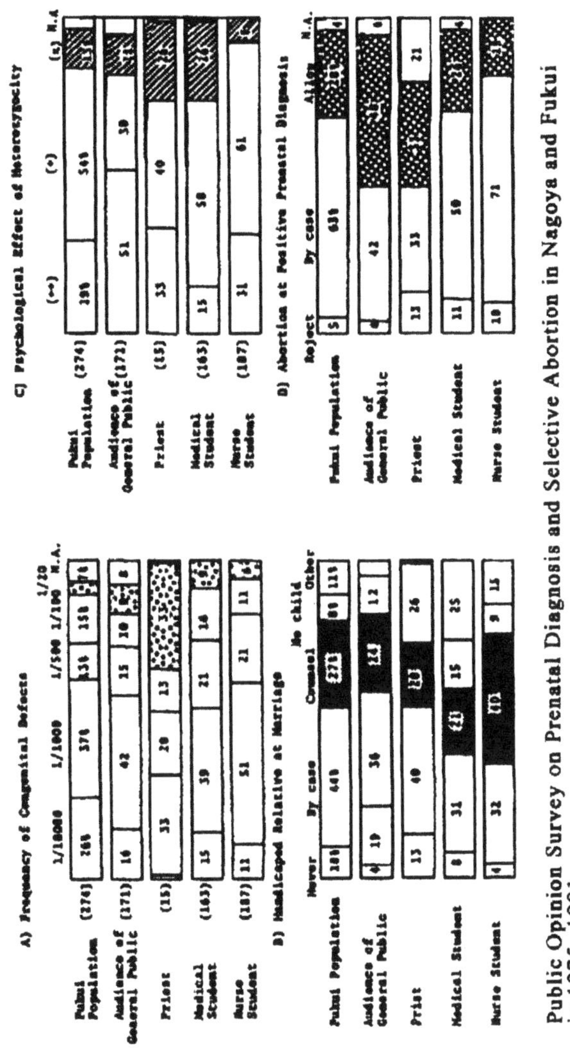
A) Frequency of Congenital Defects
B) Handicapped Relative at Marriage
C) Psychological Effect of Heterozygocity
D) Abortion at Positive Prenatal Diagnosis
Public Opinion Survey on Prenatal Diagnosis and Selective Abortion in Nagoya and Fukui in 1975-1981

Figure 5. Attitides to biomedical technology

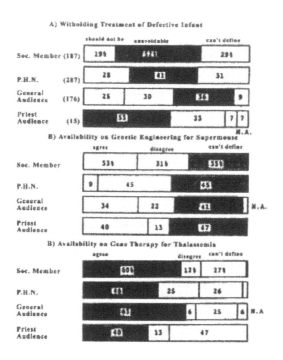

Figure 6. Bioethical Opinion Survey in Asian Countries - General Information

	India 1991	Thailand 1991	Beijing 1993	Fukui 1993
Number	1500	500	221	387
Sex (Male/Female) %	23/77	78/22	43/57	36/64
Age range (years)	20-60	20-60	20-60	20-40
Religion %	Hindu 75 Moslem 8 Christian 5 Sikh 9	Buddhism 100	Believer 10 Atheist 90	Buddhism 85
Education:				
No education	9			
Primary School or less	9	1		20
High School	31	43	15	30
College	44	50	49	40
Professional	14	6	35	10
Occupation:				
Student	17		39	43
Housewife	48	7	26	
Service	31		12	31
Business	2	49		25
Official		44	23	

Figure 7. Bioethical Opinion Survey in Asian Countries - Attitudes towards Prenatal Diagnosis

	India	Thailand	Beijing	Fukui
Acceptance of prenatal diagnosis Down syndrome	43	76	80	74
Acceptance of abortion after positive prenatal diagnosis	70	11	87	40
Preference for practising prenatal diagnosis in general	63	65	80	44
Acceptance of selective abortion of abnormal foetus	72	65	72	40
Carrier detection approved	93	88	72	82

Figure 8. Bioethical Opinion Survey in Asian Countries – 'What do you think of genetic disorders?'

	India	Thailand	Beijing	Fukui
Prefer prenatal diagnosis in General	63	65	80	44
Disagree prenatal diagnosis for sex selection	70	88	60	80
Approve selective abortion of abnormal foetus	72	65	72	40
Abnormal foetus has a right to survive	32	24	33	50
* Because life is given by God	58	2 N.D.		20
* Because life should be respected	47	46	59	50
Shocked very much if you were a carrier	62	55 N.D.		60
2% frequency seems to be very high	59	65 N.D.		40

Figure 9. Bioethical Opinion Survey in Asian Countries – 'What do you think of the handicapped?'

	India	Thailand	Beijing	Fukui
Who should take care of the handicapped - Government	42	24	60	70
Who should take care of the handicapped - Family	86	53	69	60
Spend money on both the healthy and handicapped	82	85	60	60
Image of Heredity - Good / Bad	42/32	40/60	90/10	20/40
Image of Genetics - Scientific / Mysterious	61/14	40/60	80/20	20/30
Marriage if fiancés family has a handicapped person?	76	40	72	20
Are most serious diseases inherited? (Yes/No)	29/33	41/34	90/10	40/20

Figure 10. Consensus survey among counselee, comparing with medical students

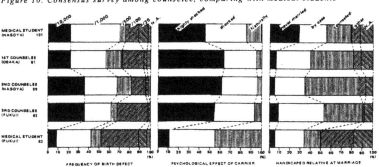

Figure 11. Consensus survey among general public in Fukui, compared with students and nurses in Fukui

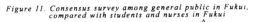

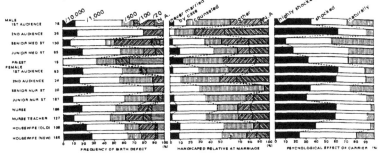

Figure 12 Consensus survey on new biotecnology in Fukui

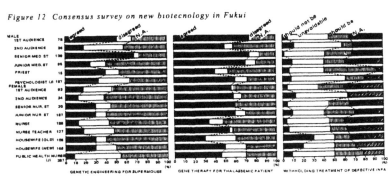

BIBLIOGRAPHY

Bernard, J., Kajikawa, K. and Fujiki, N. (eds) (1998) *Human Dignity and Medicine*, Amsterdam: Excerpta Med.

Fujiki, N. (1996) 'Medical geneticist's responsibility', in M. Okamoto, N.

Fujiki and D.R.J. Macer (eds) *Protection of the Human Genome and Scientific Responsibility*, Christchurch: Eubios Ethics Institute.

Fujiki, N. (1985) 'Genetic counselling: Clinical applications of human genetic knowledge', *Japanese Journal of Medicine*, 49: 123-138.

Fujiki, N. (1990) 'Japanese perspectives on ethics in medical genetics', in N.

Fujiki, V. Boulyjenkov and Z. Bankowski (eds) *Medical Genetics and Society*, Amsterdam: Kugler.

Fujiki, N. and Macer, D.R.J. (eds) (1992) *Human Genome Research and Society.* Christchurch: Eubios Ethics Institute.

Fujiki, N. and Macer, D.R.J. (eds) (1994) *Intractable Neurological Disorders, Human Genome Research and Society*, Christchurch: Eubios Ethics Institute.

Fujiki, N. and Macer, D.R.J. (eds) (1998) *UNESCO Conference on Bioethics in Asia*, Christchurch: Eubios Ethics Institute.

Fujiki, N., Sudo, M. and Macer, D.R.J. (eds) (2001) *Bioethics and the Impact of Genomics in the 21ˢᵗ Century. Pharmacogenomics, DNA Polymorphism and Medical Genetic Services*, Christchurch: Eubios Ethics Institute.

Lenoir, N. (1997) 'Universal Declaration on the Genome and Human Rights', Paris: UNESCO.

Macer, D.R.J. (1992) *Attitudes to Genetic Engineering: Japanese and International Comparisons*, Christchurch: Eubios Ethics Institute.

Macer, D.R.J. (1994) *Bioethics for the People by the People*, Christchurch: Eubios Ethics Institute.

Okamoto, M., Fujiki, N. and Macer, D.R.J. (eds) (1996) *Protection of the Human Genome and Scientific Responsibility*, Christchurch: Eubios Ethics Institute.

Ratanakul, P. (1992) 'A Preliminary report on an opinion survey on handicap and heredity in Thailand', in N. Fujiki and D.R.J. Macer (eds) *Human Genome Research and Society.* Christchurch: Eubios Ethics Institute.

Ratanakul, P. (1994) 'A survey of Thai Buddhist attitudes toward science and genetics', in N. Fujiki, N. and D.R.J. Macer (eds) *Intractable Neurological Disorders, Human Genome Research and Society,* Christchurch: Eubios Ethics Institute.

Shirai, Y. and Fujiki, N. (1982) 'Doctors' attitudes on prenatal diagnosis and selective abortion, *Representative Study Group in Ministry of Health & Welfare,* 1: 80-89.

Verma, I.C. and Fujiki, N. (1992) 'The common people's views on handicap and heredity', in N. Fujiki and D.R.J. Macer (eds) *Human Genome Research and Society,* Christchurch: Eubios Ethics Institute.

Verma, I.C. and Fujiki, N. (1994) 'How national are Indians in their views on handicap and heredity?', in N. Fujiki and D.R.J. Macer (eds) *Intractable Neurological Disorders, Human Genome Research and Society,* Christchurch: Eubios Ethics Institute.

Verma, I.C. (1994) 'International attitudes to genetic technology and diseases', in N. Fujiki and D.R.J. Macer (eds) *Intractable Neurological Disorders, Human Genome Research and Society,* Christchurch: Eubios Ethics Institute.

Wertz, D.C. and Fletcher, J.C. (eds) (1989) *Ethics and Human Genetics. A Cross-cultural Perspectives,* New York: Springer Verlag.

Wertz, D.C., Bulyzhenkov, V., Fletcher, J.C and Berg, K. (eds) (1987) 'Proposal on WHO Guidelines in Medical Genomic Services', WHO.

Wertz, D.C., Bulyzhenkov, V., Fletcher, G.C. and Berg, K. (eds) (1998) 'Proposal on WHO Guidelines in Medical Genomic Services', WHO.

Chapter 13

Attitudes towards Biotechnology and Bioethics in the Philippines: A Pilot Study

Mary Ann Chen Ng and Darryl Macer

INTRODUCTION

Biotechnology is a word that can be thought of in many ways. It has been defined by a number of persons and organisations. However, one can simply think of it as the use of biological systems to produce or improve goods or services. The impact and potential of modern biotechnology has been widely debated not only by the scientific community, government agencies and international organisations, but most importantly by the public. The relationship between public opinion, government policy and decision-making is crucial in the adoption of biotechnology, the nature of which is determined in context by a particular set of factors.

There are many methods used to study public opinion. One method is to use fixed response questions. Major studies include the 1986 United States Office of Technology Assessment Study (OTA 1987), the 1992 study on agricultural issues by Hoban and Kendall, and the 1991 and 1993 Eurobarometer survey on biotechnology and genetic engineering.

Another strategy is to use both set and open questions. Open comments reveal the reasoning and rationale behind various opinions of the public. Previous studies of this type include the 1993 International Bioethics Survey, in which persons from the

Philippines and nine other countries participated (Macer 1994:170-174), and the various studies done by the Eubios Ethics Institute in Japan from 1991 to 2000. These surveys were conducted in 1991, 1993, 1997 and 1999 to 2000. The respective samples were 551, 352, 297, and 297 people. The participants were randomly selected across the nation and responses were gathered by mail; except in the 1997 survey, which used random digit dialling. In 1991 and 2000, 555 and 370 scientists, respectively, were questioned about their attitudes to biotechnology to assess differences between the public and professionals (Macer 1992; Macer and Chen Ng 2000: 945-947; Chen Ng et al.2000: 106-113).

The Philippine public debate on transgenic crops, which has been covered by the media, involves a highly critical NGO front on one side and a highly optimistic and influential scientific and political block on the other (Aerni et al.1999: 18-21). But how do people actually perceive biotechnology? What are the nature and the role of the public on issues of biotechnology? What images do they have of bioethics? This paper explores the attitudes of Filipinos about biotechnology and bioethics. A pilot study composed mainly of students belonging to the middle class elicited 273 responses that reveal various concerns. This group was deliberately targeted because it includes both present and future decision makers and members of a generation who will not only have to bear the full impact of the applications of biotechnology but who will also have to respond to the ethical challenges that come with it. The results are compared with the results from the 1993 International Bioethics Survey obtained from 164 Filipino students and previous studies by the Eubios Ethics Institute. These are then interpreted in the light of questions of bioethics and the Philippine experience.

SAMPLE DESIGN AND CHARACTERISTICS

The pilot sample was obtained by distributing 1000 questionnaires with the assistance of 19 students who went to key middle class areas. The questionnaire consisted of 5 A4-sized pages with a 1-page introductory letter. The questionnaire included 14 major questions, 4 of which were open-ended questions. The respondents had a choice between a Filipino and an English version; but they all opted to answer the English version. The responses of the people who consented to answer the questionnaire were collected personally in order to avoid delay and possible loss due to the unreliability of the local postal system.

The response rate of 27 per cent was considerably lower than the 70 per cent response rate of the 1993 Philippine sample (Macer 1994:188). But this was expected since the present study has a wider range compared to the previous study. Responses were received from 24 different areas and the national capital, Manila. 78 per cent were from urban areas and 22 per cent from rural areas. 77 per cent were male and 33 per cent were female. The sample consisted of persons aged 14 years and older and the mean age was 20. Other characteristics, including marital status, number of children, education, religion, religiosity and income are presented in Table 1. The occupation of respondents was classified into the same categories as the previous surveys, and appears in Table 2. Four of these categories covered those who did not have full-time jobs: housewives, students, the retired and the unemployed.

INTEREST IN SCIENCE AND TECHNOLOGY

When asked about their level of interest in science and technology, half of the respondents answered that they were interested. On a five-point scale, 6 per cent indicated that they were 'extremely interested', and 24 per cent said that they were 'very interested'.

There were more people who said that they were 'interested' compared to 1993; but there were fewer people who said that they were 'very interested' or 'extremely interested' (see Table 3).

The highest level of interest was shown for computers and IT, followed by telecommunications. Most viewed genetic engineering and biotechnology less favourably than other areas of science and technology. Biotechnology was perceived more positively compared to genetic engineering. 21 per cent also indicated that genetic engineering could make life worse. As can be seen in Table 4, this rate reflects the same trend as the studies done in Japan (12 per cent in 1997 and 24 per cent in 2000) and most other Asian countries (Macer 1994: 194-198).

An analysis of open comments about the nature of biotechnology reveals the following themes and specific examples:

1. Biotechnology will bring about a better future for society.

    'I think modern biotechnology is a good advancement of science because it improves the quality of life'.

2. Biotechnology is synonymous to cloning and other specific examples.

    'Cloning, test tube babies, mutant plants and animals…'

    'The first thing that comes to mind is cloning. Another thing is genetically engineered soldiers, like in the movies'.

3. Biotechnology provides medical benefit.

    'It should benefit man by finding cures to incurable diseases'.

'Preventive and correctional methods to fight against genetic and hereditary disorders and ailments'.

4. Biotechnology equals genetic enhancement.

   'People can genetically engineer their kids, that is, they can control the genetic make up of their children — their resistance to disease, IQ perhaps, etc.'.

   'We will be able to make the perfect baby'.

5. Biotechnology has both benefits and risks.

   'Biotechnology may improve our way of life and may be beneficial to our society'.

6. Biotechnology can provide better food for everyone.

   'It will help us in food production to address the famine on our planet'.

7. Biotechnology raises moral issues.

   'It will actually change the way we define life itself and the real and true purpose why we live it'.

8. Biotechnology goes against nature and God.

   'It is deciding whether one is playing God or not, changing that which is natural'.

SPECIFIC APPLICATIONS OF BIOTECHNOLOGY

Based on the questions from the 1996 Eurobarometer survey, respondents were also asked whether they had heard about six applications of biotechnology. And in order to understand whether people differentiated between the various applications of genetic engineering in terms of perceived benefits and risks, respondents were asked whether each application was useful to society and how much risk they perceived.

Genetically modified food and drinks and genetically engineered animals for laboratory tests were the most familiar applications. These were also perceived to be both beneficial and risky. Overall, more Filipinos had heard of every development, consistent with their high level of interest in science and technology. Pest-resistant crops were the most acceptable application. At the same time, these were perceived to be highly risky. The least acceptable was xenotransplantation. However, this was not perceived to be as risky as pest-resistant crops. From these responses, it appears to be that some degree of risk is acceptable if it is accompanied with benefits. In fact, unlike other countries, most people indicated that they can accept some risk so long as it enhances the Philippines' economic competitiveness. This reflects the people's emphasis on economic development, which is not surprising in a country where most people live below the poverty line.

Attitudes towards products using GMOs released into the environment were explored by a question used in the OTA survey (1987) and by surveys by Macer (1992) asking about the acceptability of 'tomatoes with better taste', 'healthier meat', 'larger sport fish', 'bacteria to clean up oil spills', 'disease resistant crops' and 'cows that produce more milk'. Overall, there was an increase in the degree of support, compared to the 1993 survey, for most products except for disease resistant crops. Although it was still highly acceptable, there were fewer people who supported it compared to 1993. And there were fewer people who were not supportive of these products. There was also an increase in the number of people who answered 'don't know' (see Table 5).

The level of support was highest for healthier meat, followed by bacteria to clean oil spills and disease-resistant crops. The higher level of media exposure regarding BSE and foot and mouth disease can explain the present attitudes towards meat compared to 1993. Unlike people in other countries, the Filipinos did not object to larger sports fish. There was even a slight increase in the number of people who supported it.

Another concern that some people have is cross-species gene transfer. When asked about the acceptability of rice that contains genes from other plants, 72 per cent answered 'yes', 9 per cent answered 'no', and 19 per cent answered 'don't know'. When asked about the acceptability of rice that contains genes from animals, 31 per cent answered 'yes', 36 per cent answered 'no', and 33per cent answered 'don't know'. As in other surveys, plant-to-plant gene transfers were more acceptable than plant-animal gene transfers (Macer and Ng 2000: 947). The range of ethical concerns expressed in the open comments show that people made a differentiation between the two types. These concerns are centred upon the person's values and beliefs about what is natural and known; which, in turn, indicates the type of worldview that the person has. For example:

- 'I am not sure of the effects of using animal genes on plants'.

- 'Animal cruelty. Again, manipulating food seems unnecessary to me'.

- 'There's a reason why God separated plants and animals'!

– 'What about people who are vegetarian'?

Another application of genetic engineering that has been widely talked about is gene therapy. When asked about the acceptability of specific types of gene therapy, the respondents were supportive especially towards therapeutic cases such as cancer and AIDS. Although not as high as the ones for therapeutic use, support was shown for physical, intellectual and even ethical enhancement. This trend was also evident in the 1993 Philippine sample (Macer 1994:202-203). Compared to the 1993 sample, there was a slight decrease in support for most forms—except for genetic enhancement, which showed a slight increase (see Figure 1).

The respondents showed positive expectations of biotechnology, especially towards crime prevention and solution of crimes through DNA fingerprinting. This echoes the importance of public safety issues in the Philippines, and the concern about the seeming inability of public authorities to uphold justice. Overall, more Filipinos expressed higher expectations compared to the Japanese (see Figure 2). They were also quite optimistic about the potential of biotechnology to increase food production and reduce world hunger. However, they were not as positive about its potential to reduce environmental pollution. Filipinos were also very concerned about its potential for harm in creating new and dangerous diseases. Again, this reflects the currently increasing and seemingly insurmountable pollution and health care problems of the country.

REGULATION OF BIOTECHNOLOGY

Regulation guidelines on biosafety by the National Committee on Biosafety in the Philippines (NCBP) have existed since 1991. However, when asked what agency the public thought should regulate biotechnology, there was very little support for the government. 50 per cent of the respondents were in favour of international regulatory bodies, such as the United Nations and the World Health Organization, followed by scientific organizations (22 per cent) and ethics committees (9 per cent). Therefore, there is public support for an international regulatory system for biotechnology. Currently, this involves especially the WHO, FAO, Codex Alimentarius Commission, and UNEP (Cartegena Protocol). Because of global trading, the WTO-SPS agreements are also important.

There was also very little trust in public authorities, political parties and trade unions as sources of truthful information about modern biotechnology (see Figure 3). Most people indicated corruption of officials and lack of transparency in policy and decision-making as reasons for their lack of trust. Environmental organisations were the most trusted, followed by schools and universities and animal welfare organisations. It should be noted that people who work for NGOs tend to come from the middle class. Unlike in Japan, there was some trust in industry and religious organisations.

IMAGES OF BIOETHICS

Bioethics is a concept and a word that expresses people's concern about the ethical issues brought about by science and technology. It can be called love of life (Macer 1998:1-2). Because of the nature of these concerns, people want bioethics to be a multidimensional and thoughtful approach to decision making so that it may be relevant to all aspects of human life.

Bioethics as a word was mainly applied to issues of medical ethics in the 1970s and the 1980s, but in the 1960s and 1990s it referred primarily to environmental ethics. It focused on the ethics of genetic engineering in the late 1990s and at the start of the millennium. The word bioethics was first used in 1970, however the concept of bioethics is older, as can be seen in the ethics of great religious and cultural traditions of various civilisations (Macer, 1998:2; Tsai, 1999).

Bioethics can be viewed in three ways. Descriptive bioethics is the way people view life, their moral interactions and responsibilities to living organisms in their life. Prescriptive bioethics involves telling others what is ethically good or bad, or what principles are most important in making such decisions. It may also involve saying something or someone has rights, and others have duties to fulfil them. Interactive bioethics refers to discussion and debate between people, groups within society, and communities about descriptive and prescriptive bioethics (Macer 1998:2-3).

In the Philippines, bioethics as a discipline is mainly associated with medical ethics as done in ethics committees or as a subject in medical school. As such, it is a form of bioethics based on sources such as Beauchamp and Childress' *Principles of Biomedical Ethics*. To paraphrase what Catapusan said about Philippine sociology (Pertierra 1997:4), there is a distinction between a bioethics set in the Philippines and even practised by Filipinos, on the one hand, and a Philippine bioethics, on the other.

In addition, the ethical stance of the Catholic Church on various issues such as abortion, contraception, stem cell research, cloning and the like is highly influential in bioethics circles. This is evident when one looks at the predominance of Catholic clergy in the list of bioethics faculty in universities and speakers at national conferences. Due to the intersubjective dimension of religion and its importance in the reality of everyday life in the Philippines (Pertierra, 1997: 12), one cannot speak of bioethical policy without taking into consideration the power and influence of the Catholic Church.

Given that the word bioethics is mainly associated with an academic discipline, this might explain why, when asked what they thought about 'bioethics', a significant number of respondents in the Philippines had no answer or indicated that they don't know or have not heard of the word before.

Those who answered the question associated bioethics with moral issues that can be categorised into the following themes:

1. Bioethics deals with the ethical limitations of research and the applications of biotechnology.

   'I think that's when you consider the limits of what you are doing. For instance, would killing people be acceptable to you if it would help you in your experiment'?

   'I think of the limits of biotechnology or how far one is permitted to apply biotechnology in everyday life or in any aspect for that matter'.

2. Bioethics deals with science ethics.

   'What scientists should bear in mind when discovering/producing new things in order for their work to be named moral'.

   'Rules or ethics that scientists must keep in mind in all scientific endeavours that they undertake'.

3. Bioethics is respect for life.

   'I think of it as the respect shown to a specimen which is being used in an experiment'

'I really don't have an idea what bioethics is, but I think that you should respect life'.

4. Bioethics is love for nature and God.

'There are certain laws of nature that we must follow, or else it will backfire. We must not let our curiosity get the best of us. The perfect example being *Jurassic Park*'.

'It is deciding whether one is playing God or not'.

CONCLUSION

The majority of the pilot sample in the Philippines had optimistic views about biotechnology. They were more favourably disposed to biotechnology and genetic engineering than people from other countries. The sample was informed about scientific developments and discriminated between biotechnology and genetic engineering. People had high expectations of biotechnology's capacity to help food production, provide medical benefit and improve society in general. At the same time, there were concerns about its unknown risks and implications for morality and religion.

Products made from genetically modified organisms (GMOs) were viewed as both beneficial and risky. The most acceptable application was pest resistant crops; the least acceptable was xenotransplantation. Pest resistant crops were thought of as risky, but xenotransplantation was not considered as risky as the former. It thus seems that some degree of risk is acceptable so long as it brings about benefits, especially economic ones. Except for meat, there was an increase in the level of support for various products made from GMOs compared to 1993. Therapeutic gene therapy was viewed favourably, especially for its potential for curing fatal diseases. There was also some support for the use of gene therapy for enhancement purposes. Expectations were also quite high about the potential of biotechnology to solve crime, increase food production and improve public health.

In other countries in previous surveys such as Japan, the trend is that of increased negative attitudes towards biotechnology in general, along with high level of interest in science and technology. This is reflected in the demand for more regulations and public control. The assumption was that the decline of public trust in regulatory procedures and public authorities, and the scandals involving these bodies, have contributed to the low level of public confidence. In the Philippines, such scandals are a common phenomenon and the lack of trust towards the government and public bodies is inherent in the Philippine consciousness. The reason is structural and was best expressed by Pertierra (1995:17):

In the Philippines, the routinization of everyday life conflates these spheres of value, resulting in the structures of kinship ,locality, and association. Politics, culture, and practical life are permeated by this undifferentiated sphere of values whose coherence must be maintained... In such a structure, politics represents the political will of the powerful.

Therefore, the resolution to conflict is often sought externally. It is not surprising, then, why a majority of the people who participated in the study look to international bodies such as the United Nations to regulate biotechnology.

ACKNOWLEDGEMENT

We thank Dr Hiroko Nagai for her valuable insights on Philippine Studies. We also thank Jose Jason Villaroman, Diane Joy G. Zaragoza, Abegail Arana, Elaine M. Gaza and their classmates for their assistance in conducting the 2001 survey and to the other contributors acknowledged in previous surveys.

Table 1: Sample Characteristics in Phillippines in 1993 and 2001

	1993	2001
N	164	273
Response per cent	70	27
Time	34182	36951
Male	46	77
Female	54	33
Rural	13	22
Urban	87	78
Age		
Mean(yr)	21	20
14-20	3	78
21-30	97	13
31-40	0	4
41-50	0	3
51-60	0	1
61+	0	1
Marital Status		
Single	99	83
Married	1	16
Divorced/W	0	1
Other	0	0
Children		
None	100	84
Pregnant	0	2
One	0	0
Two	0	0
>two	0	14

...

	1993	2001
Education		
High school	0	68
2-year college	0	6
University Graduate	50	13
Postgraduate	47	7
Other	3	6
Religion		
None	0	2
Catholic	99	80
Christian	0	16
Moslem	0	1
Other	1	1
How important is religion?		
Very	89	79
Some	11	16
Not too	0	3
Not at all	0	2
Income (in Philippine pesos: 50 pesos=US$ 1		
<200,000	-	9
200,000-500,000	-	69
500,000-1,000,000	-	12
>1,000,0000	-	10

Table 2: Occupation of Respondents in Phillipines 2001

Housewife	7	Student	198
Retired	1	Administrator	(
Farmer	1	Self-Employed	1
Teacher	9	Arts	(
Government	(	Social Work	(
Company	5	Part-Time	(
University/ Research	3	Unemployed	3
Engineer	3	Others	3
Medical	5	Not Stated	34

Table 3: Levels of Interest in Science and Technology

per cent	Philippines 1993	Philippines 2001
Extremely Interested	16	6
Very Interested	49	24
Interested	33	50
Not Very Interested	1	18
Not At All Interested	1	2

Table 4: Comparisons of Attitudes of Respondents towards Five Areas of Science and Technology

per cent	Computers and IT		Biotechnology		Genetic Engineering		Telecommunications	
	Japan 2000	Phil. 2001	Japan 2000	Phil. 2001	Japan 2000	Phil. 2001	Japan 2000	Phil. 2001
Will Improve	82	96	66	82	59	67	77	94
No Effect	4	9	4	6	2	5	10	1
Make Worse	8	3	15	5	24	21	8	3
Don't Know	6	1	14	5	15	6	4	2

Table 5: Attitudes towards products produced using GMOs

per cent	Japan 1993	Japan 2000	Philippines 1993	Philippines 2001
Tomatoes with better taste				
Yes	69	59	68	71
No	20	31	27	20
Don't Know	11	10	5	9
Healthier Meat				
Yes	57	52	75	79
No	26	32	21	13
Don't Know	17	16	4	8
Larger Sport Fish				
Yes	22	20	54	61
No	54	63	40	20
Don't Know	24	17	6	19
Bacteria to Clean Up Oil Spills				
Yes	71	66	78	78
No	13	21	19	9
Don't Know	16	13	3	13
Disease Resistant Crops				
Yes	66	55	82	78
No	17	28	15	15
Don't Know	17	16	3	7
Cows Which Produce More Milk				
Yes	44	42	70	71
No	32	40	26	18
Don't Know	24	18	4	11

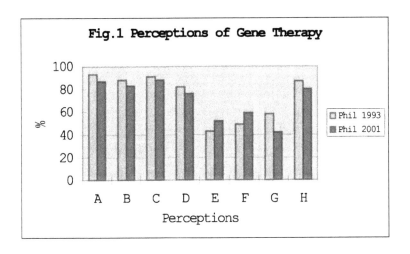

A. Cure fatal disease such as cancer;

B. Reduce the risk of developing a fatal disease

C. Prevent children from inheriting a fatal disease;

D. Prevent children from developing A non-fatal disease;

E. Improve the physical characteristics that children would inherit;

F. Improve the intelligence level that children would inherit;

G. Make people more ethical;

H. As an AIDS vaccine

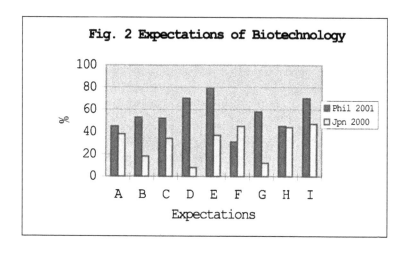

Fig. 2 Expectations of Biotechnology

A. Substantially reducing environmental pollution;

B. Allowing insurance companies to ask for a Genetic test before they set a person's premium;

C. Substantially reducing world hunger;

D. Creating dangerous new diseases ;

E. Solving more crimes through genetic fingerprinting;

F. Reducing the range of fruits and vegetables we can get;

G. Curing most genetic diseases;

H. Producing designer babies;

I. Replacing most existing food products with new varieties

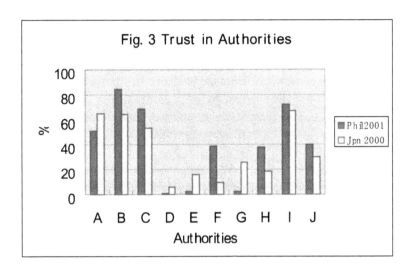

A. Consumer Organisations;

B. Environmental Organisations;

C. Animal Welfare Organisations;

D. Political Parties;

E. Trade Unions;

F. Religious Organisations;

G. Public Authorities;

H. Industry;

I. Schools or universities;

J. Mass Media

BIBLIOGRAPHY

Aerni, P., Phan-Huy, S.A. and Rieder, P. (1999) 'Indications of Public Acceptance of Transgenic Rice in the Philippines', *Biotechnology and Development Monitor*, 38: 18-21.

Biotechnology and the European Public Concerted Action Group (BEPCAG) (1997) 'Europe Ambivalent on Biotechnology', *Nature*, 387: 845-847.

Chen Ng, M.A., Takeda, C., Watanabe, T. and Macer, D. (2000) 'Attitudes of the Public and Scientists to Biotechnology in Japan at the start of 2000', *Eubios Journal of Asian and International Bioethics*,106: 106-113.

EUROBAROMETER 46.1 on Biotechnology (1997).

Hoban, T.J. (1997) 'Consumer Acceptance of Biotechnology: An International Perspective', *Nature Biotechnology*, 15: 232-234.

Macer, D.R.J. (1992) *Attitudes to Genetic Engineering: Japanese and International Comparisons*, Christchurch: Eubios Ethics Institute.

Macer, D.R.J. (1994) *Bioethics For the People by the People*, Christchurch: Eubios Ethics Institute.

Macer, D.R.J. (1998) *Bioethics is Love of Life*, Christchurch: Eubios Ethics Institute.

Macer, D.R.J. (1999) 'Bioethics in and from Asia', *Journal of Medical Ethics*, 25: 293-295.

Macer, D.R.J., Azariah, J. and Srinives, P. (2000) 'Attitudes to Biotechnology in Asia', *International Journal of Biotechnology*, 2: 313-321.

Macer, D.R.J. and Chen Ng, M. (2000) 'Changing Attitudes to Biotechnology in Japan', *Nature Biotechnology*,18: 945-947.

Macer, D.R.J.,Bezar, H., Harman, N., Kamada, H.and Macer,N. (1997) 'Attitudes to Biotechnology in Japan and New Zealand in 1997, with International Comparisons', *Eubios Journal of Asian and International Bioethics*, 7: 137-151.

Pertierra, R. (1995) *Philippine Localities and Global Perspectives: Essays on Society and Culture*, Quezon City: ADMU Press.

Pertierra, R. (1997) *Explorations in Social Theory and Philippine Ethnography*, Quezon City: University of the Philippines Press.

Tsai, D.F.C. (1999) 'Ancient Chinese Medical Ethics and the Four Principles of Biomedical Ethics', *Journal of Medical Ethics*, 25, no. 3.

Chapter 14

Chinese 'Eugenics': Definition, Practice and Cultural values

Yanguang Wang

In China, most applications and research of genetics and genomics have been under ethical, legal and social scrutiny in recent years, and some controversies are ongoing and unresolved. The 'eugenics' issue is very sensitive within China as well as elsewhere. The dispute on Chinese 'eugenics' occurred as a result of the 'Law of The People's Republic of China on Maternal and Infant Health Care', which was enacted in 1994. Afterwards, many Chinese thought about what Chinese eugenics is and why the response to the law was so negative. Part of the explanation may be that eugenics, in China, is not the same set of ideas and practices as eugenics in other countries.

Every bioethical issue must be understood within the context of particular societies, cultures and religions. In China, 'eugenics' is a term applied to preventive genetic medicine. Ethical issues include how to do genetic counselling with informed consent, how to disclose the carrier's information to relatives, whether or not social policies involving intervention can be justified, and so on. Insight into the ethical basis for the practices that in China are called 'eugenics', and into the cultural interpretations of situations in which these ethical issues arise, might be valuable not only for China but also for other developing countries in Asia and throughout the world, as they seek to develop and apply new advances in genetics for the benefit of their populations.

A PROTEAN CONCEPT OF EUGENICS AND THE CHINESE DEFINITION OF EUGENICS

As we will see, eugenics has always been a protean concept. Almost from the start, eugenics has meant different things to different people. The Chinese definition of 'eugenics' is different from Francis Galton's eugenics, and even the Chinese definition of eugenics has many different meanings.

FRANCIS GALTON'S EUGENICS AND THE EUGENICS MOVEMENT

Eugenics derives from the Greek word *eugenes* meaning 'good in birth,. In 1883, Francis Galton started using the word 'eugenics', defining it as the 'science of improving stock—not only by judicious mating, but whatever tends to give the more suitable races or strains of blood a better chance of prevailing over the less suitable than they otherwise would have had'. Galton later experimented with a variety of different formulations such as 'the study of agencies under social control which may improve or impair the racial qualities of future generations', and 'the science which deals with all influences that improve the inborn qualities of a race: also with those that develop them to the utmost advantage'.

Francis Galton's definitions on improving stock or impairing the racial qualities of future generations are not based on scientific evidence. Such eugenics relies on untenable claims in modern behavioural genetics about the inheritance of personality traits. Even though the desire to find a way of social control that may improve or impair the racial qualities of future generations was later used by Nazis and other racists, with grave consequences in countries like the United States and Germany, the eugenics of Francis Galton is rather innocuous by today's standards (Paul 1995: 3-9).

Both in the United States and Germany, a number of leading figures moved away from the kind of eugenics proposed by Francis Galton nearly five decades earlier. They combined eugenic interests with a focus on the 'unfit'. In the heyday of eugenics, sterilization, infanticide, murder, euthanasia, and a variety of other 'final solutions' were tools for the prevention or elimination of the 'unfit'. This 'eugenics' became central to Nazism and a major weapon for discrimination against minorities. Most contemporary geneticists and bio-ethicists, consequently, are concerned and warn that, by promoting genetic essentialism and determinism, eugenics leads to Nazism and racism.

Bioethical authorities provide their own definition of eugenics. In the Encyclopaedia of Bioethics, someone defined eugenics as a major scientific and pseudoscientific weapon for discrimination against minorities, a political, economic, and social policy that espouses the reproduction of the 'fit' over the 'unfit' and discourages the birth of the 'unfit' (Simon 1995: 970-972). According to this view, eugenics is nothing more than a pseudoscience in the modern world. Thus the workshop on the science and ethics of eugenics, held during the 18th international congress of genetics in Beijing, 10-15 August 1998, concluded that 'eugenics' is used in so many different ways that it is no longer suitable for scientific purposes (Dickson 1998: 711).

EUGENICS AND THE CHINESE WORD YOUSHENG

A few Chinese geneticists, who had studied and conducted genetics research in the U.S., introduced Francis Galton and his eugenics around the year 1920. From 1949 to 1980, Chinese geneticists were on the alert against the eugenics movement, and the term eugenics provoked references to nazism and racism, just as in most Western countries.

Academics subsequently redefined eugenics. A book published in 1981 gave eugenics a new meaning: it suggested that eugenics is a science of *Yousheng* for the well-being of next generations; eugenics could make the dreams of parents, families, societies and races come true. A book published in 1985 argued that the history of eugenics consisted of three phases: pre-science (ancient 'eugenics' ideas), half-science (Francis Galton's eugenics and the eugenics movement) and science (modern genetics). The author called for the revival of the term and urged people not to let the Nazi experience ruin its original meaning of 'having a healthy baby'. In the Chinese Encyclopaedia of Medicine, published in 1995, 'eugenics' was defined as a science aimed at improving human heredity, preventing birth defects, and raising the quality of the population by research on and applications of genetics theories and approaches'.

Most Chinese geneticists are unaware of the history of eugenics in the West, and of the negative connotation of the word for Westerners. Chinese use the English word 'eugenics' continuously and translate the English word to the Chinese word *Yousheng*. The meaning of *Yousheng* is the same as the Greek word *eugenes*, meaning 'good in birth', or 'healthy birth', or 'reproductive health'. The view most widely held by Chinese is that *Yousheng* implies processes of genetics designed to ensure that children who are born are, as far as possible, 'good'. This 'good' is to be achieved by way of prenatal nutrition, contraception, prenatal diagnosis and abortion, or diagnosis and treatment of newborns, which are common genetic procedures throughout the world.

The opposite of the Chinese word *Yousheng* is *Liesheng*, meaning 'inferior birth'. Some Chinese scholars refer to physical deformity or mental retardation as 'inferior birth' and are unaware that this term could easily cause discrimination against handicapped. This term was also used in some governmental documents and a minister's speech. Chinese scientists have also defined parents with severe genetic diseases as 'parents without reproductive value', which is also a term that could easily cause discrimination. Around 1994, bioethics was not a common topic of public debate and genetics education in China had not covered many ethical issues yet. But this does not mean that people using phrases like *Liesheng* or 'parents without reproductive values' intend to be discriminatory.

After the dispute on the Chinese Maternal and Infant Law during the last a few years, Chinese bioethicists have urged the public and scholars to avoid words like *Yousheng* in relation to eugenics. They suggest changing the word *Yousheng* to 'reproductive health', and most people do so now.

THE GOAL OF EUGENICS AND GENETIC COUNSELLING

Some Chinese scholars still use Francis Galton's interpretation and define Chinese eugenics as improving the stock of humankind by application of the science of human heredity. In a survey done in 1994-1996, someone provided evidence on eugenics in China, showing that 252 of the Chinese geneticists who responded agreed with the definition of eugenics as 'improving the population quality and reducing the population quantity' and agreed with the statement: 'An important goal of genetic counselling is to reduce the number of deleterious genes in the population' (Mao 1998: 692-693).

As we know, attempting to improve the stock of humankind by application of the science of human heredity, and thereby reduce the recessive gene in a population, is impossible. Most people would probably agree that means taken to directly reduce the number of a-symptomatic carriers of recessive genes is a truly coercive 'eugenic' goal. Mandatory population screening followed by mandatory sterilization of carriers could theoretically eliminate a gene except in the many disorders with high rates of new mutations. If ever implemented, the mandatory programs would remove a considerable percentage of the population or result in the sterilization of the majority of the population.

The attempts to reduce the frequency of a gene go beyond the goal of the Chinese eugenics definition, and the hope of Chinese geneticists, to prevent birth defects through clinical measures such as contraception or abortion. The survey mentioned above showed that while most Chinese geneticists would prefer directive counselling, many Chinese geneticists apparently believe that their pessimistic counsel accords with generally accepted views in most nations, which emphasize that the goal of genetics is prevention of 'birth defects'. There is no evidence showing that the majority of Chinese geneticists would advice voluntary surgical sterilization to decrease the population size. Since China has major overpopulation problems, it denies prospective parents the opportunity to make their decision on the basis of informed consent, and also denies any possibility that a child with birth defects may contribute positively to society (Wertz 1998: 501).

There is no mandatory population screening followed by mandatory sterilization in China. Doctors only recommend males or females with serious diseases visible to the naked eyes to remain childless. The compulsory pre-marital physical check-up certificates or medical appraisement certificates generally do not involve genetic analysis; only those with serious diseases undergo such gene testing.

The survey of Chinese eugenics referred to earlier did not mention the difference in genetic knowledge between the East and the West. Chinese geneticists should know that the likelihood of carriers of recessive genes marrying others with recessive genes is small, and even attempting to reduce the frequency of recessive genes in a population by voluntary non-reproduction of all affected individuals would be impossible. The development of Chinese genetics lags behind that of Western genetics: Clinical genetics services, available to all citizens in the West, are not available in most cities in China. The quality of education regarding modern genetics is also inferior.

When Chinese say 'quality of population', they do not mean a certain race or ethnic group. There is no tradition of racism in China; there are no Chinese who think that they are superior to particular minorities. Chinese geneticists do not want to clean the gene pool by precluding 'birth defects'. For Chinese, improving the human stock involves decreasing the number of babies with serious genetic diseases. The public in general also hopes to improve the Chinese population's quality by decreasing the number of deleterious genetic diseases in the population. 'Cleaning up the gene pool' and 'improving the stock of humankind' might just be a utopian dream. In the survey mentioned above, the populations in six other developing countries, facing similar economic conditions, had nearly the same ideas about eugenics as the Chinese (Wertz 1998: 497).

CHINESE EUGENIC PRACTICE AND RELATED ISSUES

Chinese eugenics involves a wide variety of practices, such as education on good birth, improvement of the environment, medical intervention before and after marriage and childbearing, genetics research, and clinical genetics. Public health services offer genetic counselling and, on occasion, abortion with informed consent if there is proof that the pregnancy will result in a seriously handicapped child.

In practice, most scientists seek to prevent birth defects. They try to avoid hereditary diseases and handicaps through the prevention of marriages between persons likely to transmit serious diseases and handicaps to their progeny. Most Chinese believe this practice is the same as the 'negative eugenics or preventive eugenics' promoted by the American scholar Dickson (1994:1-3). Chinese also agree with the ideas of Bajema about 'a new eugenics'. A Chinese scholar, for instance, quotes Bajema's words in an important book about Chinese eugenic practice: 'a new eugenics consists of genetic counselling, examination before birth and selective abortion' (Yen 1986: 4).

DIRECTIVE AND NON-DIRECTIVE COUNSELLING

Individual eugenics is achieved by deliberately providing certain information during counselling, sometimes accompanied by directive advice. Practices that place the power of decision-making in the hands of anyone other than the family or the patient may be considered eugenics. The final decision should be made by families or patients. Directive advice in genetics counselling is dangerous when the geneticist can influence people's own decisions. Some say that there is evidence for eugenics in China because most Chinese respondents in the survey would prefer directive counselling ('urge termination' and 'counsel pessimistically') for 26 terminal conditions (Mao and Wertz 1997: 102).

In practice, Chinese genetic counselling in recent years has involved non-directive as well as directive counselling. Non-directive counselling may be difficult or impossible to achieve for many reasons. There may be social factors or good clinical reasons for geneticists to recommend a specific course of action to clients. There is an inherent difficulty in separating giving information from giving advice (Elwyn, 2000: 135).

The patient's free choice depends upon full and honest information, and also on a fairly high level of public knowledge. When geneticists want a patient to terminate the pregnancy, they often emphasize the negative aspects of birth defects. Most Chinese think that we should not exclude any compulsory genetic screening or testing, because we have an obligation to the health and life of next generations. Chinese professionals apparently believe that they have a moral obligation to steer families toward termination of pregnancy in some serious cases. Those who come to clinics to seek genetic counselling are mainly couples that worry about whether their future baby will be genetically normal, particularly if they have a relative who has a genetic disease or if they have given birth to a defective child before. If a person appears to suffer from a dominant genetic disease, and if the child has a 50 per cent chance of getting the disease, the physician generally feels that he or she has an obligation to recommend screening or testing. When prenatal testing reveals a genetic disease, a doctor will generally advise an in-clinic abortion. One explanation for this attitude is that historically China was a paternalistic society. Although modern China has changed considerably, paternalism still prevails in the medical field.

Throughout the world, most genetic counselling after prenatal diagnosis is directive, although the definitions of directive and non-directive counselling vary. The 'non-directive counselling' found in English-speaking nations, with counsellors presenting 'unbiased' information and then telling people that they should make their own decisions, is an exception (Wertz 1998: 498). Another definition of 'non-directive counselling' is that clinical geneticists try to help their clients arrive at the best decisions from their own perspective and do not guide them towards any particular decision. However, whether total 'non-directiveness' is attainable remains unclear and contested.

The problem of eugenics arises only when one considers who has the power to decide what should be prevented. In other words, who defines what constitutes a 'birth defect'? Who decides on the measures for prevention? The difference between eugenics and medical ethics is that eugenics is a program imposed by the state, regardless of the preferences of the individuals involved. Although a few eugenic practices without informed consent occurred in the countryside of China many years ago, they are no longer legal. In recent years, informed consent has become the norm in the field of genetics. We prefer genetic counselling with full respect for individual rights, individual choice and informed consent. Informed consent is a criterion that distinguishes eugenics from prevention.

Informed consent and voluntary testing is not easy to get in the rural areas of China. Poor Chinese are quite deferential towards whomever or whatever they consider an authority, and personal informed consent may become communal consent or authoritative consent. Last fall, 200 international members of UNESCO's Forum of scientists, physicians, and legal experts in China debated the principle of informed consent. As the *China Daily News* (September 4, 2001) reported: 'Despite agreement on the necessity of informed consent, many questions remain open. Among the most puzzling is how to reconcile the fact that informed consent bans scientists from giving participants anything, or creating an undue influence for their willingness to volunteer'.

PROVING GENETIC INFORMATION TO FAMILIES OF CARRIERS

When geneticists transmit information about a carrier's genetic condition to other members of the family without the consent of these carriers, they engage in individual eugenics. In genetic testing and counselling, there are quite a number of situations where professional ethics and public policy have to balance individual rights with professional and public obligations, e.g., the right of the individual to confidentiality, on the one hand, and the duty of the physician to protect fellow citizens from unwarranted harm, on the other. When hereditary genetic disorders affect other members of someone's family, the bioethical principle of confidentiality may be violated in order to protect others from harm. It is well known among professionals that Polycystic Kidney Disease (ADPKD), the most frequent among severe genetic diseases, can be controlled by limiting hypertension and avoiding stress to the lower abdomen. Therefore it would be beneficial if carriers knew early enough about their status and got appropriate advice.

A cross-cultural case study has described the tendency among Chinese professionals to violate confidentiality in favour of disclosure of carrier information to relatives in the case of ADPKD. We asked the views of 182 health care professionals—including geneticists, physicians, ethicists, philosophers, nurse students, and postgraduate students—and compared them with the views of 146 health care professionals in Europe in 1999-2000 (Wang 2000: 63).

There are strong temptations among health care professionals to violate confidentiality in favour of disclosure and avoiding harm to potential patients. Participants from China voiced somewhat stronger support for the moral duty of potential carriers to seek genetic testing. Some even go so far as to support a legal obligation of health care professionals to inform the family against the patient's will. Chinese responses were more favourable towards health care policy providing free genetic testing than those from Europe. Chinese also voiced somewhat stronger support of a moral duty of potential carriers to seek genetic testing, thus being less favourable towards the 'right not to know'. Chinese also were more in favour of not limiting prenatal genetic testing to a number of severe disorders, and open to more information concerning parental choice.

This survey showed that Chinese hold stronger views on genetic information than Europeans: it is not only the patient's privacy that is important, but also the family and society. Chinese health care professionals seem to recognize the benefits of individualized and efficient drug delivery. This might not be surprising since more genetic services are provided free of charge in Europe than in Asia, and Europeans are more favourable towards the principle of autonomy. In China, the collectivist model still seems to play an essential role, particularly in regulating clinical genetic services.

Collectivist thinking bases ethical principles primarily on collective values, the common good, social goals and cooperative virtues. Such an approach will put a higher emphasis on preventing harm from others, collectives, communities and society in general than on individuals. The mass media and public education have promoted a collectivist ideology in China for a long time. Some government officials and scholars still favour a collectivist model. We should admit that such a model does not take the possible harm and danger of discrimination and stigmatisation of the individual seriously enough. It may be harmful to individuals as well as to society. In particular, the collectivist model seems to be inappropriate for regulating clinical genetic services.

Clinical genetics services are not yet available for all citizens in China or in most other countries. It is important that departments of clinical genetics and local genetic services meet the highest levels of medical and ethical standards. Chinese, moreover, should be able to clarify which 'genetic disorders' warrant disclosure and which do not. And medical ethical education should pay more attention to the confidentiality principle in drafting guidelines on ethical issues related to medical genetics and genetic services.

However, the views of Chinese health care professionals towards balancing confidentiality with obligations, and towards the right to genetic information and education are the same as in most other countries. Wertz has described temptations among professionals to violate confidentiality in favour of disclosure and avoiding harm. This is a common challenge in many countries, not just in China.

As expressed by the 'Proposed International Guidelines on Ethical Issues in Medical Genetics and Genetic Services' of the WHO, professionals in human genetics have responsibilities and obligations even towards those who have not asked for their service yet and who do not know that they are carriers of genetic disorders. The Guidelines also ask that 'the genetic service provider should encourage the individual to ask relatives to seek genetic counselling, but, in case the individual refuses, recommend that the genetic counsellor should make direct contact with relatives' (WHO 1998: no. 9).

Some scholars seem to be aware of recent controversies regarding the rebirth of eugenics. Sass recommends considering the patient as the primary moral agent responsible for disclosing genetic risk as the golden rule. The German association of human geneticists recommends treating each case individually. Given the probability of influencing the time of onset and severity of ADPKD, Kielstein and Sass value the 'duty to know' higher than a questionable 'right not to know' (Hans-Martin 2001: 130-132).

CHINESE LAW AND SOCIAL POLICY INTERVENTION

The Law of Maternal and Infant Health Care

China's Law on Maternal and Infant Health has attracted considerable criticism in Western media and scientific circles. One reason for the association of Chinese eugenics with Nazism is that the law was initially called the 'eugenics law'. Nevertheless, I would argue that China's version of eugenics is quite different from the eugenics of Nazism, racism or genetic discrimination of the handicapped.

Article 1 of the law emphasizes that: 'This law is formulated in accordance with the Constitution with a view to ensuring the health of mothers and infants and to improving the quality of the newborn population'. The intention of the Chinese government in passing the 'Law of the People's Republic of China on Maternal and Infant Health Care' is merely to warn people of the risks of inheriting genetic diseases, and to avoid them among their children. The Chinese government seeks to prevent avoidable genetic handicaps among future generations.

Article 19, moreover, states that: 'Any termination of the pregnancy or sterilisation shall be agreed to and signed by the person concerned. If the person has no capacity for civil conduct, it shall be agreed to and signed by the guardian of the person'. Surely the law stresses that such action is only admissible with the individual's informed consent. But the law is ambiguous in the wording of articles 10 and 16, which concern genetic counselling with informed consent.

Most negative responses from abroad focused on articles 10 and 16. Article 10 prescribes that: 'Physicians shall, after performing the pre-marital physical check-up, explain and give medical advice to both the male and the female who have been diagnosed with a serious genetic disease that is considered to be inappropriate for child-bearing from a medical point of view. The two may only marry if both sides agree to take long-term contraceptive measures or undergo sterilization'. Article 16 stipulates that: 'If a physician detects or suspects that a married couple in their child-bearing age suffer from a serious genetic disease, the physician shall give medical advice to the couple, and the couple in their child-bearing age shall take measures in accordance with the physician's medical advice'.

In practice, while doctors may advise two individuals at risk of passing on a hereditary disease to refrain from marrying or to undergo sterilization, the ultimate decision is left to these adults. According to Chinese government officials, the law seeks to provide a wide range of pre- and post-marital services; they suggest that the commotion outside of China is primarily the result of the ambiguous wording of articles 10 and 16 (Dickson 1998: 711). The Chinese government would like to revise the law, and at present it does not include any penalties and is apparently not enforced.

In May 2000, Chinese bio-ethicists and the ELSI Committee of Human Genome recommended the Chinese government to change article 10 into the following: 'Physicians shall, after performing the pre-marital physical check-up, explain and give medical advice to both the male and the female who have been diagnosed with a serious genetic disease, which is considered to be inappropriate for child-bearing from a medical point of view; and advise the two to take long-term contraceptive measures or undergo sterilisation'. They suggested revising article 16 to: 'If a physician detects or suspects that a married couple of child-bearing age suffer from a serious genetic disease, the physician shall give medical advice to the couple, and the couple of child-bearing age can take measures in accordance with the physician's medical advice, but any measures taken by the couple shall be based on mutual consent'.

Social Policy Intervention

A major criticism of the 'eugenics law' is that the Chinese seem to favour social policy interventions restricting the freedom of the female who has been diagnosed with a serious genetic disease. In the law, though, there are also some social policy interventions restricting the individual choice of the male. When Chinese register for a marriage license, both male and female applicants must produce their pre-marital physical check- up certificates or medical technical appraisement certificates.

Other Chinese laws prescribe social policy interventions that prohibit marriage between close relatives. In the 'marriage law' promulgated on September 10, 1980, it is stipulated that: 'Marriage can be prohibited in the following cases: 1. Directly-related members of one's family and indirectly-related family members within three generations; 2. Those who have contracted incurable leprosy or any other disease that medical professionals consider harmful'. According to a critic outside of China, all above social policy interventions belong to 'eugenics', as defined by ethical authorities. But similar social policy interventions related to genetics exist in various other countries as well.

Economics and national health issues are part of the context in which Chinese social policy interventions have evolved. Let me give some basic facts about China, indicating the big challenges and pressures facing the Chinese population. In 1994, China's population reached 1.2 billion and it will soon reach 1.3 billion. According to a national survey in 1987, moreover, there were 51.64 million disabled people (4.9 percent of the total population) in China. More than 35 percent of these disabilities are due to birth defects and genetic diseases. The rate of infants born with inherited genetic diseases was 99.62 of 100,000. Between 1997 and 1999, the rate of infants born with a serious heritable genetic disease was 23.96 of 100,000 infants. In the category of 7-14 year olds, there are about 1 million Chinese whose IQ is below 50, half of which due to genetic diseases.

The cost of looking after those with hereditary handicaps is enormous, imposing a heavy burden on the state and on families, and causing a grave social problem regarding their livelihood. Because of the underdeveloped economy and poverty in China, the social support network for a defective infant is minimal. All of these make the life of a defective child and his or her parents miserable.

The public generally wants to reduce the number of people with deleterious genetic diseases— for the good of the nation, the families, and of course the individuals themselves. Consequently, there was wide popular support for Chinese eugenics and a eugenics law with effective measures to reduce the rate of infants born with serious inherited genetic diseases.

From this point of view, the Chinese do not discriminate against the handicapped child or adult; they just want to prevent the misery faced by handicapped people. It is unreasonable to expect any major improvements in the treatment of handicapped children and their mothers in China in the near future. Consequently, many feel that these children and their mothers would be better off if the handicapped infant is never born.

In Chinese culture, Confucianism is dominant. Confucianism is an ethics or philosophy that teaches us how to be moral persons. There are a number of ethical principles in Confucian ethics, which regulate interpersonal relationships. In Confucianism, *Ren* means loving people, caring for others. Ren is an extension of the natural compassion that everyone feels in view of the hardship and misfortune of others. Ren can be, and has to be, cultivated and developed in interpersonal or social relationships, first and foremost in the family. Love, compassion and care for parents and siblings are at the root of this Confucian concept. The affection that is assumed to grow naturally in the family should also become the model for treating others in society at large. Paternalism together with Ren guide the behaviour of Chinese government officials and health care professionals, and they justify interference with people's liberty by referring to the welfare, good, happiness, needs, interests, and values of the person involved.

In any case, few of us are entirely free of the eugenic notion 'good birth'. An adult, for instance, generally delays having a child until he or she is financially and emotionally ready to be a good provider and parent. Most modern governments hope that their people will be energetic, ingenious and enterprising. However, eugenic thinking and practice should balance the interests of all sides. Nations with social policy interventions and government involvement are mostly developing nations. In the future, when the family and society are able to support handicapped infants, these nations may become less concerned with 'birth quality' as a social issue.

CONCLUSION

The cultural background behind the Chinese definition of eugenics has major implications for genetic practice in China. Chinese should recover the core meaning of eugenics: good birth and voluntary prevention of birth defects. It is important to have a contemporary definition of eugenics for the application of genetics. This new definition of eugenics can make conceptual thinking clearer and justify the medical measures involved in contemporary genetics. What is right depends not just on the facts, but also on how eugenics is defined. Eugenics cannot, and should not, be understood without an analysis of the moral, political, and social implications of advances in science and technology at particular times, in particular places and for particular individuals or groups in society.

BIBLIOGRAPHY

Dickson, D. (6 January 1994) 'China's Misconception of Eugenics', *Nature*, 367: 1-3.

Dickson, D. (20 August 1998) 'China's "eugenics" law still disturbing despite relabelling', *Nature*, 394: 711-720.

Elwyn, G., Gray, J., Clarke, A. (2000) ' Shared Decision Making and Non-Directiveness in Genetic Counselling', *Journal of Medical Genetics*, 37: 135-138.

Mao, X., Wertz, D.C. (1997) 'China's Genetic Services Providers' Attitudes Towards Several Ethical Issues: A Cross-Cultural Survey', *Clinical Genetics*, 32: 100-109.

Mao, X. (1998) 'Chinese Geneticists' View of Ethical Issues in Genetic Testing and Screening: Evidence for Eugenics in China', *American Journal of Human Genetics*, 63: 688-695.

Paul, D. B. (1995) *Controlling Human Heredity—1865 to Present*, Humanities Press.

Sass, H.M. (2001) 'A Contract Model for Genetic Research and Health Care', *Eubios Journal of Asian Intern Bioethics*, 11: 130-132.

Wang, Y. (2001) 'A Study of Chinese View on Carrier Information in Pharmacogenetics Genetics and Disorders', in *Bioethics and the Impact of Genetics in the 21st Century*, Eubios Ethics Institute.

Wertz, D.C. (1998) 'Eugenics Is Alive and Well: A Survey of Genetic Professionals around the World', *Science in Context*, 11: 493-510.

World Health Organization (1998) *Proposed International Guidelines on Ethical Issues in Medical Genetics and Medical Services*, Geneva: WHO.

Yen, R. (1986) *Applied Eugenics*, Ren Min Medicine Press.

Chapter 15

Genomics, Health, and Society: A View from the South[1]

Chan Chee Khoon

INTRODUCTION

On June 27, 2001, the Advisory Committee on Health Research (ACHR) of the World Health Organisation (WHO) conducted hearings in Geneva for a Special Report on Genomics & Health. Initially intended as a document to address the ethical, legal and social implications of the gathering genomics revolution (ELSI), the ACHR's terms of reference were subsequently modified to give primary emphasis to a scientific and technological assessment of the implications of genomics for human health, in particular, the prospects and challenges arising from these developments for countries of the South. The Citizens' Health Initiative (CHI), one of two NGOs invited to make submissions at these consultations, suggested that no less important than the scientific and technical assessment was a perspective which gave due attention to the social context and political economy of scientific/technological development and its deployment. The article below touches upon neglected health priorities of the South, intellectual property rights and patents, risk management, insurance and discrimination, and predictive (prenatal) testing, reproductive choice, and eugenics.

The Citizens' Health Initiative (CHI) is a coalition of NGOs based in Malaysia, which has extensive international links. We thank the World Health Organisation for this opportunity to express our views on genomics and health, and we wish to state the following as among our concerns.

Justified Exuberance or Genohype?

Dr Francis Collins, director of the US National Human Genome Research Institute has stated that the benefits from mapping and sequencing the human genome 'would include a new understanding of genetic contributions to human disease and the development of rational strategies for minimizing or preventing disease phenotypes altogether' (Collins 1999), with further prospects of 'genetic prediction of individual risks of disease and responsiveness to drugs...and the development of designer drugs based on a genomic approach to targeting molecular pathways that [have] been disrupted in disease [pharmacogenomics]' (Collins and McKusick 2001).

We believe that a balanced assessment of the relative importance of genomics for human health is much needed, and this need not be confined to a developing world context. This debate is far from settled as is evident from the widely divergent views appearing lately in leading biomedical journals and the importance now attached to the interplay of diverse etiological factors, to the social determinants of health and disease, and to health equity (Evans *et al.* 2001; Braveman *et al.* 2000; Leon and Walt 2000).

Re-instating the Social Context

Over and above our deliberations on the potential and limitations of genomics for human health, we are no less concerned with the political and economic forces that have vast influence in shaping the priorities of its development and its subsequent deployment. This is especially so given a pervasive policy posture, which favours privatisation of health care and its financing and the retrenchment of the public sector. This fundamental dilemma, between need and economic demand, was recently dramatised by the campaign for affordable essential drugs, in particular, for anti-retroviral treatment for people living with HIV/AIDS. We have seen how a profit-driven, market orientation can sacrifice a humane, lifesaving mission in order to cater to the dictates of shareholder interests and market pricing strategies. Genomic-based enterprises will undoubtedly follow the same trajectory unless a pro-active campaign intervenes effectively to re-direct them more towards needs-based priorities.[2]

Neglected Health Priorities of the South

The *10/90 Report on Health Research* of the Global Forum for Health Research (Geneva 2000) documented the gross imbalance between the health needs of poorer countries and the pitiful scale of research geared towards these needs. The imbalance in health-care spending for services overall was equally bleak—nearly nine-tenths of the global burden of disease occurs in the poorer countries, where only 1 in 10 healthcare dollars are spent.

In a recent interview in Lyon, France, Dr Tikki Pang, Director for Research Policy and Cooperation at the WHO, contrasted the enormous investment in genomics research with the funding levels for research on tropical diseases such as malaria. Dr Pang further remarked that what was needed to cope with the three leading killers in the developing world—malaria, diarrhea and AIDS—were mosquito netting, cheap re-hydration therapies and condoms, none of which would become more available as a result of advances in genomics research.

It is doubly alarming that the very same forces pushing for privatisation, for cost recovery in public health outlays, are undermining disease control efforts in developing countries. In Gambia, for instance, villages that were provided with insecticide free of charge for bed-net impregnation, recorded a five-fold higher use of this proven malaria-preventive measure when compared to villages where user charges were introduced (Weissman 2000). Households consistently cited lack of money as the main reason for families not dipping their bed-nets. User charges introduced in Kenyan STD clinics similarly resulted in dramatic declines in patient attendance (Moses *et al.* 1992).

INTELLECTUAL PROPERTY RIGHTS (IPR) AND PATENTS: LEGAL ARTEFACTS OF A CORPORATE-DRIVEN AGENDA

Intellectual property rights and patents have been declared indispensable prerequisites for innovation and the introduction of new and useful commodities. Recent experience in the South, however, suggests that intellectual property law encourages not so much innovation as theft. We refer of course to the unrelenting efforts of biotechnology entities to privatise indigenous knowledge and genetic resources, appropriating what is essentially an evolved, cumulative heritage of human ecology. Among these instances of biopiracy are the following:

The granting of a patent (US patent no. 5,663,484) for South Asian-derived *basmati* rice to RiceTec, Inc. of Texas, and the trademark *jasmati* for a potential hybrid between the long-grained aromatic *basmati* with the equally renowned jasmine-fragrant rice of Thailand. The patent applies to breeding crosses involving 22 farmer-bred *basmati* varieties from Pakistan and India, and lays claim to such strains grown anywhere in the Western Hemisphere and marketed under the brand name *basmati*.

Basmati, sadly, is merely one instance of an escalating trend of biopiracy that has now engulfed plant materials from diverse sources—Mexican yellow beans, Bolivian *quinoa*, Andean *nuna* beans, Amazonian *ayahuasca*, West African sweet *(brazzein)* genes, Indian and Iranian chickpeas, among others which have been well-documented by the Rural Advancement Foundation International (RAFI).

– The failed attempt by University of Mississippi scientists to patent the oral and topical use of *turmeric* powder for ulcers and surgical wound healing, a long-established *Ayurvedic* medical practice.

– The extraction and processing of *azadirachtin* from the *neem* tree for pesticide and other usage (another Indian traditional practice, which WR Grace, Inc. successfully patented).

More directly pertinent to human source material and genomics-related intellectual property claims are the following:

– The aborted attempt by the US National Institutes of Health to patent a cell line derived from the *Hagahai* people of Papua New Guinea.

– Aside from cell lines with commercial value, gene sequences from populations with unusual disease frequencies are highly sought after in hopes of isolating disease-linked genes. On the South Atlantic island of Tristan da Cunha, for example, about 50 per cent of the isolated and inbred population are either asthmatic or asthma-prone. The inhabitants of Kosrae, a Micronesian island in the South Pacific, have a high prevalence of obesity. Together with the Pima Indians of Arizona, who have high prevalence of both obesity and diabetes, they are prime targets for the 'obesity gene' hunters. As early as the 1980s, Dr Cesare Sirtori of the University of Milan had discovered an unusual allele among residents of a small Italian village, which seemingly conferred low risk of cardiovascular disease despite the subjects' low levels of the protective high-density lipoproteins (HDL). This allele (*apo A-1 Milano*)[3] was subsequently isolated, cloned and patented in an attempt to develop a genetically engineered product to treat heart disease.

– With the completion of mapping and sequencing of the human genome,[4] the focus will now shift from genomic organisation and its generic structure to studies of genomic diversity between and within populations, down to the level of single nucleotide polymorphisms (SNPs), and studies of multiple gene expression in healthy and diseased tissue samples using DNA microarrays. A prime objective of course is to correlate genomic differences (and gene expression data) with disease occurrence, a hugely expanded effort to identify putative disease-linked genes (and gene ensembles) with commercial potential. With or without the controversy-plagued Human Genome Diversity Project (HGDP), efforts will continue to collect genetic source material from diverse populations for research on genomic diversity.

In parallel with the development of biotechnology and genetic engineering, a legal armamentarium has emerged to bring the human body and its parts within the ambit of capitalist property relations. One significant milestone was the case of *John Moore*, a leukemia patient who underwent surgery in 1976 at the University of California for removal of his cancerous spleen. The *Council for Responsible Genetics* (Cambridge, Massachusetts) noted that:

> the University [of California] was later granted a patent for a cell line called 'Mo', removed from the spleen, which could be used for producing valuable proteins [cytokines, including ones which mediate antibacterial and cancer-fighting activity]. The long-term commercial value of the cell line was estimated at over one billion dollars. Mr. Moore demanded the return of the cells and control over his body parts, but the California Supreme Court decided that he was

not entitled to any rights to his own cells after they had been removed from his body.

This principle was re-affirmed in the New Jersey state legislature in 1996 when it enacted legal protections against genetic discrimination in employment and health insurance. This same legislature, however, also rejected a draft clause which would have declared *individual genomic information* to be *individual, private property*, with obvious implications for royalties and other benefits.

It is increasingly clear that 'intellectual property rights' have largely become corporate-defined artefacts of law in capitalist society, often at the expense of individual as well as of community. As George Annas, professor of law and public health at Boston University remarked in *Nature* (21 November, 1996): it is 'bizarre that other people can own your genetic information [and body parts], but you can't'.

RISK MANAGEMENT, INSURANCE AND DISCRIMINATION

In October 2000, the Genetics and Insurance Committee (GAIC) of the UK Department of Health approved the use of genetic screening tests for Huntington's disease in the assessment of life insurance premiums. According to committee chairman John Durant, 'this decision will mean that those with a negative test result will not be asked to pay more for life insurance because of their family history of Huntington's disease'. This puts a nice gloss to it, but on further reflection those who test positive (and those who decline to be tested despite having a family history of Huntington's) would have the entire risk premium loaded onto them. In effect, we're back to the dilemma of risk-rated healthcare insurance: disaggregating an existing risk pool into sub-groups with differing risk profiles, so as to allow for profit-maximising differential premiums for low-risk groups ('cherry-picking'), while marginalising high-risk sub-groups as uninsurable. *The net result is that those people at highest risk of falling ill and requiring treatment will be those least able to afford premiums, and therefore treatment.*

These concerns take on added urgency with the worldwide trend towards privatisation of the *financing* of healthcare, concomitant with an increased reliance on risk-rated health insurance. This fragmentation of community will be greatly exacerbated if insurance-mandated genetic testing is sanctioned and widely adopted.[5] It would be complacent to treat this as idle or alarmist fantasy. Hard on the heels of the UK decision, health insurers in Hong Kong are pushing for similar provisions under which

> people shown in genetic tests to have a higher risk of developing specific diseases can have their insurance cover rejected or be forced to pay higher premiums. The [Hong Kong Federation of Insurers] said its members were not yet asking clients for the results of genetic tests, but they might soon start doing so as allowed under the code, which is based on the British version and was adopted last May (*South China Morning Post* 2001).

The deputy chairperson of the federation's life insurance council, Sarah Ho Sook-ming, further added that 'once genetic tests for breast cancer and other diseases have proved to be technically reliable, we will have to ask for those results...'

The Council for Responsible Genetics has quite correctly pointed out that genetic (disease) risks in a population, which are fairly stable (unlike the less predictable risks for infectious outbreaks),

> are already reflected in the actuarial tables used by insurers to establish [premiums]. It is misleading for insurers to suggest that their financial solvency will be jeopardized if

they are obligated to insure people at risk for genetic conditions. In fact, insurers have always insured people at risk for genetic conditions. Previously, however, it was not possible to identify those people before they became ill with the disorder. There is no reason for insurers to begin to use this new predictive information now, merely because it is available."[6]

What we observe in practice however is opportunistic (reciprocal) poaching of low-risk subscribers by competing insurers (identified by ever-more discriminating risk markers), which continually threatens to undermine any existing risk pool. This unfortunately is almost unavoidable with every new and more discriminating technology (such as DNA testing) that is introduced into a competitive, profit-driven setting. *CHI is convinced that a sensible and civilised way of avoiding this deplorable situation of stigmatised discards and social exclusion, is to move towards a re-affirmation of community through non-discriminatory social insurance, if not NHS-type nationalised or socialised healthcare.*

PREDICTIVE (PRENATAL) TESTING, REPRODUCTIVE CHOICE, AND EUGENICS

These are clearly among the most difficult and troubling issues raised by the imminent proliferation of prenatal genetic diagnostics. Philip Kitcher (1996), the American bioethicist, has authored a very nuanced and courageous book, suggesting that some form of eugenics is inevitable. Provided that it is voluntary and practised on an individual basis without social coercion, the 'utopian eugenics' that Kitcher envisages would attempt a fine balance between 'compassionate abortion' (following upon prenatal diagnosis of severely disabling conditions and a very restricted future life) and maximally enabling services for the lives of future people with even the most severe medical conditions. He is sensitive to the interplay of social versus genetic constructions of 'disability', and to the dangers and contingencies illustrated by these hypothetical but not far-fetched scenarios of excess—if a genetic basis for left-handedness, for example, were ever demonstrated, would the higher mortality associated with this trait (plausibly from social more than physiological causes) dispose some parents to abort a 'less-than-perfect' or 'defect- free' child? Could foetuses bearing a 'homosexuality gene' suffer the same fate?

These are clearly very contentious issues over which consensus may only emerge, if ever, after protracted, iterative deliberations, and even then they will be highly contingent on social and historical context. Crucial to this will be the social circumstance and process adopted in seeking a popular consensus that does not ride roughshod over minority rights.

GENETICALLY MODIFIED (GM) CROPS

We note the ACHR's request that further discussion on genetically modified crops be deferred to other occasions and settings. While biosafety and environmental impacts of GMOs are also addressed by other agencies such as FAO, we consider it quite appropriate for WHO to evaluate and advise upon the health aspects of genetically engineered food. On this issue, CHI takes note of the very legitimate concerns raised by scientific and lay communities. In line with the precautionary principle, we support an indefinite moratorium on the further dissemination of genetically modified crops to allow time for more inclusive consultation and public inputs in policy and regulatory processes.

A POLICY RE-ORIENTATION FOR RESPONSIBLE AND EQUITABLE GENOMICS

We urge the WHO to lend its moral authority in support of all the above concerns.

We call on the WHO to re-assert its international leadership in crucial areas of health policy such as the organisation and financing of healthcare. Healthcare must remain as a collective social responsibility, not a service to be delegated to the market as arbiter of access. CHI notes that Director-General Dr Gro Harlem Brundtland affirmed in the 1999 World Health Report that 'not only do market-oriented approaches lead to intolerable inequity with respect to a fundamental human right, but growing bodies of theory and evidence indicate markets in healthcare to be inefficient as well'. In the few years since then, even more evidence has emerged to confirm the poor track record of market-driven healthcare (and of its soft-edged cousin, managed competition), judged on equity as well as on efficiency grounds (Light 2001; Woolhandler and Himmelstein 1999: 444; Chan 2000). It is deplorable that international agencies such as the World Bank, International Monetary Fund, and the World Trade Organisation can continue to advocate the dismantling of public sector healthcare out of an obsessive faith that market-based solutions will invariably deliver higher efficiency and lower unit costs, clearly not the case in many instances.

We also call on the WHO to take all necessary steps to promote access to primary care led health services on the basis of need, and not on the ability to pay. This is the only meaningful stance consistent with a declaration of healthcare as a human right. We are mindful of the reality that healthcare, up to a point, will be rationed, but we are equally firm in our view that rationing by the market is completely unacceptable. Recognising that the WTO threatens to ride roughshod over health concerns in international trade, the WHO should support any moves to take health-related services out from under the ambit of WTO-GATS regimes, and to further loosen the grip of WTO-TRIPS on access to essential drugs and other lifesaving items.

We finally call on the WHO, an organisation of member states, but increasingly subject to corporate influence, to create more space for the meaningful participation and inputs of popular organisations in international health policy advising and agenda setting. We believe that these are some of the important pre-requisites for an equitable harvest of benefits that are possible from a humane and responsible development of genomic technologies.

GENOMICS AND THE SOUTH: PREPARING FOR THE CHALLENGE

In preparing to meet the challenges of the gathering genomics revolution, and to ensure that they are better positioned to reap the positive potential of these developments rather than suffer the consequences and unfavorable terms dictated by hegemonic technological powers and a market-oriented system, countries of the South should:

– Build up their independent national capacities in genomics, coupled with a widely disseminated, popularised understanding of the key issues at stake. The accent is on a *democratisation* of awareness, meaningful popular inputs into decision-making, building of national consensus so as to negotiate from positions of greater strength, and cooperation in research and development when it is mutually beneficial.

- Identify, document and protect natural genetic resources, and develop national and regional guidelines on the transfer of genetic materials.

- Identify mutually beneficial exchanges and collaboration in research and development, and pool regional resources with a view towards effective regional negotiating blocs.

- Learn useful lessons (pros and cons) from country case studies (e.g. Iceland) and community experiences so as to negotiate effectively for equitable benefits for their local populations in return for access to genetic source materials.[7]

- Establish trust institutions at various levels to ensure that the benefits that may accrue from the genomics revolution are equitably distributed. Most importantly, there must be adequate, effective and credible representation of popular organisations and transparent, publicly owned and publicly managed institutions committed to a needs-based orientation.

NOTES

[1] An earlier draft of this paper was presented at the World Health Organisation's global consultations for a Special Report on Genomics & Health (June 27, 2001, Geneva) and has since been published in *New Solutions: A Journal of Environmental & Occupational Health Policy*, 12, no. 2: 109-119. *[Year of publication? Reprinted with permission of?*

[2] The HIV genomic sequence, known since the mid-1980s, brought little benefit to impoverished HIV-infected persons in the South, until an effective campaign was mounted by *Medecins sans Frontieres, South African Treatment Action Campaign,* and *Oxfam* for affordable anti-retroviral treatment.

[3] Coding for a mutant *Apolipoprotein A-1,* which turned out to be efficient at scavenging cholesterol from arteriosclerotic plaques for disposal via the liver's metabolic processes.

[4] The Human Genome Project sequenced an 'average' genome of a 'typical person'. This 'typical person' is a compilation (composite) of 20 to 30 individuals anonymously selected from hundreds of subjects who, given the demographics of the volunteers used for this project, are thought to be primarily of Western European descent.

[5] Over and above this atomisation of society, fear of genetic discrimination can also deprive people of the real benefits of genetic testing. Unless there is effective protection against post-test discrimination, many people may avoid genetic testing out of fear that the test results would be used against them. This could result in their missing out on the benefits of early diagnosis, treatment or prevention (e.g. risk reduction through avoidance of etiological co-factors).

[6] See 'Genetic Testing and Life & Disability Insurance'. Online. Available HTTP: <http://www.gene-watch.org/programs/GD-FAQ-Life_Ins.html>.

[7] One such instance is the formal granting of intellectual property rights to the *Kani* tribe of Agasthiyar hills in Kerala, India in recognition of their traditional development and use of *jeevani* (the Indian *ginseng*), a non-steroidal stimulant for combating stress and fatigue.

BIBLIOGRAPHY

Braveman, P., Krieger, N. and Lynch, J. (2000) 'Health Inequalities and Social Inequalities in Health', *Bull World Health Organisation*, 78: 232-234.

Chan, C.K. 'Privatisation, the State and Healthcare Reforms: Global Influences and Local Contingencies in Malaysia', paper presented at the 9th International Congress of the World Federation of Public Health Associations, Beijing, People's Republic of China, 2-6 September, 2000.

Citizens' Health Initiative (CHI) '13 Myths About Genetic Engineering'. Online Available at HTTP: <http://www.ipcb.org/news/myths.html>.

Citizens' Health Initiative (CHI) 'Frequently Asked Questions About Genetically Engineered Food'. Online. Available at HTTP: <http://www.gene-watch.org/programs/FAQ-Food.html>.

Collins, F.S. (1999) 'Shattuck Lecture—Medical and Societal Consequences of the Human Genome Project', *New England Journal of Medicine*, 341: 28-37.

Collins, F.S. and McKusick, V.A. (2001) 'Implications of the Human Genome Project for Medical Science', *Journal of the American Medical Association*, 285, no. 5.

Evans, T., Whitehead, M., Diderichsen, F., A. Bhuiya and Wirth, M. (eds) (2001) *Challenging Inequities in Health: From Ethics to Action*, Oxford: Oxford University Press.

Kitcher, P. (1996) *The Lives to Come. The Genetic Revolution and Human Possibilities*, New York: Simon & Schuster.

Leon, D. and Walt, G. (eds) (2000) *Poverty, Inequality and Health*, Oxford: Oxford University Press.

Light, D. (ed.) (2001) 'Comparative Studies of Competition Policy', *Social Science & Medicine*, 52, no. 8 (special issue).

Moses, S., Manji, F. and Bradley, J.E. (1992) 'Impact of User Fees on Attendance At a Referral Centre for Sexually Transmitted Diseases in Kenya', *Lancet*, 340: 463-466.

Murray, C.J.L. and Lopez, A.D. (eds) (1996) *The Global Burden of Disease*, Geneva: WHO.

New York Times, 'Lifting the Curtain on the Real Costs of Making Aids Drugs', 24 April, 2001.

South China Morning Post, 'Insurers review gene-test code', 23 April, 2001.

Washington Post, 'A Turning Point That Left Millions Behind', 28 December, 2000.

Weissman, R. (December 2000) 'Phasing Out User Fees', *Multinational Monitor*.

Woolhandler, S. and Himmelstein, D.U. (1999) 'When Money Is the Mission: The High Costs of Investor-owned Care', *New England Journal of Medicine*, 341, no. 6.

LIST OF CONTRIBUTORS

Dr Chan Chee Khoon (Citizens' Health Initiative, Malaysia) is an Associate Professor in the Development Studies Program of the School of Social Sciences, University Sains Malaysia. He earned his Doctor of Science degree in epidemiology from Harvard University, and is currently on sabbatical as Visiting Lecturer in Medicine at Harvard Medical School. Chan has published extensively on cancer epidemiology, eugenics and bioethics, health care financing policy and environmental health and development.

Prof Fujiki Norio is Professor Emeritus at Fukui Medical University and the President of the International Bioethics Seminars in Fukui. Besides a notable career as Medical Advisor to the Gene Analysis Laboratory (Toyobo Tsuruga), and as Head of the Department of International Medicine and Medical Genetics at Fukui Medical School, Fujiki served as Vice President of the IBC (UNESCO) (1993-8). He is a member of the Advisory Panel on Human Genetics, (WHO) (1978 to date) and has presided over the International Association of Human Biologists (1993-8) and many other committees.

Dr Gursatej Gandhi obtained her Ph.D. from Haryana Agricultural University (Hisar) in genetics, and is a senior lecturer at the Department of Human Genetics at Guru Nanak Dev University, Amritsar. Apart from being active in publishing and lecturing on the Human Genome Project, her most recent achievements include the estimation of DNA damage in individuals living near the sewage disposal drain of Mahal village, using the single cell gel electrophoresis (SCGE) assay.

Dr Soraj Hongladarom (Chulalongkorn University, Thailand) earned his Ph.D. in philosophy from Indiana University

(Bloomington, USA), and is specialised in epistemology, modern Western philosophy, philosophy of science and the philosophy of culture. He has published on medical ethics, Theraveda Buddhism, human rights and modern technology.

Prof Lee Shui Chuen is professor at the Graduate Institute of Philosophy of National Central University at Chungli. He serves as the Director of the Graduate Institute of Philosophy and is the founder and chief editor of The Newsletter of Applied Ethics (1997). He is also chief investigator of a group project on the ELSI of the Human Genome Project, which is part of the national project on Genetic Medicine of the ROC. Lee has published extensively in philosophy and education, among others a book on Confucian Bioethics (1999).

Prof Morioka Masahiro is professor of philosophy and ethics at the College of Integrated Arts and Sciences, Osaka Prefecture University, and is currently a Visiting Professor at the University of Tokyo's Graduate School of Humanities and Sociology (2001-). Morioka has published an impressive number of books and articles in the fields of bioethics, on topics like life studies, brain death and ethics in the post-religious era.

Darryl Macer has been director of the Eubios Ethics Institute in New Zealand since 1990 and is an associate professor teaching bioethics at the Institute of Biological Sciences, University of Tsukuba. Macer is founding director of the International Union of Biological Sciences (IUBS) since 1997 and was member of the UNESCO Bioethics Committee from 1993 until 98. He is also member of the HUGO Ethics Committee since 1995, board member of the International Association of Bioethics since 1999, secretary of the Asian Bioethics Association and editor of the Eubios Journal of Asian and International Bioethics since 1990. And finally, he is the author of many papers and books on a large range of issues related to bioethics.

Prof Min Jiayin is a Research Fellow at the Institute of Philosophy of the Chinese Academy of Social Sciences. He is member of the 'General Evolution Research Group' and consulting editor of World Future, the journal of general evolution. He is also the president of the Chinese Branch of the Club of Budapest. Min's main books are The Evolutionary Pluralism—A New System of Systems Philosophy and The Chalice & The Blade in Chinese Culture: Gender Relations and Social Models.

Dr Anwar Nasim earned his Ph.D. in Biochemical Genetics (University of Edinburgh) and is currently serving as adviser to COMSTECH (Islamabad, Pakistan). Internationally, he occupied many eminent positions, for instance, Principal Scientist and Head of the Molecular Genetics Group in the Biology and Medical Research Department; King Faisal Specialist of the Hospital and Research Centre (1989-93); and executive secretary of the Pakistan Academy of Sciences (1994-6).

Mary Ann Chen Ng (Eubios Ethics Institute, The Philippines) earned her Master in Science in Biosystem Studies from the University of Tsukuba (Biosystems Program) and lectured at the Department of Biology (Ateneo de Manila University) (2000-2001) and the Tsukuba Institute of Science and Technology (Japan) (1999-2000). Ng has conducted research and surveys into the attitudes of the public and scientists towards biotechnology in Japan and the Philippines. She is currently head of the Philippine Office of the Eubios Ethics Institute (Quezon City).

Dr Santishree Dhulipudi Pandit earned her Ph.D. in International Relations from Jawaharlal Nehru University, School of International Relations, in1990. Currently, she is University of

Pune's director of the Department of Politics and Public Administration and director of the Centre for Gender and Society.

Prof Sakamoto Hyakudai is Professor Emeritus at Aoyama-gakuin University (Tokyo) and founder (and former president) of The Japanese Association of Bioethics (JAB) (1996-1999). He is also founder (and president) of the Asian Bioethics Association (ABA) (1995-), founder (and president) of the East Asian Association of Semiotics (EAAS) (1997-) and former director of the International Association of Bioethics (IAB) (1997-2001). Sakamoto has written extensively on the mind-body problem, philosophical anthropology and bioethics.

Dr Tanida Noritoshi, is Associate Professor of the Department of Gastroenterology, Hyogo College of Medicine. Dr Tanida graduated from the Faculty of Medicine, Hirosaki University. Tanida teaches medical ethics and infectious diseases to medical students and has published on Japanese religions' views on euthanasia and extraordinary treatments.

Dr Wang Yanguang is Honorary Professor at the Centre for Applied Ethics (Beijing University) and teaches at the Centre for Applied Ethics of the Chinese Academy of Social Sciences in Beijing, where she received her Ph.D. Wang's numerous publications deal with family planning, reproductive ethics, geriatrics, eugenics and AIDS. She has taught various courses on Genetic Ethics, Health Insurance, Nursing Ethics, Bioethics and Law, Social Medicine, Bioethics and the History of Medicine.

Dr Yu Kam Por received his Ph.D. degree in moral and political philosophy from the University of Hong Kong. Yu is a senior lecturer in the General Education Centre of the Hong Kong Polytechnic University and has written widely on bioethical issues such as organ transplantation, human cloning and homosexuality.

He is also a founding member and council member of the Hong Kong Bioethics Association.

9 780415 560641